THE BEST OF
PRACTICAL POINTERS

Sponsored by the
Adapted Physical Activity Council of the
Association for Research, Administration,
Professional Councils & Societies

An association of the
American Alliance for Health, Physical Education,
Recreation, and Dance

ISBN 0-88314-437-9

ISBN # 0-88314-437-9

AAHPERD Publications © 1989 • The American Alliance for Health, Physical Education, Recreation and Dance, 1900 Association Drive, Reston, VA 22091

THE BEST OF PRACTICAL POINTERS

Contents

THE BEST OF PRACTICAL POINTERS

Introduction

From 1977 through 1982 the Information and Research Utilization Center, Unit on Programs for the Handicapped of the American Alliance for Health, Physical Education, Recreation and Dance published a series of monographs entitled PRACTICAL POINTERS. Dr. Julian U. Stein, then Director of the Unit, compiled a vast array of teaching techniques, activity adaptations, equipment modifications, programming information, coaching hints, skill development strategies and curriculum data. He searched for practitioners in the field to author POINTERS in their particular area of expertise. Where a need for information existed and no author was available, Dr. Stein researched and wrote material himself. The result was sixty monographs published in five volumes.

PRACTICAL POINTERS were written by teachers for teachers. They contained information directly applicable to activity situations. They were a result of real life teaching experiences with special populations. They are as useful today as when they were originally written. It is for that reason that this publication is presented. It contains the BEST OF PRACTICAL POINTERS.

The Adapted Physical Activity Council of the Alliance, with the cooperation of the Alliance Publications Office and Alliance Archives, presents this publication to assure that his valuable information remains available to the profession. Sincere appreciation is expressed to Dr. Stein for his time, talent, and expertise in developing the original series. Gratitude is also due to original POINTER authors, pioneers in their field, who not only had creativity and innovative spirit to develop techniques, but also willingness to share with others. THANK YOU one and all!

The BEST OF PRACTICAL POINTERS editorial committee:

Susan J. Grosse, Chair
Milwaukee Public School System
Milwaukee, WI

Carol Cooper
University of Northern Iowa
Cedar Falls, IA

Sue Gavron
Bowling Green State University
Bowling Green, OH

Julian U. Stein
George Mason University
Fairfax, VA

About the Authors

HEZKIAH AHARONI, PhD.—formerly on staff with the Columbus, Ohio Public Schools, Dr. Aharoni is independently employed as a consultant in physical education programs for special populations.

DAN BAUER—developed these fitness activities while on the staff of the San Bernadino Unified School District, California.

DONALD G. BORNELL Ed.D.—is Health, Physical and Adaptive Physical Education Coordinator for the Santa Barbara County Schools, California.

JANE SILVERMAN BRADTKE—wrote and illustrated several POINTERS while AAHPERD/IRUC Information and Materials Assistant.

JOYCE M. BUIS—contributed these adapted aquatic techniques while an instructor-trainer for the Metropolitan Atlanta Chapter of the American National Red Cross, Atlanta, Georgia.

SUSAN J. GROSSE—formerly on staff at Gaenslen Orthopedic School in Milwaukee, Wisconsin, Ms. Grosse teaches at the Milwaukee High School of the Arts.

CORDELIA GRAVES HARRIS—introduced these dance adaptations to the orthopedically handicapped students at Sunbeam School, Cleveland, Ohio.

MICHAEL MARSALLO—is an itinerant physical education teacher in the physically handicapped program of the Fairfax County School System, Virginia.

TOM MARSH—developed these relays while a physical education instructor at the Devereau Foundation, Santa Barbara, California.

CHRISTINE D. MCGILL—developed these aquatic teaching techniques while a paraprofessional at Gaenslen Orthopedic School, Milwaukee, Wisconsin.

CATHERINE S. SCHANE—teaches in the Department of Health, Physical Education, Recreation and Dance, Georgia State University, Atlanta.

HOWARD M. SORRELL—is retired from the Arlington, Virginia public schools.

BRUCE THIELE—developed these relays while a psychomotor specialist at the Devereau Foundation, Santa Barbara California.

KATHLEEN THOME—developed these aquatic activities while teaching at Fryk Center, Torsby, Sweden.

SALLY WARNER—developed these relays while a recreation therapist at the Devereau Foundation, Santa Barbara, California.

UNAUTHORED MATERIAL—many of the "pointers" in this collection are unauthored. They represent the work of Dr. Julian U. Stein, currently Professor of Physical Education at George Mason University, Fairfax, Virginia and formerly Director, Information and Research Utilization Center, Unit on Programs for the Handicapped, American Alliance for Health, Physical Education, Recreation and Dance.

Content Reference Matrix

The information contained in POINTERS in this collection can be applied to a wide variety of teaching situations involving individuals representing a great diversity of handicapping conditions. This Content Reference Matrix has been designed to assist readers in locating needed information quickly. Primary application of a POINTER is indicated by a "1". Secondary application is indicated by a "2". These distinctions are not meant to be exclusive. Rather, they are merely a guide in focusing attention and interest.

	Page No.	Mental Retardation	Multiply Handicapped	Orthopedically Handicapped	Severe & Profound Retardation	Equipment	Aquatics	Mainstreaming	Movement Fundamentals	Organization & Administration	Perceptual-Motor	Physical Fitness	Rhythms/Dance
SECTION I—PRACTICAL POINTERS FOR FITNESS													
Circuit & Station Activity Approaches	1	2	2					2		1		1	
Rope Activities for Fun, Fitness, and Fonics	8	2	2			2		2	1	2		1	
Desk and Chair Activities for Fun and Fitness	18	2	2	2	2	2		2		2		1	
Isokinetic Physical Fitness Activities with Bicycle Innertubes	31	2	2			2		2				1	
Aerobic Fitness for the Mentally Retarded	52	1			1	2	1	2	2	2	2	1	2
SECTION II—PRACTICAL POINTERS FOR MOVEMENT FUNDAMENTALS AND DANCE													
Innovative Perceptual Motor Activities: Programming Techniques that Work	73	2	2					2	2		1		
Innovative Perceptual Motor Activities: Programming Techniques that Work—Part 2	87	2	2					2	2		1		
Innovative Developmental Physical Activities for Early Childhood and Special Education Students	101	2	2					2	1		1		
Movement Discovery Linking the Impossible to the Possible	120	2	2					2	1		1		
Motor Development Relays	139	1						2	1	2	1		
Dance for Students with Orthopedic Conditions—Popular/Square/Folk/Modern/Ballet	155		1					2					1
SECTION III—PRACTICAL POINTERS FOR ACTIVITY PROGRAMS FOR THE SEVERE AND PROFOUND MULTIPLY HANDICAPPED													
Physical Activities for Children with Severe Multiple Impairments	173			1	1		2				2		
Games and Activities for Severely Handicapped Students Utilizing Small Space and Minimal Equipment	191			1	1		2				2		
SECTION IV—PRACTICAL POINTERS FOR ADAPTED AQUATICS													
Adaptive Devices for Aquatic Activities	213		2			1	1						
Independent Swimming for Children with Severe Physical Impairments	227		1	1	1		1				2		
Movement Exploration as a Technique for Teaching Pre-Swimming Skills to Students with Developmental Delays	241						1		1		1		
Adapting Aquatic Circuit Training for Special Populations	262	2					1	2				1	
SECTION V—PRACTICAL POINTERS FOR ORGANIZATION AND ADMINISTRATION													
Tips on Mainstreaming: Do's and Don'ts in Activity Programs	277	2	2					1					
Organizing Playdays and Large Group Activities	293									1			
Making Outdoor Play Areas Usable for All Children	307		1	2	2	1		2		1	2		

Section I—
Practical Pointers for Fitness

PRACTICAL POINTERS

CIRCUIT AND STATION ACTIVITY APPROACHES

Circuit and station activity approaches make it possible to provide individualized programs and activities to students of all ages regardless of type or degree of impairment, disability, or handicap. These approaches can be adapted to any type of activity--physical education, recreation, sports, swimming, general education--used in any setting--gymnasium, playfield, playground, swimming pool, athletic field, classroom--and organized so individuals can take part whether they can read or not. Basically this approach requires very little space. Stations where specific tasks are performed can be set up indoors as well as outdoors, in classrooms as well as gymnasiums, on blacktop areas as well as playfields. Systematic ways to control activities at individual stations and participant movement from one station to the next are additional factors that must be considered for successful implementation of these approaches. With flexibility a circuit or station approach can be used to attain goals, objectives, and skills in various program areas--basic motor skills, perceptual-motor skills, physical fitness, specific sports skills, aquatic skills, readiness skills, academic skills. In establishing a circuit or series of stations (the current educational in word is learning centers!), all of the factors that have been discussed must be considered.

1

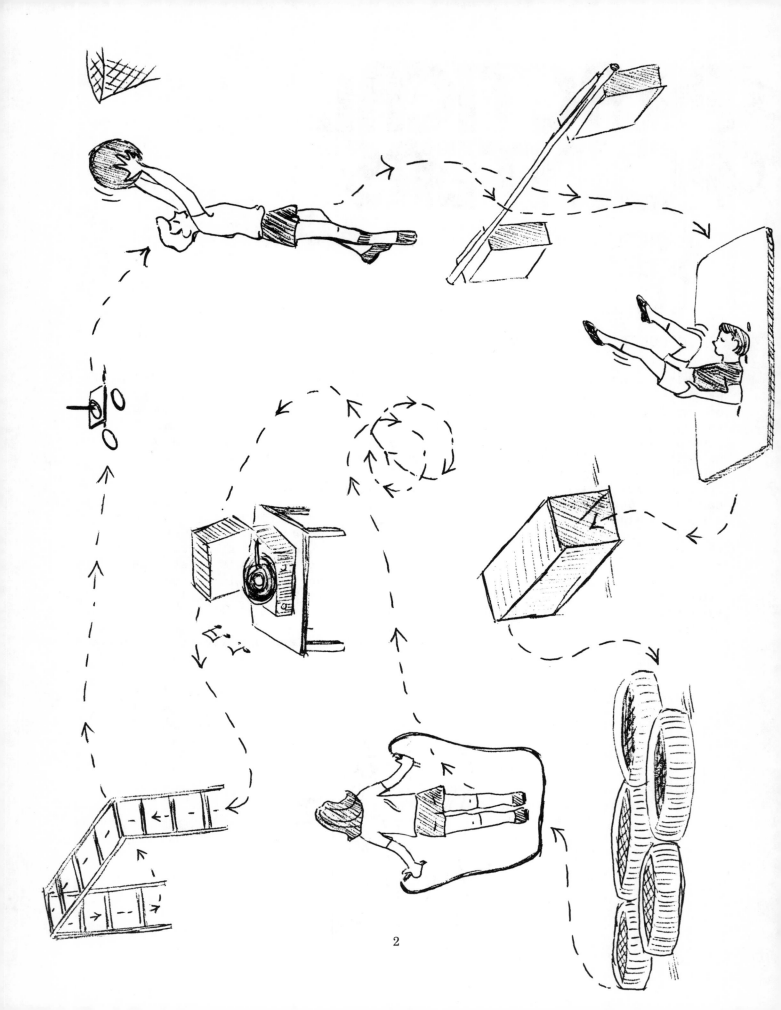

PRACTICAL POINTERS

* Tape appropriate music for length of time each activity is to be per-
formed--when music stops activity stops and participants move to the
next station, repeating the process until all stations are completed.
Gradually increase activity time and reduce movement time.

* Use records in the same manner described for taped music. An obvious
disadvantage of records is necessity to have someone constantly
operating the phonograph.

* Use taped musical accompaniment with instruments such as piano, accordian, harmonica, banjo, or guitar.

* Pre-teach activities, movements, patterns, and skills, before introducing
them in a circuit or through stations. For example, teach specific
resistance or weight training movements with broom sticks or wooden
dowels before having individuals apply them in a circuit or on a multi-
station apparatus. This applies the principle of having only one new
element in a learning task or situation. In this instance a familiar
activity is used in a new setting. When this setting becomes familiar,
a new process or approach can be introduced.

* Have stick figures, drawings, photographs, loop films, or other means
of visualization for participants with hearing difficulties and to reinforce
what is to be done at each station. The graphic display can be as simple
or complex as desired. Pictorial materials can be attached to a wall
near the station or put on black bottles filled with sand or dirt and
placed at stations.

* Have a leader--teacher, aide, volunteer, buddy, advocate, another student--
  go through the entire circuit with individuals who need additional assistance
  or support--psychological or emotional as well as physical.

* Keep a leader--teacher, aide, volunteer, buddy, advocate, another student--
  at stations with activities that need additional supervision and
  mastering because of the difficulty of the activity as well as for
  safety purposes.

* Use contact paper, masking tape, or tempra paint to make lines and
  arrows on the floor to assist individuals in moving from one station to the
  next.

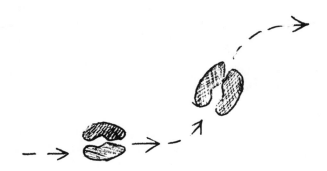

* Number stations when this type of identification adds to and reinforces ability of participants to recognize specific stations and activities to be done at each.

* Have participant carry a specially marked card from station to station so that he/she has another way to identify activities for each station and the specific number of repetitions to be done at each station. Combinations of pictures (at stations and reproduced on individual cards), symbols (to indicate differential tasks for those at different functional levels or of different ages), and color codes (for specific number of repetitions to be done by the individual) provide additional ways for nonreaders to have circuit or station activities tailored to their individual needs. For individuals with less reading difficulties, conventional circuit or station cards can be utilized.

* Use audiocassettes with brief instructions and descriptions of activities for individuals with visual impairments and to reinforce procedures for other participants.

* Have each participant perform a specified number of repetitions at each station before moving to the next station. To add challenge and further individualize an activity according to participant needs, repeat two or three sets of the activity before moving to the next station.

* Plan highly controllable circuits or station activities so that number of stations and number of participants are the same. In planning other circuits, no relationship need exist between number of stations and number of participants.

5

* Use stations as an obstacle or confidence course in which each participant performs an activity, movement, or pattern at a station and then moves onto the next, continuing in this way until all stations have been completed.

* Use traditional circuit approaches in which participants are timed for a maximum all-out effort over the entire circuit. Establish individual training times based on the all-out effort of each person--i.e., one-and-one half or two times the all-out time as a training time for the circuit. Move through the circuit at less than all-out effort seeing how many stations can be completed in the training time; when the last station is completed, return to the first station continuing in this manner until the total training time has elapsed. Another approach is to maintain all-out time striving to increase number of stations completed in that time. Regardless of approach, periodically reassess the all-out effort and adjust training times accordingly.

* Plan stations so that more than one piece of apparatus is available, especially when using stations in a traditional circuit approach, as an obstacle or confidence course, or in other less controlled ways. This procedure reduces jam-ups and lines at these stations and provides opportunities for participants to select size of apparatus that provides most appropriate individual challenge at each station.

* Plan stations so that pieces of apparatus requiring the same movements, patterns, or skills, are of different sizes to accommodate participants of different ages and functional abilities. For example, different sizes of horizontal ladders provide similar experiences and opportunities for individuals with different abilities. Obstacle course stations can be made one size for adults, another for adolescents, and still another for younger children. Leap frog tires can be made from truck, regular car, and compact car tires.

6

* Add challenge and variety to stations in ways they are constructed. For example, make horizontal ladders out of rope rather than wood.

* Obtain input and ideas from participants regarding specific activities, movements, and patterns for stations and additional approaches to provide interesting and challenging ways to complete the circuit.

* Use each station as a learning center with longer blocks of time spent at each. In such an approach, rotate or move among stations on a day-to-day basis or cover two or three stations in a single period depending upon its length.

* Provide check lists with individual sequences for each participant for each station so that a self-testing approach is used. Check lists can be developed so that performance goals are attained before the individual moves to the next stop in the progression. Participants can work in pairs to encourage, assist, monitor, and evaluate each other.

* Place a card, graphic description, or audiocassette describing movements or patterns at each station. Each participant follows the progression, attaining one step or level according to performance goals before moving to the next step or level. Be sure that sequences provide for a wide range of abilities among participants.

* Plan and implement circuit and station approaches so that participants continually function more independently in increasingly difficult tasks and challenges.

* Plan and adapt station devices and activities so individuals in wheelchairs, on crutches, or with leg braces can participate actively. For example, gym scooters can be used by everyone; many individuals in wheelchairs can take part in many of these activities with minor modifications.

* Use, adapt, and apply station or circuit approaches in aquatic/swimming activities, highly organized team practices, recreational activities, perceptual-motor skills, as well as in more traditional physical education and physical fitness activities.

. Combine two or more of these specific approaches according to activities themselves and abilities of participants.

* Take your mark .... set ....

PRACTICAL POINTERS

ROPE ACTIVITIES FOR FUN, FITNESS, AND FONICS

Rope--old or new, short or long, small or large, strong or weak, straight or curved--can be used in various ways to provide stimulating and challenging activities for boys and girls, men and women of all ages and abilities. Individuals with different handicapping conditions can participate in and enjoy most of the same rope activities and personal challenges as their nonhandicapped classmates. Individuals on crutches, persons with braces, and those in wheelchairs need not be left out as each can participate in his or her own way. Rope activities can be done individually, in pairs or small groups, and in large gatherings. They can be vigorous or not too strenuous; done with lots of space or in very confined areas; tasks can be easy and simple or difficult and demanding. Rope activities provide opportunities for everyone to participate together while responding to individual challenges. Rope activities provide excellent opportunities to satisfy demands of individualized education programs in least restrictive environments through a medium that is appealing, well received, and fun. The only limitations in using rope activities are those imposed by lack of immagination exhibited by teachers/leaders and participants. So, hitch your rope to a star and swing to who knows where.

Ropes

Ropes can be obtained from a variety of sources--

. Commercially made ropes for jumping, turning, twisting, climbing, tugging, and using in exploratory and problem-solving activities.

. Made from three-eights inch clothesline, sash cord, and other easily obtained and inexpensive sources.

. Commercially available ropes made from plastic and other synthetic materials that are elastic or nonelastic depending upon proposed uses; they can be used in straight lines, circles, and in a variety of shapes and patterns.

Obviously, ropes come in a wide range of materials and colors--

. Individual jump or short ropes should be from six to nine feet long depending upon the user's height. A rule of thumb is to have ends of the rope just long enough to reach the shoulders while the individual stands on the middle of the rope.

. Long ropes for group jumping should be heavier than individual ropes and can range from ten to twenty feet in length.

. Circle ropes can be made from clothesline, sash cord, or other easily obtained ropes. Although commercially made circle ropes can be obtained, caution should be exercised in using them for this purpose for safety reasons; i.e., overstretching the rope, letting go of the catch, being hit by recoiling rope.

Long ropes can be used in straight lines as well as placed in circles and in various shapes and patterns for many different kinds of vigorous and interesting activities. When long ropes are used for jumping and leaping activities in particular, elastic rather than firm ropes are recommended for safety reasons--if an individual trips or gets a foot hung, the rope will give making it less likely that a participant will trip and fall.

Activities, patterns, and approaches that follow are among the infinite number of ways ropes can be used in physical education and recreation programs for fitness, motor development, and fun. By changing emphasis, the same activity can be used for different purposes--focus on quantity of movement for fitness purposes, quality of movement for perfection of patterns, and personal interaction and working together for social goals. Music provides an excellent background for many rope activities. This accompaniment can be from special records, current favorites of the group or individual participants, piano, banjo, guitar, accordian, harmonica, auto harp, recorder, or rhythm band. Music can be taped on reels or casettes in advance to free the teacher/leader and other staff personnel for working directly with activity participants.

Sample Rope Activities

With the rope on the ground in a straight line, have youngsters--

. Walk forward (backward, sideward) along the rope (keep feet on either side of the rope).

. Jump (hop) forward (backward, sideward) along (over) the rope.

. Do a standing (running) jump over the rope (hold it at different heights).

. Stand astride the rope, jump and click heels (once, twice) while above the rope.

With the rope on the ground in a circle, have youngsters--

. Run, jump, and land in the circle in a crouch (standing) position; follow with various stunts while in the circle and jump out of the circle in different ways (standing long jump, frog jump).

. Jump in and out of the circle (forward, backward, sideways).

. Jump and click the heels (once, twice) while above the circle; start either standing astride or in the circle.

. Walk forward (backward, sideways) around the circle.

. Do a cartwheel over the circle.

Basic Individual Rope Activities

Individual jump ropes or six to nine foot sections of clothes line or sash cord are all needed to introduce basic individual rope activities.

. Place rope in a straight line on the floor and--

--Walk along the rope with one foot on either side of the rope.
--Walk on the rope using the same patterns as done on a balance beam (forward, backward, sideward, knee to heel, bounce a ball, step over objects, duck under objects, keep a bean bag on top of the head, carry weighted objects, keep eyes closed).
--Face the rope and jump (hop) over it forward (backward).
--Run, (jump, hop, gallop, skip, leap) back and forth along (around) the rope.
--Stand with feet together on one side of the rope, jump sideward over the rope, jump back over the rope, continue down the rope and back in this alternate manner.
--Hop back and forth over the rope in the same patterns described for the jump above.
--Use various animal walks (crab, spider, lame dog, seal, walrus, inch-worm, bear, elephant) to move back and forth along (around) the rope.
--Use various imaginative ways (airplane, train, dragon, giants, midgets) to move back and forth along (around) the rope.
--Balance with body parts in different combinations (one foot, foot and hand, head and feet) and numbers (one, two, three, six parts) on the rope (on either side of the rope).
--Provide opportunities for students to be creative as they explore and solve movement problems over (around) the single straight rope.
--Increase difficulty and challenge by raising the rope for activities where appropriate.

. Place rope in the shape of a circle on the floor and--

--Do all activities for single straight ropes discussed above.
--Jump (hop) in and out of the circle in as many different ways as possible (forward, backward, sideward, one foot, straddle, heels, tip toes).
--Get all the way inside the circle and then move around in the circle.
--Put body parts in different combinations and numbers in and outside of the circle.

. Place the rope in various shapes (triangle, square, rectangle, pentagon, diamond) as numbers, letters, or in creative combinations and have students perform movements and patterns as discussed above.

. Have students made creative patterns with the rope and then reproduce these patterns with their bodies.

. Reverse the procedure above--make a pattern with the body and then reproduce this pattern with the rope.

. Use the body and rope together to form specified shapes, letters, numbers, other patterns, or creative shapes.

. Work with a partner using one or two ropes and bodies of each participant to form specified shapes, letters, numbers, other patterns, or creative shapes.

Circle Rope Activities

Have members of the class space themselves evenly around a circle rope. Twenty-five or fifty foot sections of clothes line work well depending upon the size of the class. Rope loops can be tied into the main circle rope as hand holds to assure even spacing around the rope. Some teachers have reported success in circle rope activities with hyperactive and distractible children having short attention spans by looping the rope around the waists of these children. Nonelastic materials are preferred for types of circle rope activities presented for safety reasons. Representative of endless activities that can be introduced with circle ropes follow.

. Stand in place with feet shoulder width apart (together, astride) and--

--Pull back on the rope at waist (thigh, knee, shin, foot, stomach, chest, shoulder, chin, nose, eye) level; have palms up (down, one up and one down).
--Push the rope forward (backward, up, down) from each of the levels listed above.
--Pass the rope this (right) way, that (left) way, fast (faster, slow, slower) at each of the levels listed above.
--Move the rope back and forth like pumping a bicycle.
--Push the rope forward with one hand and pull it back with the other; reverse hands and arms, continuing to alternate in this manner (slowly, faster, still faster, even faster).
--Hold the rope at different levels with hands various distances apart and try to move hands together (push hands apart).
--Hold rope at thigh level with palms facing toward (away from) center of circle and bend one (right), then the other (left) arm until arm is fully flexed; return to the starting position, continuing in this alternate manner. Perform with both hands/arms simultaneously.

. Turn around so the rope is behind participants; maintain grasp on rope with both hands, and--

--Run (fast, faster, knees high).
--Perform selected and appropriate activities from listing above.

. Lift the rope up, take one step to the inside, bring the rope down to belt or waist level, and--

--Push back against the rope hard.
--Walk (run) backwards against the rope; increase (decrease) force against rope and the speed of the run.
--Turn around so the back is toward the center of the circle and walk (run) slowly (fast, faster).
--Have participants alternate so that one faces the center and the next has his/her back to the center and repeat activities listed above.

13

. Sit down on the floor, place the rope over the feet and supported on
  the insteps; extend the knees, lie back, and--

  --Sit up, grab the rope, and stretch the legs; lie back, continuing
    in this alternate manner for a given number of repetitions (length
    of time, music sequence).
  --Sit up, grab the rope, pull hard, and don't let yourself slide along
    the floor (the more slippery the floor, the more difficult this is
    to accomplish).
  --Sit up, grab the rope, pull hard, and let the body slide quickly
    (slowly) under the rope--FUN!!!
  --Raise the legs and keep the rope supported a few inches off the floor;
    raise the rope gradually higher, returning it to the floor in a
    coordinated way.
  --Place the rope over one ankle and under the other heel so that the
    rope can be raised as high as possible with the one foot while being
    held down as far as possible with the heel; reverse and raise with
    the other foot; use time or music sequences to control the length of
    time for this activity.
  --Hold the rope on the soles of the feet and move them in a bicycling
    motion, starting with the legs close to the floor, leaning on the
    elbows, and gradually moving the legs upward to a traditional bicycle
    position.

. Lie on the stomach, head toward the center of the cirlce, extend the
  arms fully, grasp the rope with the hands and--

  --Raise one (left), other (right), both arms as high as possible;
    keep the chin, toes, and knees in contact with the floor.
  --Raise one (left), other (right), both legs as high as possible; keep
    the chin in contact with the floor; do initially with the knees,
    also maintaining contact with the floor, then with the knees not in
    contact with the floor (make sure the legs are straight throughout the
    pattern at this level).
  --Raise one (left), other (right), both legs as high as possible; keep
    the hands and arms in contact with the floor; get the head and chin
    as high up into the air as possible.
  --Raise one (left), other (right), both legs, one (left), other (right),
    both hands and arms, and the head and chin as high into the air as
    possible.

. Stand beside the rope, hold it with one (left, right) hand and--

  --Walk (slowly, quickly, fast, faster, backwards, loudly, quietly,
    knees high, knees low; on toes, tip toes, heels, one heel and one
    toe, outsides of the feet, insides of the feet, one outside and one
    inside of the feet; scissors steps, giant steps, baby steps; as the
    music dictates.
  --Run (vary in similar ways as listed above).
  --Jump (forward, backward, variations as listed above).
  --Hop (one foot, other foot, even patterns/uneven patterns, similar
    ways as above).
  --Gallop (put one foot forward, keep it there, now move forward, back-
    ward, change lead foot, change speeds).
  --Skip (forward, backward, slow, fast).
  --Leap (high, low, long, short).
  --Perform movements suggested by music (swing, sway).

. Hold the rope with both hands and--

--Do locomotor movements into and out of the center of the circle.
--Introduce basic square dance movements such as circle right/left,
  all to the center and back, ladies/gents to the center, star formations,
  and variations of do-si-do, allemande and grand right and left.
--Introduce circle and folk dances such as Hokey Pokey, Bunny Hop,
  Seven Jumps, Virginia Reel, La Raspa, and Hora.
--Perform original physical fitness movements, activities, and sequences
  as well as those in patterns such as Chicken Fat.

. Provide opportunities for students to respond in original and innovative
ways through exploratory and problem solving techniques.

Long Rope Activities

    Have two individuals hold opposite ends of a long rope that is extended
across the middle of a room, gymnasium, hard top area, or indoor or outdoor
open space. It is possible to attach one end of a long rope to a chair, table,
or other stable object while the opposite end is held by an aide, another
teacher, a parent, or a student. Have class members go to one end of the room
so that they can face the middle of the room and the rope.

    In small settings, class members can be divided so that half is at each
end of the space being used. When this pattern is used, students on one side
perform the designated activity, movement, or pattern at the rope, continue
across the area, and then perform a specified activity with a specific partner
or someone on the other side of the area. For example, partners could salute,
bow or courtsey, shake hands, do one/two hand/arm/elbow swing, perform do-si-
do right/left, touch certain body parts, churn the butter, leap frog, do
a combative activity, follow the leader, add-on, or perform creative movements
before returning or having the other person go back to the other side; the original activity, movement or pattern is performed at the rope on the return activity.

    Another possibility in these situations is to have the first performer take
the second one back to the other side in various ways--crawl, creep, walk, run,
jump, hop, gallop, skip, leap together; carry piggyback, saddle back, in arms;
wheelbarrow. When the partners reach the other side, then the second student--
the visitor--returns to his/her starting side while performing the basic activity,
movement, or pattern at the rope.

    Activities can be made increasingly difficult by gradually raising or lowering
the rope for students to go over or under it. Additional challenges and fun can
be introduced by gently shaking the rope from side-to-side or in up and down
motions so that the rope may be given the appearance of a wiggling snake. Individual differences can be met by angling the rope so that one end is wider or
higher than the other, much in the same way done in games like Jump the Creek. An
elastic or stretch rope is recommended for these activities for safety reasons.
Elastic ropes give if a student catches a foot or trips so that falls are less
likely than in situations where a nonelastic rope is used. Representative of
the countless number and type of activities and personal challenges that can be
introduced with long ropes follow.

. Hold the rope across an area, have students run and go over the rope,
  taking off and landing in the following ways--

    --Step over the rope with regular (big, small, giant, baby, scissors,
      bold, timid) steps.
    --Take off both fee and land on both (one, then the other, right, left)
      feet (foot).
    --Take off one (right,left) foot and land on the same (opposite, other,
      right,/left, left/right) foot.
    --Perform each of the activities described above executing a quarter
      (half, three-quarter, full) turn before landing.
    --Have partners (groups of three, four) perform activities, movements,
      patterns as coordinated groups.

. Hold the rope across an area, have students go under the rope in the
  following ways--

    --Crawl (creep) slowly (slower, still slower, fast, faster, still faster).
    --Do animal walks (crab, spider, seal, walrus).
    --Lead with the head (arm, hand, elbow, chest, stomach, back, buttocks,
      side, knee, leg, foot, chin, ear).
    --Go under the rope forward (backward, sideward).
    --Go under the rope with back (chest, stomach, side) toward the ceiling.
    --Combine movements from the above listings, such as move forward on
      all fours with the back toward the ceiling.
    --Roll under the rope (roll still a different way, still another way).
    --Pretend you are a bear (worm, kangaroo, row boat, swimmer) and go
      under the rope.
    --Go under the rope in ways suggested by the music.

. Double the rope so that one person holds the two ends and another person
  holds the rope near the middle so that two rope lines are parallel to
  each other and the floor and then have students--

    --Go over (under) both ropes in ways listed above for single long rope
      activities.
    --Use patterns listed above to go over one rope, land between the ropes,
      and then go over the other rope.
    --Use patterns listed above to go over one rope and under the next rope.
    --Have one rope high and the other low so that students go under (over)
      the high side and over (under) the low side.

. Stand with both feet between the ropes and--

    --Jump over one rope to one side, return to the middle, and continue
      in this manner.
    --Jump so that one foot lands outside of each rope.
    --Jump from both feet and land on outside (inside) foot over left (right)
      rope.
    --Jump and do a half (full) turn landing between (outside) both ropes.
    --Do activities with music, such as a march with a good solid beat.

. Stand with one side next to one of the rope lines when they are held in the
  double pattern as above and--

--Jump sideward so as to land between the ropes, and jump back to
   starting point (over the other rope).
--Hop on one (right, left) foot over ropes in the same pattern as
   described for the jump above.
--Hop so as to land on inside foot after clearing nearer rope, change to
   the other foot in the middle, hop over the other rope landing on the
   other foot, return over the ropes in the same pattern, and continue
   in same alternate pattern which is both left, right change to left,
   left change to right, right.
--Do with music for Tinikling, Philipine Stick Dance, or Bamboo Hop.

Double the rope so that one person holds both ends and another persons
holds the rope near the middle so that the two ropes are parallel to
each other and perpendicular to the floor to form a window and--

--Go through the window in the same ways as discussed for going over
   single ropes.
--Lead with the hands and arms (reach closer and closer to the
   floor until a forward roll results).

Story Activities

   Use ropes for props in dramatic stories, so that students can take part in
either structured or creative movement activities. For example--

. Mount your horse and ride away from camp (use rope as bridle for the
   horse, a whip, lasso, or the horse itself).

. Tie the horse to a tree.

. Get in a canoe and row across the river (use rope for oars, the boat
   itself).

. Bring the boat out of the water on the other side of the river and tie
   it to a tree.

. Hike toward the mountain, swing the rope overhead (at the side as a
   lasso, in big/small circles) and/or bring it down against the ground
   with much (little) force.

. Look up into the sky and watch eagles flying (use the rope as wings
   and fly).

. Place the rope in the shape of a mountain and walk (crawl, creep, run,
   jump, hop, gallop, skip, leap, spider walk, crab walk, bear walk, lame
   dog walk) around the mountain.

   --Jump (hop) over the mountain in different ways and patterns (forward
      backward, sideward, high, low).
   --Jump (hop) in and out of the mountain in different ways and patterns
      and combinations.

PRACTICAL POINTERS

DESK AND CHAIR ACTIVITIES FOR FUN AND FITNESS

Jane Silverman Bradtke

It is mid-afternoon at Emanon Elementary School--your fifth grade class (or first, second...) has just finished an arithmetic test. Restlessness is pervasive. Alan pulls Debbie's hair; Rich's geography book keeps accidentally falling on the floor; white spots continue to flash before your eyes before you realize they are moisture missles (spit balls, paper wads...)!! It is definitely time for a break--time to chanel pent-up energies into constructive activities. The gymnasium is being used by the sixth grade for basketball activities; a good softball game outside would be perfect. That's what you'll do! Then, you see a flash of light, followed by a loud clap of thunder, and a downpour. Now what?!!!

*   *   *

Grahamwood Elementary School is small and located in the heart of downtown. Not only is there no playground, but no gymnasium or formal physical education program. Having a classroom full of children for hours on end is not proving to be healthy for students-- or for you. Arts and crafts and music help break up the day, but vigorous activities are essential. What can be done?!!!

*   *   *

These examples are not uncommon and can leave teachers with frustrating situations. Children need physical activities. It is fundamental to success in other school areas and productive classroom experiences. Physicians and child growth and development specialists agree that a first grade child needs four to five hours of physical activity a day. How attentive can a child be who has done nothing but sit for hours on end? Some games provide diversion, but generally not essential vigorous physical exercise or activity. This Practical Pointer--Desk and Chair Activities for Fun and Fitness--attempts to help relieve some of these problems by presenting physical activities designed for typical classroom settings. These suggestions should not only help keep teachers from pulling their hair out on rainy days--and keep children from climbing the walls--but also provide vigorous, challenging physical activities that every growing body needs for intellectual, social, and emotional growth as well as physical and motor development.

Desk and chair activities can be used successfully with children possessing various handicapping conditions. There is no reason why children with mild or moderate mental retardation can not perform these tasks and participate actively in all individual activities, relay races, and games. When instructions are clear and concise, everyone understands what is expected so that activities move along smoothly.

Children in wheelchairs can participate actively. The only modification necessary is to provide extra room to allow maneuvering around desks or up and down aisles. Some of these students may not be able to stand on chairs or seats of desks, or hop on one foot, but all other activities mentioned are quite suitable. Students in wheelchairs should be encouraged to devise their own interpretations of movments they cannot do in conventional or usual ways. Many students in wheelchairs jump, hop, leap, gallop, ... In other situations students in wheelchairs can crawl, creep, or perform activities on gym scooters or scooter boards.

Hearing impaired, including both deaf and hard of hearing children, should experience no problems at all as long as instructions are clear and concise. Demonstration and active participation are great teachers for all children, especially those who have receptive communication difficulties.

Partially sighted and blind students can also take part in desk and chair activities. Clear explanation are musts for these children; once concepts are understood, maneuvering around desks should become a matter of feeling out situations. For relays, a partner can be assigned to run along and verbally direct or lend an elbow for physical assistance. One way to equalize competition is to blindfold children on other teams. This is also an excellent learning situation so that sighted children in a class experience blindness.

Equipment

Questions arise--what kinds of real physical activities can be done in classrooms? There is no room for equipment, no space to run--just desks, tables, chairs of all types, and books! Exactly!!! Answers lie in the questions!!! Equipment for most of these activities consits of desks, tables, chairs, and books. Additional equipment may be required for some games, but nothing that can not easily be found at home in a garage or quite inexpensively at a store.

19

Desk Activities

Let's **look** at a typical schoolroom desk. What sort of physical activities can be enjoyed by each child at his/her desk? The following problems to solve and opportunities to explore evoke much activity, enthusiasm, and maybe a bit of giggling from a classroom of children who are ready to move.

. Stand* on the seat of your desk; step back to the floor! Up to the seat again! Back to the floor!...

. Squeeze underneath the table of your desk.

. Walk around your desk (forward, backward, sideward).

. Take giant (baby, scissor) steps around your desk.

. Jump around your desk (fast, slow, big, small).

. Hop around your desk (alternate feet, two on one foot, three on the other).

. Hop like a frog (rabbit, kangaroo, cricket, grasshopper) around your desk.

---

*Problem solving or exploratory techniques use positive statements, not introductory words such as "Can you..." which can back you as an instructor or leader into an untenable corner!

. Show me how a dog (horse, cat, cow, turtle, butterfly, mouse) would go around your desk.

. Run around your desk as fast/slow (loud/quiet) as your can!

. Skip around your desk.

. Put your right/left foot on the seat of your desk and then the left/right foot so that you are standing on the desk seat. Do this five (ten, twenty) times.

. Balance on the one foot, eyes open/closed, hands high/low.

. Pick up your desk and hold it ten (twenty) seconds.

Varations. Have the class repeat above activities while clapping, whistling Dixie, singing a song, being happy (sad, mad, silly), fast, slow-motion, quietly, loudly.

Let's Add More Desks

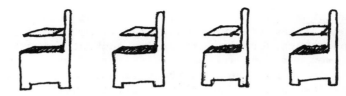

. Stay in line and walk (run, skip, jump, hop, crawl, creep) around your row of desks.

. Follow-the-leader around the row of desks; change leaders frequently.

. Walk (run, skip, jump, hop, crawl, creep) around row of desks moving in and out between desks (like in and out of the windows).

. Pretend to be dogs (horses, cats, cows, turtles, butterflies, mice) as you walk around a row of desks.

. Put your right foot on the seat of your desk and step up onto the seat; move to the next desk in the row and repeat; person at the last desk should quickly come to the front desk.

    <u>Variations</u>. Use variations mentioned with single desk activities. Do these same activities moving in lateral files rather than forward and backward rows.

<u>Even More Desks</u>!!

    As numbers of desks increase, so do possible activities. With several rows of desks, a variety of relay races and games can be introduced--use your **imagination**

  . <u>Running race</u>. Children line up at the front of their rows. At the sound of the teacher's clap, the first person for each team runs (jumps, hops, skips, crawls, creeps) in and out between each desk to the end of the row and back in the same/different way. Each person on the team goes in turn. The first team to have all members complete the task wins the relay. Keep each team relatively small so that emphasis is on active participation, not standing in line and waiting for turns.

  . <u>Book relay</u>. Using the same formation for teams as in running race, collect one book per desk--in a row of six desks, there will be six books. The first person of each team holds all books; at the sound of "<u>Go</u>" he/she places one book on each desk in the row. At the end of the row, he/she changes directions and comes back, this time collecting books, handing them to the next person in line who repeats the process.

    <u>Variations</u>. Have half the members of teams at opposite ends of each row. In this situation half the team members distribute books on desks to the end of a row. After which awaiting members of teams begin to pick them up alternating in this manner until all team members have taken turns, a given number of laps are completed, or a specific time period has elapsed. In large classes, this eliminates long waits in line.

    Have students set books on their sides as they are placed on desk tops.

    Have first student place books on desks, next one picks them up, alternating in this manner until the relay is completed.

- <u>Jump rope relay</u>. Are jump ropes available? If so, use the basic formation already discussed, but have each team member jump rope to the end of the row and back. Make jump ropes from clothes line if actual jump ropes are not available. Introduce and include appropriate variations for children who for whatever reason cannot jump rope.

- <u>Newspaper relay</u>. Divided into teams, individuals walk with each foot on a piece of newspaper to the goal line and back while holding a piece of newspaper in each hand. A variation for this is to use show boxes or other cardboard boxes on each foot. This relay is good for mentally retarded, visually impaired, and hearing impaired children. Keep directions simple. It might be helpful for a teacher to demonstrate this activity to the group. Even better, be an <u>active</u> participant yourself!!!

These relay approaches can be used in as many ways as teachers--and students--can think of ideas. Additional variations include skipping, galloping, scissors walking, hopping, running backwards, skipping backwards, leaping sideward, balancing a book on the runner's head, putting hats on and off, and imitating various animals.

Still at a Desk

The following exercises are intended to be done while students are seated at their desks. This entire series can be accomplished in approximately seven minutes. Since these exercises can be performed at a desk while students are seated, they disrupt classes very little, and are recommended for times of days when children are restless, but too much time or commotion are neither appropriate nor desirable.

All positions should be held to counts of six and repeated several times unless otherwise indicated. Obviously, children in wheelchairs can easily take part in these activities with little or no adaptation.

. Place hands and arms under the desk and force upward as hard as possible; do with palms up/down.

. Grab the bottom of the desk seat with both hands; pull up with shoulders and hands as hard as possible.

. Push up with upper legs on bottom of the desk and push down with lower arms on top of the desk.

. Place outsides of feet against insides of front chair legs and push out forcibly; reverse with insides of feet against outsides of front chair legs and push in forcibly.

. Lift lower legs up, pull toes back and stretch arms forcibly back, stretching, stretching, stretching!

. Lean over desk, keep back straight, and grasp front edge of desk with arms extended over top of desk; pull back hard.

. Wrap legs around legs of desk and pull forward/push backward.

. Lift legs and reach out with stiff arms to touch toes.

24

Grasp the back legs of the desk and pull upward and forward--keep shoulders locked.

. Grasp hands behind the head, keep the neck straight, force head back and hands forward.

. Flutterkick as in swimming for one (two, three) minutes.

. Place both hands inside desk and push out on the inside of the desk; place palms/backs of hands against sides of desk.

. Rotate head in one direction for about thirty seconds; repeat in the opposite direction.

. Place both arms out to the side and force shoulders back, turn palms of hands up and rotate whole arm (stiff armed) in small circles; start with backward motion.

A good way to lead these exercises is for teachers to do them right along with the students--they are good fitness exercises for teachers too!!! These isometric exercises are performed by astronauts and others who are confined to small areas for long periods of time. This might be of interest to your students. They can name different kinds of people who need to do such exercises then pretend to be these people as they perform the exercises. Kids love to be astronauts!!

Circle Activities

Have class members arrange their desks into a large circle to allow much activity space for interesting circle games and activities. All activities mentioned for individual desks and chairs can be done with this formation.

- Place a mat in the middle of the circle and have individuals perform stunts or other activities when they are called. Many variations are possible--have a student leader decide stunts to be performed; add-on so that each participate does a new stunt in addition to ones performed by those who preceded him/her; free choice by each participant.

- Introduce circle games such as follow-the-leader, musical chairs, and duck-duck-goose.

- Guess Who. One person is asked to leave the room so that a leader can secretly be chosen. This leader gives different gestures and motions at his/her discretion while the rest of the group follows exactly as the leader directs. The person who has left the room gets three guesses to select the leader.

Obstacle Courses

Scatter chairs throughout the classroom and use them for various obstacles so that students can perform basic movement activities around the area. Chairs and desks can become mountains to climb, tunnels to crawl through, bridges to go under, detours to go around, girders on which to balance, dangerous people-eating monsters to squeeze between!! The classroom can become an exciting jungle that a safari of children must go through successfully.

Circuit and Station Activities

Using chairs and desks, set up around the classroom various stations in a circuit so that each child can go to specific stations and perform designated tasks. Two separate circuits can be set up with a class divided into teams. The first team which completely finishes tasks at each station within its circuit is the winning team. For variation of responsibilities and activities among the classmates, assign students to man stations and call out tasks; have different students decide tasks to be performed at each station. For more detailed ideas on circuit and station activities see Practical Pointer Volume 1, Number 2, Circuit and Station Activity Approaches (available from AAHPER/IRUC, 1201 16th Street, N. W., Washington, D. C., 20036, for $2.00).

Miscellaneous Activities and Games

One idea for a desk or chair activity will spark ideas for other activities. The following ideas are presented for use, modification, adaptation, and fuel for further thought and innovation.

. Who says a desk or chair can only be used right-side up? Try this--turn a chair up-side down and toss quoits--rubber quoits, rope rings, or garden hose made into rings of different sizes--toward legs of the chair. A challenging game is made when a scoring system is devised.

. Place 2x4's, broom handles, wooden dowels, or other kinds of poles between rungs of chairs and/or across chair seat--crawl/creep under, step over, move under and over in various combinations.

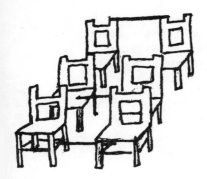

. Place obstacles in a series with each stick or pole at a different height.

. Use scooter boards or gym scooters to go under and around these obstalces in different combinations.

OVER!   UNDER!

. Approach so that an individual has to go over and under obstacles in combinations after (1) demonstrations involving visual input and stimuli, and (2) auditory input as direct commands or problems to solve using exploratory approaches. Increase the number of tasks in the series that the individual must perform as a means of improving sequencing. Interrupt this process by using signals for <u>stop</u> and <u>go</u>. Introduce relationships of red lights and stop, green lights and go.

Chairs and desks can be arranged for use in games requiring throwing skills and hand-eye coordination.

. <u>Flying Saucers</u>. This simple tossing game is designed for four or five participants. Equipment includes paper plates stapled together; circles cut out of paper or made with string—these resemble planets and the moon and should be set up on chairs at various distances from the throwing line. Toss three flying saucers and try to get highest score possible. Closer planets have lower scores.

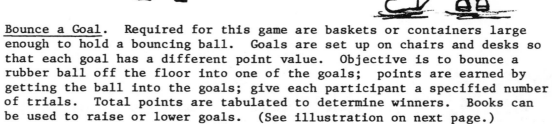

. <u>Bounce a Goal</u>. Required for this game are baskets or containers large enough to hold a bouncing ball. Goals are set up on chairs and desks so that each goal has a different point value. Objective is to bounce a rubber ball off the floor into one of the goals; points are earned by getting the ball into the goals; give each participant a specified number of trials. Total points are tabulated to determine winners. Books can be used to raise or lower goals. (See illustration on next page.)

28

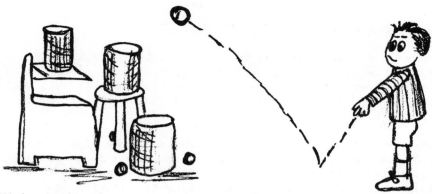

   With simple adaptations these games are suitable for <u>all</u> children. A
child confined to a wheelchair derives just as much pleasure from participating
in these games as anyone else. For activities requiring crawling and creeping
under broom handles, have a child restricted to a wheelchair devise his/her own.
ways for going under an obstacle. Use <u>limbo</u> approaches for participants in
wheelchairs to go under ropes or sticks held by classmates or teachers near the
chair.

   For games requiring tossing objects to a particular goal, moving goals
closer may make the difference between successful and frustrating participation.
If a blind child is trying to toss to a goal, have another child make a noise,
place a radio, or use some other sound device near the goal so that the blind
child can aim by sound. This might be fun and challenging for sighted children
to try blind-folded.

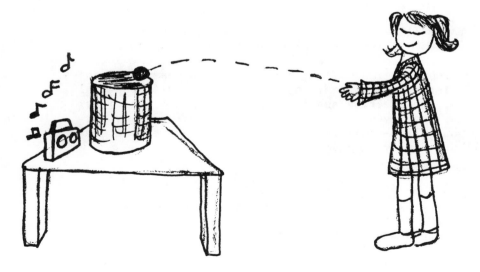

Do You Like to go to the Circus?

Probably no one under the sun doesn't love a circus with its animals, acrobats, flying trapeze artists, tightrope walkers, lion trainers, clowns, and .... When a teacher mentions circus to a classroom full of children, watch for loud and excited responses. If the teacher suggests that all might be in a circus, watch out!!!

Hold a short discussion about circuses. Have members of the class name different people and animals that appear in circuses; list them on the chalk board. Assign or let the class and/or individuals chose what they want to be in the circus. Use desks and chairs to form a three-ring circus with animals and trainer in one circle, acrobats and flying trapeze artists in another circle, and clowns in the third circle. Lively music adds to the spirit and rhythm of performances as the circus parade moves around the room and members of the troupe go to their performing circles. When the circus is ready to present, after a few practices, perhaps teachers and students from other classrooms can be invited to watch. After all, everyone loves the circus!

A Few Final Thoughts

Remember, all of these activities, even basic exercises, should be fun. Keep in mind KISS-MIF!!!!--Keep it super simple--make it fun. Presentation is of utmost importance. Instead of saying "All right class, we're going to exercise now!! They're good for you!!" Why not try this approach--"That was a long arithmatic test, and you all worked very hard. I'll bet you're ready to have some fun, so how about a game of Atlas says!" Then Atlas can say to do all those physical exercises! This is even more effective when the children take turns being Atlas. Activities then become rewards for hard work, not hard work themselves.

Music does much to liven up these activities. Fast and slow music used strategically provides variety in speed, exertion, and fun for ordinary exercises. Add variations to activities by playing records slow to get flow and continuity of movements and give more time to think about what has to be done--or fast for added challenge and fun.*

So, the next time it rains all day or the class and you need breaks, be prepared with various activities. This Practical Pointer has opened some doors, provided some ideas, but is not intended to be all-inclusive. If these activities stimulate your own creative thought, innovation, and resourcefulness and enables you to think of more and different activities, major purpose of this Practical Pointer will be accomplished. Be creative and invent new games and exercises; let your children be creative and invent their own games. Paper-wads may not completely disappear from your class--children will be children--but attitudes and levels of fitness will definitely improve.

---

*Choosing and Using Phonograph Records for Physical Education, Recreation, and Related Activities (AAHPER Publication Sales, 1201 16th Street, N. W., Washington, D. C., 20036, $3.50) provides descriptions of 181 records that have been used successfully in programs and activities involving participants with handicapping conditions.

PRACTICAL POINTERS

ISOKINETIC PHYSICAL FITNESS ACTIVITIES WITH BICYCLE INNERTUBES
FOR ABLE-BODIED AND DISABLED PERSONS

Throughout history different attitudes have affected programs and activities designed to develop and maintain specific components of physical fitness. Such attitudes have ranged from active antagonism and apathy to fitness activities considered as entire physical education programs. In earlier days less attention had to be given to developing and maintaining certain fitness components; life itself required more physical activity.

As lifestyles changed so did needs for more attention to specific components of physical fitness. Such needs permeate all ages and individuals in every community, affect able-bodied and disabled alike, and know no bounds in terms of race, creed, color, national origin, or sex. In fact, many individuals have difficulties in performing certain motor skills and participating in given sports because of insufficient muscular strength and endurance, inflexibility, and inadequate range of motion. These factors along with a variety of other considerations indicate need today for concerted efforts and special attention to physical fitness activities.

Individuals are finding fitness outlets in diverse settings--educational and recreational as well as commercial and personal. Various methods and different approaches are often used in these settings. Many kinds of equipment and vastly different devices can be found in use.

This Practical Pointer deals with physical fitness--muscular strength and endurance, flexibility, and range of motion. A very special and complicated device is used--a bicycle innertube, in fact an old bicycle innertube! This device fits well into most budgets, and enables each individual to have his/her own personal piece of equipment. Qualities found in expensive equipment and costly devices are present in bicycle innertubes.

- Isotonic, isometric, and isokinetic activities can be developed.
- Dual, partner, small group, and individual uses can be explored.
- Games and relays can be devised.

The sky is the limit. Only limitations in student and teacher/leader initiative and creativeness restrict beneficial activities which can be generated with free and fun bicycle innertubes.

Principles and Practices for Successful
Fitness Programs With Bicycle Innertubes

This _Practical Pointer_ focuses on isokinetic physical fitness activities
with bicycle innertubes. Activities presented--not even scratching the scratch
that scratches the surface--can be used to develop and maintain general and
specific components of fitness, to further certain sport skills, and for rehabilitation purposes. Bicycle innertube activities can be tailored to meet
individual needs. To get started--

. Obtain bicycle innertubes--local bicycle shops are glad to find
  constructive uses for their old innertubes; individuals are happy
  to provide innertubes which can no longer be used on their bicycles.

. Review this publication to become familiar with the exercises in
  general and how each is executed with an innertube.

. Review other publications and articles on weight or resistance
  training, isotonic/isometric/isokinetic techniques, and related
  topics.

. Determine general and specific fitness needs with various assessment and observation approaches, formal and informal techniques
  alike.

. Develop specific programs and activities according to the needs of
  each individual; determine specific muscles and muscle groups
  appropriate for and needed in each individual's personalized
  program.

. Include periodic evaluation to show progress and for making
  necessary changes in programs and activities for each individual.

Additional principles and practices to add variety, assist in individualizing according to participant needs, and promote personal progress include--

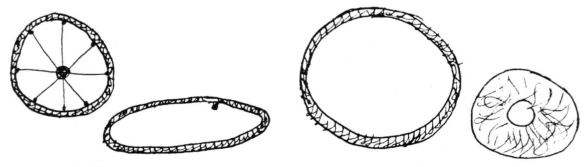

. Use different size innertubes--large and stretched for less resistance;
  small with a great deal of tension for more resistance (wheelchair
  innertubes are super for this).

. Consider other materials for specific program participants--bands cut from automobile innertubes for especially strong individuals; waistband elastic for individuals needing considerably less resistance.

. Cut off the valve stem or tape it to the innertube for safety purposes.

. Paint bands or place masking tape of different colors at regular distances around the innertube to control resistance systematically; use the valve stem as the point of reference when painting bands or placing masking tape on an innertube.

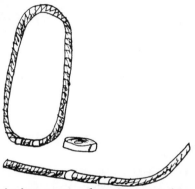

. Vary foot and/or hand positions on the innertube to change resistance--move feet and/or hands closer together to reduce resistance and further apart to increase resistance.

. Attach small bar--wooden dowel, cut off broom handle, lummi stick--as a means of easily changing and controlling resistance.

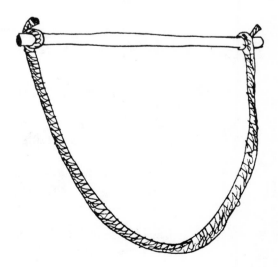

Loop portions of the innertube around the bar or cut diagonal slits into the bar to hold the innertube securely.

. Cut the innertube so it is one long piece rather than a closed loop. One way to accomplish this is by cutting on either side of the valve stem so as to remove it with a small section of the innertube. Tape ends on the innertube with friction, adhesive, masking, or strapping tape. Virtually all exercises described can be done when the innertube is in one long piece. Greater flexibility can be attained with a one piece innertube, especially when performing certain side-bending and twisting exercises. Greater variations in resistance can be attained with the innertube in this form as compared to an uncut innertube.

. Control number of repititions and amount of resistance according to desired end results...

   ...fifteen or more repetitions with low resistance for body tone and definition;

   ...eight to twelve repetitions with medium resistance for body definition, muscular endurance; and

   ...three to five repetitions with high resistance for muscular strength, bulk, and size.

. Work up to two or three sets of each exercise. One way to accomplish this is by doing one set, resting a specified time-- ten, twenty, or more seconds--doing the next set, and continuing in this manner until reaching the desired number of sets. In this gradual process, do not exceed specified maximum number of repetitions on first and/or second sets--the key is in attaining specified maximum number of repetitions on each set.

. Start off slowly, gradually increasing repetitions and sets to avoid unnecessary soreness and tightness while becoming familiar with this training device.

. Be sure to warm up properly and adequately by following usual and appropriate warm up regimens.

. Be sure to warm down properly and adequately by following usual and appropriate warm down regimens.

. Progress slowly, cautiously, and intelligently for whatever purposes the innertube is used.

. Use the innertube as a means of working on and improving certain sport skills as well as for developing specific components of physical fitness.

. Devise and use appropriate forms to record progress and control progressions of individual participants.

. Analyze individual movement needs and devise innertube exercises
to meet these needs--experiment, create, innovate.

. Attach a portion of an innertube on the hinge side of a closed
door, secure the innertube to a heavy standard by looping it
around the standard, or loop and secure the innertube to

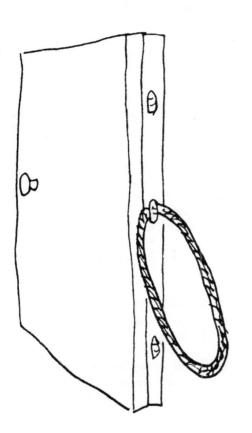

horizontal supports or lattice portions of a fence to expand
uses of this versatile device. When using a standard, be sure
to work with partners or in small groups so the standard, no
matter how heavy, can be held physically. Tape the portion of
the innertube to be held in the door to reduce wear and tear
on the innertube; use friction, adhesive, or strapping tape,
preferably around the area of the valve stem, for this purpose.
Position the innertube at different heights or levels in the
door, around the standard, or to the fence according to exercises, movements, patterns, or skills being performed.

. Adapt interval and circuit training techniques to make the
innertube even more appealing and functional for individual
participants. These techniques can also be adapted and
modified' for promoting cardiorespiratory/cardiovascular
endurance from innertube activities.

. Use background music to add to appeal and versatility of the
innertube.

35

. Change pace by having individuals perform exercises as many
  times as possible in specified numbers of seconds or see how
  long it takes to do a given number of repetitions.

. Insist that movements be performed correctly and through the
  full range of motion. Whenever possible have participant
  start each movement from a fully extended position attained
  with a pre-movement stretch of involved muscles and muscle
  groups.

. Control breathing by inhaling during exertion and exhaling
  during relaxation phases of exercises. Reduce force of effort
  and exertion by reversing this breathing pattern--i.e., exhale
  during exertion and inhale during relaxation. For some participants, natural breathing throughout execution of exercises
  may be most appropriate and effective.

. Execute each movement so that two or three seconds are used on
  exertion and four or five seconds on relaxation phases of exercises. This not only facilitates proper execution of exercises
  but helps in further developing weaker extensor muscles.
  Rhythmic execution of this type adds to benefits derived.

. Use a wide base with feet parallel and shoulder width apart for
  most exercises.

. Use a grip in which hands are approximately a shoulder width
  apart unless directions to the contrary for specific exercises
  are indicated.

. Change grips to bring in and work more actively with muscles and
  muscle groups antagonistic to those basic to described exercises
  and movement patterns.

. Use partners working alternately as a means of increasing the
  number of participants at any given time, especially when space
  is limited or when doing exercises with the innertube attached
  in a door, looped around a heavy standard, or attached to a
  fence. This procedure can also be used when interval techniques
  are incorporated in innertube exercise programs.

The Exercises

Following are innertube exercises designed for many different purposes.
A basic and simple format has been used which includes...

...name of the exercise;

...starting position;

...movements for execution;

...variations where appropriate.

Exercises have been listed alphabetically. A Handy Use Index of all exercises included is provided to help readers select exercises in terms of specific needs--i.e., arms, legs, shoulders, trunk, back, abdomen; flexion, extension; abduction, adduction. (See page 22 for the Handy Use Index.)

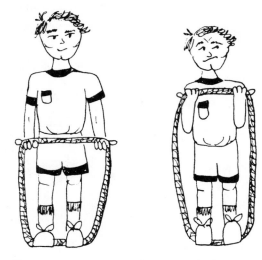

Curls--Regular

Starting Position--Stand on inner-tube so that palms of hands face away from the body with thumbs to the outside; be sure arms are fully extended and elbows touch the body; rest inner-tube against thighs.

Movements--Bend elbows and bring innertube up until elbows are fully flexed and innertube is just below chin level and against upper portions of chest.

Return to starting position.

Variations--Do one arm at a time. Alternate one arm and then the other.

Stand on middle of a cut innertube and perform exercise movements with ends of the innertube.

Curls--Reverse

Execute exactly as Curls--Regular except grasp innertube so that palms of hands face toward body with thumbs to the inside.

Dead Lift

Starting Position--Stand on inner-tube or on ends of cut innertube.

Grasp innertube so that palms of hands face toward body, thumbs to the inside, and arms extend down from shoulders.

Bend forward from the waist until upper body is approximately parallel with floor or ground.

Use high tension for maximum

resistance in this exercise.

Keep elbows straight by using a small bar and rolling innertube down; if no bar is used, position hands on innertube so they are about six inches above floor or ground.

Movements--Keep arms and legs locked and move to standing position.

Return to starting position.

Variations--Start in a seated position on the floor and move to a supine position.

Flys

Starting Position--Attach an intact innertube or middle of a cut innertube into a closed door, loop it around a heavy standard, or attach it to a fence so ends are free to use.

Stand with back toward door, standard, or fence.

Grasp innertube or ends with palms of hands facing forward, thumbs up, and arms extended to side so that they are slightly back and behind the body.

Movements--Bring arms forward until hands meet in front of the body making sure arms remain straight and at shoulder level throughout the exercise.

Return to starting position.

Variations--Reverse positions so the individual faces the door standard or fence, has palms of hands out, thumbs down, and holds the innertube together in front of body with arms extended; bring arms back as far as possible and then return to starting position.

Stand on middle of cut innertube, bend forward until back is parallel with floor or ground, grasp ends of innertube with palms of hands first in down then in up positions, and bring ends of innertube backward and away from sides as far as they will go; return to starting position.

Front Raises

Starting Position--Stand on innertube or on ends of cut innertube.

Grasp innertube with palms of hands facing down and thumbs to the inside.

Extend arms forward so that they make a 45 degree angle with the body.

Movements--Raise the innertube so that it goes directly over head keeping elbows fully extended throughout the exercise.

Return to starting position.

Variations--Start from position in which hands and innertube rest against the thighs.

Perform in a supine position on the floor.

Reverse positions of hands so that palms face up and thumbs are to the outside.

Kicks

Standing Position--Attach innertube in a door, around a heavy standard, or to a fence.

Position body and place portion of foot in the innertube according to desired movements--

. Stand with back toward door, standard, or fence, and toe down for front kicks.

Face the door with heel down for back kicks.

. Stand with side toward door and toe in innertube for

side kicks.

Use stool, chair, or another person to assist in maintaining balance as needed.

Movements--Move leg from hip in desired direction--forward, backward, sideward--keeping knee straight throughout the exercise.

Return to the starting position. Change back position in relation to door, standard, or fence to emphasize segments of muscles and muscle groups important during different stages of kicking movements and patterns.

Lateral Raises

Standing Position--Stand on innertube or in middle of cut innertube.

Hold innertube or ends out to side and away from the back so arms make an approximate 45 degree angle with the body; palms of hands are up with thumbs back.

39

Movements—Bring arms up until
  hands meet with arms fully extended overhead.

  Return to starting position.

Variations—Start with hands at
  sides and arms extended
  straight down.

  Reverse positions of hands
  so palms are down and thumbs
  forward.

Leg Lifts

Starting Position—Attach innertube in door, around a heavy
  standard, or to a fence.

  Take a supine position with
  head away from the door,
  standard, or fence, and
  innertube resting across tops
  of ankles.

  Keep small of back depressed
  and flat against floor
  throughout this exercise;
  extend arms down from
  shoulders; place and keep
  hands flat on floor next to
  thighs throughout the exercise.

Movements—Raise innertube into the air keeping legs fully extended throughout
  the exercise.

  Return to starting position.

Variations—Raise legs alternately.

  Raise one leg for a given number of repetitions and then the other leg.

  Increase distance innertube is raised off floor.

  Bend knees and bring left/right/both knees back to the chest.

Press--Alternate

Starting Position—Stand on innertube or in middle of cut innertube.

Grasp innertube or the two ends with palms of hands up facing away from the body, and thumbs to the inside.

Hold one hand at about waist level and extend the other arm over head until the elbow is fully extended.

Rotate lower arm so that palm of the hand is up and thumb to the outside while the innertube is being raised by the other arm to extend effectiveness and range of motion of this exercise.

Movements--Extend the arm at waist level over head while bringing the arm starting overhead down to waist level so that starting positions of arms have been reversed.

Reverse movements returning to starting position.

Variation--Extend the overhead arm toward the opposite side to add some side bending to the exercise.

Press--French

Starting Position--Stand on innertube or on ends of cut innertube.

Grasp innertube with palms facing forward, thumbs to the inside, and hands close together although not touching.

Bring innertube up and over-the-head so that it is behind and below the neck at about shoulder level.

Keep elbows facing up and close to head and ears.

Movements--Move innertube to extended position overhead.

Return to starting position.

Variation--Do one arm at a time.

Press--Regular

Starting Position--Stand on innertube or on ends of cut innertube.

Grasp innertube with palms
facing away from the body,
thumbs to the inside, and
palms slightly up so innertube starts at chest level.

Movements--Move innertube above
the head until elbows are
fully extended.

Return to starting position.

Variations--Start movements
from a position behind the
neck rather than at chest
level in front of the body.

Alternate between positions in front of the body and behind the neck.

Press--Standing

Starting Position--Attach innertube in door, around a heavy standard, or to a
fence.

Grasp ends of cut innertube with palms facing down, thumbs to the inside, and
hands touching the armpits; or

Stand inside of innertube if
not cut holding the innertube
with palms facing down, thumbs
to the inside, and hands
touching the armpits.

Movements--Move arms forward
until elbows are fully extended keeping elbows high
throughout the execution.

Return to starting position.

Press--Squat

Starting Position--Stand on innertube or on ends of cut innertube.

Take a half-squat position so thighs are no more than parallel with the
floor or ground.

Grasp innertube with palms slightly up, thumbs to the inside, and innertube
just below chin level.

Movements--Move from squatting to standing position fully extending the innertube overhead.

Return to starting position.

Pull Downs

Starting Position--Attach innertube in door, around a heavy standard, or to a fence; attach a cut innertube so middle is in door, around standard, or to fence so that ends extend.

Grasp innertube or ends with palms facing down, thumbs to the inside, and arms extended so hands are virtually touching each other.

Movements--Pull innertube down between the legs keeping arms straight throughout the exercise.

Return to starting position.

Variations--Grasp innertube with palms facing up and thumbs to the outside.

Rowing--Regular

Starting Position--Stand on innertube or on ends of cut innertube.

Grasp innertube with palms facing toward the body and slightly downward, and thumbs to the inside. Bend forward from the waist until upper body is approximately parallel with the floor or ground.

Use a stick and/or roll the innertube down to keep elbows straight.

Movements--Bring innertube up to the chest keeping elbows high.

43

and pointed outwards throughout the exercise.

Return to starting position.

Rowing--Upright

Starting Position--Stand on inner-
    tube or on ends of cut innertube.

    Grasp innertube with palms
    facing toward the body, thumbs
    to the inside, and hands touch-
    ing each other so innertube
    rests against thighs.

Movements--Bring innertube straight
    up until it is at chin level
    keeping elbows above the inner-
    tube throughout the movement.

    Return to starting position.

Variation--Do in a supine position on the floor.

Shoulder Abduction

Starting Position--Attach innertube in door, around a heavy standard, or to a
    fence. Stand so left or right side of the body is toward door, standard,
    or fence.

    Grasp innertube with palm of hand away from the door, standard, or fence
    facing by side toward door, standard or fence, thumb facing forward and so
    arm is extended down and at midline of body.

    Keep innertube parallel with the
    body throughout the exercise.

Movements--Move innertube up and
    away from midline of body so
    arm remains extended throughout
    abduction movements.

    Return to starting position.

    Reverse positions and repeat
    for abduction of the other
    shoulder.

Variations--Do with arm starting
    from different levels and in
    various positions in relation
    to midline of body.

44

Reverse position of hand so palm of hand faces away from door, standard, or fence and thumb is down

Shoulder Adduction

Starting Position--Attach inner-tube in door, around a heavy standard, or to a fence.

Stand so left or right side of the body is toward door, standard, or fence.

Grasp innertube with palm of hand closer to the door, standard, or fence down, thumb forward so arm is extended at shoulder level and parallel to floor or ground.

Keep innertube parallel with body throughout the exercise.

Movements--Move innertube down and toward midline of body so arm remains extended throughout adduction movements.

Return to starting position.

Reverse positions and repeat for the adduction of other shoulder.

Variations--Do with arm starting from different levels and in various positions in relation to initial parallel starting positions.

Reverse position of hand so palm of hand is up with thumb pointing back toward the body.

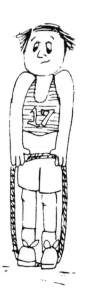

Shoulder Shrugs

Starting Position--Stand on inner-tube or on ends of cut innertube.

Grasp innertube with palms facing the body, thumbs to the inside, and arms extended directly down from the shoulders.

Use high tension for maximum resistance in this exercise.

Movements--Move (shrug) shoulders up and toward ears.

45

Return to starting position.

Variations--Bring innertube up and over the head so the top portion of the innertube rests on the shoulders; from this position do shoulder shrugs as
   described above.

Reverse hand position so palms face away from the body with thumbs to the
   outside.

Side Bends

Starting Position--Stand on innertube or in middle of cut innertube.

Grasp innertube so palms of
hands face toward sides of body
and thumbs are forward.

Bring one side or end of innertube up to thigh or armpit
level, leaning or bending sideward toward the other side.

Movements--Reverse positions bring-
   ing low side or end of innertube to thigh or armpit level, leaning or bending
   sideward toward the other side.

Reverse positions.

Variation--Start movements with innertube at different levels between foot and
   waist.

Sit-Ups

Starting Position--Attach innertube
   in door, around a heavy standard,
   or to a fence.

Sit with back to door, body at
approximately 45 degrees, and
innertube over shoulders.

Grasp innertube with palms of
hands facing away from the body,
thumbs together, and so innertube
comes over the shoulders and
is parallel to the floor.

Movements--Move forward toward
   straight-up sitting position.

Continue to bend forward bringing nose, chin, and face to knees.

Variations--Have someone hold extended legs at ankles.

Spread legs and bring nose, chin, and face to the floor.

Sport Skills

Starting Positions--Attach innertube in a door, around a heavy standard, to a fence, or place middle of cut innertube in door, tie around a standard, or secure to a fence.

Place innertube at a level appropriate for specific skills being considered.

Stand in positions to facilitate movements and at stages desired in movements themselves.

Movements--Virtually any skills in specific sports can be simulated using the innertube including--

   . Angling--casting

   . Archery--draw and anchor bow

   . Badminton--serve overhand, drive, forehand, backhand

   . Baseball and Softball--batting, throwing from different positions

   . Basic Skills--run, throw, kick

   . Basketball--passes of various kinds

. <u>Bowling</u>--roll ball

. <u>Cross-Country Skiing</u>--arm movements

. <u>Football</u>--pass, punt, place kick, block

. <u>Golf</u>--drive, approach shots, long iron shots

. <u>Handball</u>--serve, forehand, backhand, overhead

. <u>Hockey and Field Hockey</u>--pass, face-off, or bully

. <u>Lacrosse</u>--throwing, goal shooting, passing

. <u>Raquetball</u>--serve forehand, backhand, overhead

. <u>Rowing</u>--using oars

. <u>Soccer</u>--heads, kicks of different types

. <u>Swimming</u>--arm and leg movements for all strokes

. <u>Tennis</u>--serve, forehand, backhand, overhead slam

. <u>Track and Field</u>--running, putting, shot, throwing discus, throwing
javelin, arm action in long jump, lead leg action in high jump

. <u>Volleyball</u>--serve, spike

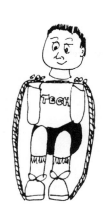

Squats

<u>Starting Position</u>--Stand on innertube
or on ends of cut innertube.

Grasp innertube with palms of hands
facing away from the body, turned
slightly up, and thumbs to inside.

<u>Movements</u>--Squat down to a sitting
position so thighs are no further
down than parallel with the floor
or ground; use a chair or bench if
necessary to prevent going too far
down in squat movements.

Return to starting position.

Toe Raises

<u>Starting Position</u>--Stand on innertube
or on ends of cut innertube.

Grasp innertube with palms facing
toward the body and thumbs to inside.

Bend forward from the waist until
upper body is approximately parallel
with the floor or ground.

To keep elbows straight it may be
necessary to use a stick and roll

the innertube down; if no stick is used, position hands on innertube so they are about six inches above the floor or ground.

Movements--Lift on the stick or pull on the innertube while simultaneously raising up on the toes.

Return to starting position.

Trunk Twister

Starting Position--Attach middle
of cut innertube in door, tie
around a heavy standard, or
secure to a fence.

Grasp ends of innertube or
innertube with palms facing
down, thumbs to inside, and
one arm extended directly
forward from the shoulder
and the other arm bent
with hand turned toward the
body and resting on the waist.

Movements--Twist trunk so extended arm crosses in front of the body and as far to the other side as possible.

Keep arm straight and elbow extended with innertube riding across the arm between elbow and wrist.

Return to starting position.

Variations--Execute all movements to one side and back and then repeat to the other side.

Alternate movements first to one side and then to the other throughout the exercise.

50

Handy Use Index

Exercise*	Page	Arms	Legs	Shoulders	Abdomen	Trunk	Back	Chest	Flexion	Extension	Abduction	Adduction
Curls-Regular	8	x							x			
Curls-Reverse	8	x								x		
Dead Lift	8						x			x		
Flys	9			x			x	x			x	x
Front Raises	9			x								
Kicks	10		x		x				x	x	x	x
Lateral Raises	10			x							x	
Leg Lifts	11				x				x			
Press--Alternate	11						x			x		
Press--French	12	x								x		
Press--Regular	12			x			x			x		
Press--Standing	13							x		x		
Press--Squat	13		x							x		
Pull Downs	14						x					
Rowing--Regular	14						x		x			
Rowing--Upright	15			x								
Shoulder Abduction	15			x							x	
Shoulder Adduction	16			x								x
Shoulder Shrugs	16			x								
Side Bends	17				x	x						
Sit-Ups	17				x				x			
Sport Skills	18			Specific Sport Skills								
Squats	20		x							x		
Toe Raises	20		x							x		
Trunk Twister	21				x	x	x					

*Index information and classifications are based on
described executions of basic exercises; variations
and modifications make it possible to extend and
expand these uses.

PRACTICAL POINTERS

AEROBIC FITNESS FOR THE
MENTALLY RETARDED

Dan Bauer

A widely-held belief is that the mentally retarded can benefit from a planned physical activity program. Studies by Julian Stein have shown that physical fitness and motor development of the mentally retarded do not need to be adversely affected by slower mental development. The fact that motor development is affected in many instances is probably not so much a primary effect of the retardation but a secondary effect caused by limited opportunities for instruction and participation. When the level of activity declines, fitness also declines, and if the individual has limited opportunity for instruction and participation in games, then specific coordinations will not normally develop. Thus, a vicious cycle is set into motion: the lack of endurance and skill puts the child at a disadvantage and for those reasons alone, may not be accepted in the active games being played by peers.[1]

While there are few laboratory studies of fitness among different handicapped groups, a growing body of research substantiates the low cardiovascular fitness of handicapped persons. This coupled with other high risk factors such as obesity, physical inactivity, poor nutrition, fear of failure, and medication, make many handicapped individuals prime candidates for heart disease.[2]

The physical educator is challenged to provide a comprehensive instructional program which will permit exposure, improvement, and success in levels of motor performance and physical fitness. The following material will deal with one area of the total physical education program, aerobic fitness. The goal of the aerobic fitness program is to develop, improve, and enhance the aerobic fitness of the moderately retarded through a varied program of conditioning and play activities.

THE ORGANIZATION OF THE AEROBIC FITNESS PROGRAM

One of the greatest services an Adapted Physical Education teacher or any physical educator for that matter, can render to a community is to care for the physical fitness of children. In addition to maintaining the fitness of the students, the teacher should seek to identify the sub-fit child, to determine the causes of low fitness, and ameliorate them by designing an individualized exercise program for each child. The teacher can use a modification of Clarke's Case Study approach as a guide for designing and implementing a fitness program to meet the individual needs of the students.[3]

The procedures used by Clarke for improving the fitness levels of students below accepted standards are more than just theory. Clarke's procedures have evolved through use in over a third of a century in school and college physical education programs. Following are some suggested steps:

1. Have the students be given an adequate health checkup. This is the proper starting point of any physical fitness program. The physical examination by a medical doctor should establish the activity tolerance level and the type of activities for which the student can benefit.

2. Select those who are below predetermined standards of strength, stamina, and other basic physical fitness elements through the administration of valid tests available to the physical educator.

3. For the students who are sub-fit, conduct physical activities selected to improve their condition. For example, obese students can begin a walking program; a blind student can ride a stationary exercise bike.

4. After six weeks, review individual programs to determine those students who are making progress and to identify those who are not responding favorably to exercise. For those students who are improving at a satisfactory rate, the exercise program can be continued with progressive dosage. For those students making little or no progress, their individual program may have been poorly conceived and may have to be altered or changed completely. Repeat reviews of the student's programs at intervals of about six weeks in order to continue checking on the progress made by each sub-fit child. This will entail chart and record-keeping by the instructor.

HOW LONG TO EXERCISE - HOW HARD

An important consideration in planning exercise or activity periods for aerobic fitness improvement is the length of time to exercise and the intensity needed.

There is much controversy over how long a person should exercise. To illustrate two extremes, Dr. Lawrence E. Morehouse, Ph.D. suggests 10 minutes, three times a week; while Dr. Thomas Bassler, M.D., suggests 60 minutes, six times a week. [4]

Somewhere between the two above-mentioned extremes lies the optimal amount of exercise for most people. Part of the confusion stems from failing to take intensity into account when comparing these estimates.

The use of the exercise heart rate is a simple and practical method of monitoring the intensity of exercise. It is safer and better than using distance or time alone during the early phase of training. It is the intensity of exercise that has the greatest significance in fitness training. If the student is exercising at only 20% of his actual capacity there will be no training effect. On the other hand, if he exercises at 100% of his capacity he may collapse.

Dr. Cooper has published a table which may help the teacher get some idea of what intensity the student has to exercise at to achieve a training effect.

Table 5. Cooper's heart rates.[5]

	Training Effect				
Daily time requirements (minutes)	180	90	45	20	10
Heart rate (beats per minute)	110	120	130	140	150

A student with a heart rate of 110 would have to exercise for 180 minutes to achieve a training effect, but a student with a heart rate of 150 only has to exercise for 10 minutes to achieve the training effect.

The Borg Scale given below in Table 6 gives an estimate of exertion put forth according to heart rate. The educator charting heart rates can use the scale as a guide as to how much effort the student is putting out.

Table 6. Borg scale perceived exertion.[6]

Rating		Pulse
6- 7	very-very light	60-70
8- 9	very light	80-80
10-11	fairly light	100-110
12-13	somewhat light	120-130
14-15	hard	140-150
16-17	very hard	160-170
18-20	very-very hard	180-200

AEROBIC FITNESS ACTIVITIES

Meeting the needs of the retarded student for aerobic fitness is not simple. Many of the students will voluntarily participate; others if left alone, will sit and do nothing. Motivation is necessary to make the student want to participate. Participation in the activities should be encouraged, but there should be no resort to pressure tactics. The mentally retarded student needs and seeks approval, and can often be led to cooperate and participate if he/she knows that this is what the teacher desires and approves.

The mentally retarded are a very heterogenous group. Among the moderately retarded there will be many different skills and motivational levels. Many different techniques of instruction may be necessary to solicit a desired response.

Those who develop programs for the moderately retarded should remember that social or mental age is more important than chronological age. At the lower level of mental ability or social age the moderately retarded child may show little interest in play. However, those with high levels of intelligence or social behavior can participate in group activities and games if slowly and carefully taught.

Although the range of activities in physical education programs for the severely and profoundly retarded is necessarily limited, the activities listed on the pages that follow will contribute to increasing cardiorespiratory endurance or increased tolerance to exercise. Many of the activities listed contribute to more than just cardiorespiratory endurance and could be used in an agility or strength-building program also. The activities offered build on basic motor skills such as walking, running, crawling, etc., and after these skills have been mastered, new activities building on these skills may be introduced.

What follows is a discussion of individual and group activities and games that can be used to increase the aerobic fitness levels of the moderately retarded student.

WALKING

In their book, Creative Walking for Physical Fitness, Harry Johnson, M.D., and Ralph Bass stated that walking is perfect for achieving physical fitness. According to Dr. Johnson, walking is beneficial to cardiovascular health, weight control, figure control, mental activity, and overall health. [7]

The YMCA walking program recommends a ten-week conditioning program of walking that gradually increases distance covered and pace walked. The ultimate objective of the YMCA program is sufficient fitness to walk two miles in thirty minutes. At this pace the walker's energy expenditure will increase four to six times the basal metabolic rate. [8]

Walking is an excellent activity for the mentally retarded. Walking can be done at school, at home, or in the neighborhood, and is helpful in building endurance and weight control. According to Astrand,

It is particularly important to stimulate young individuals to regular physical activity, for such activity will in the long run effectively counteract obesity by keeping the individual within the range where spontaneous caloric intake is properly regulated by the caloric output. The amount of work (e.g., distance moved) is more important for the caloric expenditure than the intensity of work. Walking about 2 miles a day during a 10-year period demands an amount of energy contained in about 180 lbs. of adipose tissue. [9]

In initiating a walking program with the moderately retarded it is important to begin the walking program at each student's tolerance level and attempt to build upward from that point using the overload principle. Some obese and poorly conditioned students may only be able to walk 220-440 yards when first beginning the program.

Cooper recommends the following walking exercise program for people just beginning to exercise:

Table 3. Walking exercise program [10]

Week	Distance (Miles)	Time (min.)	Freq/Week
1	1.0	15:00	5
2	1.0	14:00	5
3	1.0	13:45	5
4	1.5	21:30	5
5	1.5	21:00	5
6	1.5	20:30	5

Teaching Suggestions

1. Record distance covered or time walked by each student and gradually try to increase that amount. A good goal is to have the student walk at least two miles a day.

2. Set up a small circuit, track, or designated course for the students

3. It is important to have a track or designated area for the students to run or run-walk on. This can be a sidewalk, gym area, or a field marked with rope or lines. The course should be designed so that each lap or circuit is a convenient unit. One hundred and ten yards seems to work well with the mentally retarded. By knowing the distance around the track the teacher can easily chart distance run or walked.

4. To add the needed structure it is probably best to always begin the running at the same end of the course or track and always have the students run in the same direction. Reward and praise those who stay on course.

5. Students with certain types of handicaps, such as cardiac abnormalities, asthma, and diabetes should run within stipulated medical limitations. Also, progression in running programs should be slow. The development of endurance is the result of a deep systematic capacity, which changes slowly in response to the demands put on it.

6. Distance run can be charted and motivation increased by giving out certificates or rewards for certain distances covered during the semester or year, e.g., for 10 miles run, 25 miles, 50 miles etc.

JUMPING ROPE

Jumping, or skipping rope, can be an easy exercise or an extremely demanding one. The ability to provide different intensities of exertion makes jumping rope a flexible and useful exercise. In addition, jump ropes are inexpensive, portable, and compact. Jump ropes can be used alone, or with other students, indoors or outside. Once proficiency is obtained, very little space for jumping is needed.

Rope jumping can be used to develop agility, balance, rhythm, and in particular, aerobic fitness.

The table below gives an idea of the energy cost of jumping rope. [11]

Table 4. Energy cost of jumping rope.

Number of Turns (per minute)	Calories Spent (per minute)
50-60	6.67
70-80	7.25
90-100	8.58
110-120	11.75
130-140	15.67

Not all of the moderately retarded will learn how to jump rope, but many can be taught this skill. As an introduction to jumping rope the teacher may want to use the following activity as an introduction.

For equipment a 15-25 foot rope is needed. Have two students hold either end of the rope and use the following progression:

1. Hold center of rope on the ground and move it slowly back and forth on the ground while the student jumps over it as the rope moves along.

2. Increase the speed at which the students move the rope along the ground so the student has to jump faster.

3. Have the children holding the rope swing it back and forth slightly above ground so the student has to jump over it.

4. Swing the rope back and forth in a slow circle while students jump over it.

5. See which student can jump over the rope 5 times in a row, 10, 20, etc.

Once the students have the idea of jumping over a swinging rope held by others the concept of jumping rope individually can be introduced. Teaching this concept may require time and much patience on the part of the teacher, but many of the moderately retarded will be able to learn this skill.

Teaching Suggestions

1. The rope must fit the student. The correct length should reach the armpits when held beneath the feet.

2. To learn jumping without the rope, have the student stand with forearms down and in rear of the ribs and hands 8-10 inches out from the hips. With both feet together, have him/her hop an inch or so off the floor, with a slight bend at the knees.

   Have the students do about 20 such bounces to get the rhythm and then have them make a forward circle of the hands by moving the wrists, pretending that they are turning a rope as they bounce off the floor.

3. Once the idea is grasped by the student, start the student working with the jump rope.

4. Start by having the student hold both ends or handles of the rope in one hand; have the student hold the rope at the side and swing the rope rhythmically in a circle to the side of himself/herself in time with the bounce. Explain or show that the rope should hit the floor when he/she is off the floor. Once the student can do this or grasp this concept, he/she should have no trouble passing the rope under the feet when airborne.

5. The student can be taught to put the rope behind him/her and as he/she

brings the rope forward say outloud, "turn and jump." This gives the student the idea of jumping as the rope comes forward. At the beginning level the student may bring the rope forward and forget to jump as the rope hits the feet. They should then step over the rope and bring the rope forward again, repeating out loud, "turn and jump." Eventually the student will get the idea to turn the rope forward and jump at about the time the rope passes near the feet.

6. Allow plenty of room for each child.

7. Avoid overfatigue; as the students practice they will be able to sustain the activity for a longer period.

8. Music, e.g., top ten tunes, disco, may help the student to enjoy the activity more.

9. Manual guidance as a method of instruction may be necessary with some children.

10. Rewards may be used as a means of motivation. They can take the form of two, or five-minute jump clubs--the student can get a shoulder patch, certificate, or candy award for making the club.

11. Demonstration can be an effective teaching device. Once students see the instructor jumping rope they may be able to mimic the skill.

ROLLER SKATING

Roller skating is a good activity for improving cardiovascular fitness. Since skating burns 295-350 calories (leisure skating) or 520 to 620 calories (vigorous skating) it can also play an important part in weight control.

Roller skating is an activity in which most normal children have at some time participated. Skating can be enjoyed on the playground, sidewalk, alone, or at the local arena with friends or family. The moderately retarded child, who may be over-protected by his family, can learn the roller skating skill in physical education class, and practice it at home or around the neighborhood. Roller skating is a lifetime sport and can be enjoyed by individuals of all ages and skill levels.

While roller skating is a reasonably safe sport, safety rules and close supervision are necessary. Therefore, prior to beginning the roller skating unit the instructor may want to explain safety rules to the students. Some suggested safety rules are:

1. No pushing or shoving.

2. No touching other skaters.

3. Watch where you are going.

4. Let other skaters pass.

5. Slow down at corners.

6. If your skate comes off, go to the side of the skating area and put it back on.

Before any actual skating is attempted, students need to know how to put on and remove their own skates. This task may at first seem time-consuming, but its accomplishment in the long run will provide for more organized skating sessions. The instructor's time will be utilized in the skating lesson and not on putting on skates.

Teaching Suggestions

1. Problems will arise in starting a skating program and teaching the basics. Some methods to help the beginning skater can include:

   A. Provision of a carpeted area or mats so that those learning to skate will not fall on a hard surface. This also slows the skater down.

   B. Placing masking tape on the wheels can slow down those with balance problems.

   C. Provision of skate aids, chairs, or carts with wheels to give those learning, skate support.

   D. The teaching of fundamentals with the student having one skate on at a time.

   E. Beginning progressions with:

      1) Getting up safely from the floor with one skate on (right foot).

      2) Hanging on to a skate aid or chair with both hands for assistance in maintaining balance while shifting weight to the right skate and pushing with the left foot.

      3) Sliding forward on right skate while holding left foot off the ground.

      4) Skating on two skates with teacher aid, or a cart with wheels for support.

      5) Skating over the gym floor or area in a circle formation unaided.

2. As the students gain skill and confidence, game activities can be introduced. Some examples might include:

   A. Relays can use a number of combinations between teams (skating backwards, around obstacles, carrying a ball); the possibilities are numerous.

   B. Broom or floor hockey played on skates.

60

C.   Dodge ball.

3. Many of the students will enjoy skating to music, e.g., top ten, disco, etc.

4. Certificates or rewards may be given to those students who may want to skate for distance, e.g., 10 miles, 50 miles, or 100 miles.

STATIONARY BIKE RIDING

Stationary bike riding can be used for those moderately retarded students who may need extra exercise or whose associated handicaps may make other aerobic activities difficult. Use the stationary bike for the mentally retarded blind students and for those who are so obese that walking is difficult or hard on legs or ankles.

Stationary bicycles are produced as expensive, calibrated models, either mechanically or electrically braked or as inexpensive uncalibrated models. The calibrated models have levels of resistance that read out in watts, KgM (kilogram meters), or KpM (Kilopond meters).

Good exercise bicycles have a calibrated resistance knob or level with definite settings on it. The settings consistently provide the same exercise challenge, so that, for example, if the bicycle is calibrated at 300 KgM for one day, it will hold that setting the following day, or for an even longer amount of time. Less adequate and expensive exercise bicycles have settings that are not reproducible and slip or have no numbers on the resistance knob at all, so that it is almost impossible to know if the student is exercising at the same KgM of resistance from day to day.

Teaching Suggestions

1. The bicycle should be fitted to the exerciser. The seat height should be adjusted correctly so that the leg muscles can function most efficiently. With the toe on the pedal, there should be a small bend at the knee when the pedal is in the fully down position and the seat is at the correct height.

2. Handle bars should be positioned so that the body is relaxed and leaning slightly forward, since hanging onto awkwardly placed handlebars alters the mode of exercise from isotonic to partly isometric.

3. Progression can be programmed by increasing the length of time of each exercise period, increasing the tension level of the braking device or resistance against which the student is working; gradually shortening rest pauses.

4. Motivation may be increased by letting the student exercise to music or in front of a television set watching an interesting program.

5. The mileage pedaled by each student can be recorded and awards or certificates handed out for riding 50, 100, or 200 miles, etc.

Bike Riding

        Bike riding is an excellent activity for children and young adults. It has the advantages of conditioning the cardiovascular system and being fun at the same time.

        Another advantage is that bicycling subjects the body to little trauma. The obese, overweight, or the very unfit sometimes find that running causes some leg problems. Bike riding is not hard on the legs and is excellent for improving the strength of the leg and back muscles.

        Tricycling, or bike riding, is good for the student as soon as he can support his trunk in a sitting position whether he can walk or not. There are harnesses that come with some tricycles so the child's sitting balance can be supported while riding. The child's feet may be fastened to the pedals and the tricycle pulled about. This sets the alternating pattern necessary for walking and also serves to loosen tension in the knees.

A blind student pedaling a stationary exercise bike.

Teaching Suggestions

1. Determine the suitable size bike or trike for the student, one that allows the student to reach the pedals comfortably and have a good grasp on the handle bars.

2. To entice the student to move while on the bike, the teacher may hold a reward, such as a piece of candy in front of the student. Reward anytime the student makes any effort at all to turn the pedals. Through drills and rewards the student should eventually learn to pedal the bike.

3. Use a front wheel drive trike for those students who are just starting to learn. In this type of trike, the pedals turn when the wheels are turning. This is important because the student's legs will move when the bike is pulled or pushed. The student then gets the idea of moving his legs from the trike.

4. Foot clamps that can be attached to the pedals help hold the student's feet on the pedals; thus, when the student's feet are fastened to the pedals and a front wheel drive trike is used, the student will get the feel of his legs and feet moving in the proper motion as the instructor pulls or pushes the trike.

5. Once the student has learned to pedal the trike or bike, teach them to pedal around the track or designated course in a counter-clockwise or clockwise direction so that trike and bike riding is incorporated with other track fitness activities.

6. There are many good bikes and trikes on the market. A good bike for older students is a 3-wheeler with a 24" wheel size, especially designed for adult use. It is easy to ride and almost impossible to tip over. The bike comes with regular gears or a 3-speed gear and has front caliper brakes.

Air Flow Mat Movement

This large mattress is inflated by air supplied by a power inflator housed in a fiberglass console. The mattress or mat is constructed of reinforced vinyl. The amount of air in the mattress can easily be controlled to vary its softness or firmness while maintaining equal surface pressure.

These air flow mats can have many uses in an aerobic fitness program. The mat is a safe trampoline, a place to crawl, roll, and a place to walk on changing surfaces.

Teaching Suggestions

1. Permit the students time to familiarize themselves with the air mats. This can be done by having the student sit on the mat as the teacher bounces it up and down. Have the children experiment with crawling, creeping, walking, rolling, or bouncing on the mat.

2. Before the children learn to jump on the mat they should master the following skills:

   a. Bouncing while on hands and knees. The teacher can help by pushing the mat up and down so the student gets the up and down rhythm. The children will soon feel the rhythm and bounce on their hands and knees by themselves.

   b. Bouncing while standing. The teacher can hold the child by the waist or arms and bounce him up and down manually, until the child gets the idea of jumping on his own. With some children this may have to be repeated over and over until they get the idea of jumping.

   c. Maintaining balance on the mat. The teacher can help the child reach this level by putting a spot trainer or inflated log on the mat for the child to hold onto while jumping. With practice the child at some time should be able to jump and maintain standing balance on the mat unaided.

63

Air flow mat jumping.

3. Once the child has learned to jump on the mat the teacher can use the air flow mat activities to build aerobic fitness.

   a. Jumping is not only good for balance and self-confidence, but a few minutes of jumping raises the heart rate and develops the heart, lungs, and muscles.

4. Some suggested jumping activities:

   a. Each student jumps up and down on the mat for 2 minutes or 50, 75, or 100 jumps.

   b. Each student jumps around in a circle. Occasionally have them reverse directions.

   c. Jump and land on stomach; jump and land on back. Repeat for two minutes.

   d. Jump and land on knees; jump and land on back. Repeat for two minutes.

   e. Have each student jump as high as he/she can, attempting to touch the tip of a stick or bat the teacher holds above his/her head.

5. For more activity use two air mats at once.

6. The above activities are only a suggested sequence. There can be no standard progression or sequence for the mentally retarded since the range of performance levels are so varied. Goals are to develop increased fitness through jumping, crawling, rolling, or walking on the mats and also, to develop generalized motor abilities in changing situations on the mat.

7. Have the students remove all objects from their pockets before getting on the mat.

8. Have the students remove their shoes and jump in their socks or bare feet. This will save wear and tear on the mats.

9. Safety factors and bounce control are first and foremost in the teaching sequence and may need continual reinforcement. Make sure the area around the mats is padded.

10. Make each activity period on the mat brief. Permit as much time for rest as needed. Several short turns are better than one long turn.

11. See that balance and control in jumping are achieved before permitting more advanced moves.

SWIMMING FOR AEROBIC FITNESS

Swimming is one of the best physical activities for people of all ages and for many people who are handicapped. Vigorous water activities can make a major contribution to the flexibility, strength, and cardiovascular endurance of individuals. With the body submerged in water, blood circulation automatically increases to some extent, promoting deeper ventilation of the lungs and increased heart rate.

Dr. P. O. Astrand, the noted Swedish physician and exercise physiologist, studied young girls who were training very intensely for swimming competition. He found that they have larger hearts and higher vital capacities and maximum oxygen uptakes than more sedentary girls of the same age and size. It seems that early athletic training, particularly in swimming, can favorably influence lifelong exercise capacity if begun during adolescence.

Physical education swimming classes provide a unique opportunity to improve and maintain physical fitness. Historically, swimming classes have taught people to swim safely and skillfully, and this should always be the first consideration; once students can swim safely, fitness techniques can be incorporated into the swimming program.

Some possible aerobic activities that can be incorporated into the swimming program with the moderately retarded might include the following:

1. Kicking. The student can hold onto the side of the pool and kick. The teacher might use the following sequence:

Kick for 30 seconds

Rest for 30 seconds

Kick for a minute

Rest for 30 seconds

Kick for a minute

Rest one minute

Repeat

Kicking, if done vigorously can be very tiring. It is better to have short periods of kicking, followed by rest, than one or two long periods.

2. Distance swimming for endurance. It takes roughly as much energy to swim 440 yards freestyle as to run a mile.

Students can swim laps for rewards. Awards can be given out for distance covered, 2-mile club, 5-mile club, etc. Students who have trouble swimming a freestyle or other stroke can swim laps with the aid of a flutter board.

3. Relay races. For students who can't swim relay races can be done in the shallow end of the pool with the students walking through knee- or waist-deep water.

4. Walking in water. Walking in knee- or waist-deep water is an excellent way to build aerobic fitness. Exercise, including walking, performed in the water is frequently used in the initial stages of cardiac rehabilitation programs. A recent study stated:

> ...water resistance makes movement through waist deep water by walking or jogging more strenuous than comparable exercise in air. Relatively high levels of respiration, circulation, and oxulative metabolism are required to move through the water at slow speeds. Furthermore, the buoyant effect of water greatly reduces the weight bearing stress on muscles and joints. This information suggests that walking and jogging in water can be a valuable mode of conditioning for developing or maintaining physical work capacity and cardiovascular fitness, particularly for individuals with joint problems.[12]

Aqua-dynamic conditioning. This consists of sequences of exercise
that can be performed in water approximately shoulder-deep. The exercises are presented in a way that provides for a change of pace. That
is, a stressing and easing-off of strenuous exercise to less vigorous
ones to permit recovery periods. Following a period of warmup activities out of the water, a series of exercises lasting from 15-60 minutes,
depending on the degree of difficulty selected, can be performed in
the pool. 13

Aerobic Activities for the Non-Ambulatory

Some of the profound and severely retarded will be inefficient in locomotion. This inability to perform fundamental locomotor functions, in some
cases, has resulted in contractures of the muscles affecting the joints of
the upper and lower extremities. The muscle contractures, due in some cases
to a lack of activity, further impairs motor function and leads to limited
sterotyped patterns of activity.

However, many of these students and children can be helped and ambulation or movement achieved with an intensive program tailored to each child's
needs. To determine these needs, the student must be observed to ascertain
in what ways he/she is capable of moving. A period of trial and error may be
necessary before the best movement plan is formulated which will provide the
child with the best opportunity to achieve better physical fitness.

Before starting a program for the non-ambulatory child the teacher
should check the medical records of the student to acquire some idea of
limitations and possible contraindications. The physical educator cannot
assume that virtually any kind of physical activity, if vigorously engaged
in, will be good for the child. Some apparently useful physical activities
may lead to less than helpful outcomes with a physically handicapped child.
The teacher must be aware of safety concerns and should work in concert with
physical and occupational therapists who are working with the same children
so that the fitness program is not counteracting helpful therapies which are
being applied to the child at other parts of the day.

The non-ambulatory need physical activity in a planned progressive program to help their basic movement skills and to develop at least minimal levels
of fitness. In such a program, the first consideration of the educator should
be the safety of the child, yet at the same time normal risk-taking is also
essential to the development of all children including the non-ambulatory.
These children must not be over-protected to the extent that they are prevented
from exercising their gross skeletal muscles and practicing new motor or ambulation skills. In addition, no child can learn about the relationship of his/
her body to other objects in the environment or acquire the basic self-
proctective skills without receiving a few minor bumps or bruises.

Through a planned, progressive program of vigorous activities the fitness levels of the students can be increased and body mechanics improved. In addition, the student can become more skilled in the use of previously unused portions of the body and in the use of walkers or wheelchairs.

Often the physical educator, new to working with the non-ambulatory, will be at a loss as to how to get the students to move. Increased fitness can only come through movement, preferably at a sustained rate for a good period of time. It is important for the teacher to make full use of the many aides that are available, many of which are designed to assist the handicapped child to move around as independently as possible.

Movement Activities and Teaching Suggestions

1. Scooter board movement. The scooter board is a flat board to which four caster wheels are attached for easy movement. Either a sitting, supine, or prone lying position may be taken on the scooter board; movement is created by pushing with the arms and legs. Commercial scooter boards are usually 14 by 18 inches in size, but longer ones can be purchased or made at home or in school.

   Scooter boards, especially those of longer length, are excellent means of providing mobility to the non-ambulatory student. Use of the board greatly extends the opportunities for participation in physical education activities for those students with disabilities of the lower parts of the body.

   a. Rewards or toys may entice the lazy student to move.

   b. The teacher may have to manually move the limbs through the desired movement pattern needed to move the board.

   c. May need a one-to-one pupil-teacher ratio to keep the student moving in the desired direction.

2. Roller walker. Using this device the student just learning how to walk, or needing some hand and arm support, can move forward or on a direct course. The teacher can pull with a rope to help the student learn to move with the walker.

3. Tricycles. Tricycles provide an opportunity for exercise among the non-ambulatory as well as opportunity for fun.

   a. A good place to start for younger non-ambulatory children is a small wooden or metal tricycle without pedals. The child has to move the legs to push himself/herself around.

   b. Bikes can be purchased with hand drive; these can be used by students who cannot push or pedal with their legs.

   c. A Whiz-Wheel, a sitting platform with large wheels, can be used by the non-ambulatory also. The student sits and pushes the wheels with his hands, thus moving the device forward or backward. Builds fitness as well as shoulder, arm strength.

4. Full body suspension walker. This device consists of an overhead frame with suspension straps that holds the student in a standing position while freeing him/her to walk. Handles on the side provide a good grasping surface.

    a. A one-to-one ratio of teacher to pupil is needed when using this piece of equipment.

    b. The physiological benefits of standing and walking are so great that this piece of equipment is extremely useful. According to Astrand,

> It appears that man, through evolution, has become adjusted to his upright, two-legged, gravity-stressed existence, and ambulatory activity is necessary to maintain normal functions.[14]

5. Wheelchair pushing. The wheelchair provides a means of movement to those who are so severely immobilized by their condition that they cannot stand or walk with the aid of ambulatory devices.

    Wheelchair bound mentally retarded students can be taught to push

    a. While the ambulatory students run or walk around the track during the activity period, those students in wheelchairs can push their chairs around the track.

    b. Wheelchair pushing helps to build fitness and attending skills, and gives the student practice in pushing the chair, which has carry-over value for daily living skills.

    c. To increase the difficulty and to bring the overload principal, weights can be added to the chair.

6. Log rolling. At times this may be the only way a severely handicapped child can move.

    a. Log rolling can be done across:

        1) Air Flow Mats-these have give and make it easier for the child to roll.

        2) Up and Down Ramps and Wedges--a reward may be placed at the top to motivate the student to move. Must make sure the incline isn't too steep. This is a good way to overload a student who can roll with ease across a flat surface.

        3) Across Floor Mats

    b. Measure the distance rolled, or the number of times the distance was covered. Record this and try to increase either gradually.

    c. Rolling also promotes motor coordination, head control, directionality, and body image.

7. Crawling-creeping. The terms crawling and creeping are sometimes used interchangeably but there is a difference between the two. Crawling is primarily an arm action which pulls the body along while the stomach and legs drag along behind. Creeping is primarily a movement pattern in which weight is distributed equally to the hands and knees and movement occurs with a cross-lateral pattern.

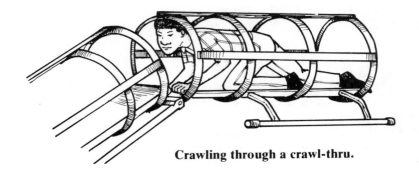

Crawling through a crawl-thru.

   a. Crawling-creeping is excellent for building aerobic fitness as well as shoulder and arm strength.

   b. Scooter board activities can be used as a lead up to creeping.

   c. A shoulder and trunk harness attached to a suspension walker can help hold up the student who is learning to crawl or creep.

   d. The principle of overload can be brought into play by having the student creep up a ramp, or over a wedge or obstacle placed on the mat or floor.

   e. Students can be taught to crawl around a circuit, track, or designated course so the distance they cover can be measured.

A FINAL THOUGHT

Studies have shown that a well-planned vigorous fitness program can have positive effects on the mentally retarded population. The teacher must be concerned with the individual needs and exercise tolerance of each student.

To enchance the aerobic fitness program it is important to pre-plan effectively by: arranging class according to ability (if possible); getting maximum use out of the time permitted for fitness; providing facilities and equipment that will stimulate interest and increase the capabilities of developing fitness; developing motivational strategies which will increase positive attitudes toward fitness; designing and modifying games and activities that will allow each individual to attain a maximum level of fitness.

Many of the severely and profoundly retarded non-ambulatory students will have low or minimal levels of aerobic fitness. Many of these students have not been engaged in any kind of fitness program at any time during their lives. Movement and exertion for any length of time may be foreign to these students.

Teachers who work with these non-ambulatory children must realize the importance that fitness can play in their lives. The life spans (as well as the quality of life) of many of these students are substantially reduced by cardiovascular and/or cardiorespiratory problems. Claudine Sherill in her excellent book on adapted physical education writes,

It is disconcerting that fitness is so poorly understood that 140 teachers and administrators recently ranked fitness as

the least important competency area for teachers of the severely mentally retarded.[15]

Inactivity is completely unnatural to the human body. With inactivity comes overweight, high blood pressure, and high heart rate. With inactivity any kind of fitness becomes impossible. Many of the non-ambulatory severely and profoundly retarded have remained inactive much too long. Through vigorous movement these students can gain the degree of fitness that will enable them to enjoy health and a better life.

FOOTNOTES

[1] Stein, Julian V. "Physical Activity and Its Contribution to the Mentally Retarded." _Journal of the Association for Physical and Mental Rehabilitation_ 20, No. 2:56.

[2] Sherill, Claudine. _Adapted Physical Education and Recreation_, 2d ed. Dubuque, IA: Wm. C. Brown Company, 1981, p. 183.

[3] Clarke, H. Harrison and David H. _Developmental and Adapted Physical Education_. Englewood Cliffs, NJ: Prentice-Hall Inc., 1978, p. 98.

[4] Kuntzleman, Charles T. _Rating the Exercises_. New York: Penguin Books, 1980, p. 56.

[5] Cooper, Kenneth H., M.D. _The New Aerobics_. New York: Bantam Books, 1970, p. 155.

[6] Sheehan, George, M.D. _Dr. Sheehan On Running_. Mt. View, CA: World Publications, 1975, p. 128.

[7] Kuntzleman, p. 117.

[8] Myers, Clayton R. _The Official YMCA Physical Fitness Handbook_. New York: Popular Library, p. 13.

[9] Astrand, Per-Olaf, M.D., and Rodahl, Kaare, M.D. **Textbook for Work Physiology**. New York: McGraw-Hill, 1970, p. 419.

[10] Cooper, Kenneth H., M.D. _The New Aerobics_. New York: Bantam Books, 1970, p. 53.

[11] Zehman, Lenore R., M.D.; Katlus, Albert A., M.D.; and Softness, Donald G. _The Cardiologist Guide to Fitness and Health Through Exercise_. New York: Simon and Schuster, 1970, p. 134.

[12] Evans, Blanche W.; Cureton, Kirk J.; and Purvis, Jamie W. "Metabolic and Circulatory Responses to Walking and Jogging in Water." _Research Quarterly_ 49, No. 4:442-449.

[13] "Youth Physical Fitness." _President's Council on Physical Fitness and Sports_. Washington, DC: U.S. Government Printing Office, July, 1976, p. 60.

[14] Astrand, Per-Olaf, M.D., and Rodahl, Kaare, M.D. _Textbook for Work Physiology_. New York: McGraw-Hill, 1970, p. 419.

[15] Sherrill, Claudine, Ibid., p. 168.

Section II—
Practical Pointers for Movement Fundamentals and Dance

PRACTICAL POINTERS

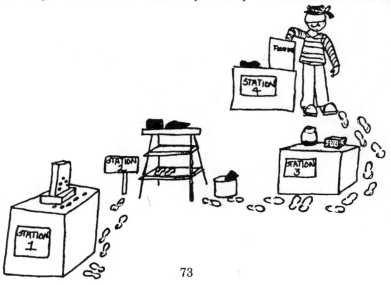

*Learning is best achieved in the environment of
fun and laughter.* Marie Montessori

INNOVATIVE PERCEPTUAL MOTOR ACTIVITIES: PROGRAMING TECHNIQUES THAT WORK

Howard M. Sorrell

What is education? So often learning experiences have been approached in
terms of teacher/leader interests, backgrounds, and experiences. Here is an
approach that is child-centered with the focus on learning not teaching. The
nature of learning is concentrated on with the understanding that the more
experiences and opportunities given a child, greater the chances for use and
application.

Think of all possibilities for these activities--small motor and manipulative
activities requiring dexterity; tracking and visual discrimination and depth
perception; tactile discrimination; concepts of laterality, directionality,
space, shape, color, and numbers; opportunities to follow directions, work
together, read, solve problems, and have fun while being successful. The
details and approach can be modified according to participating youngsters
regardless of ages, functional abilities, or impairments. Activities are
appropriate for school, recreation center, home, or wherever children are found.

73

High interest, self-motivating, programed materials are designed to spark children to learn when traditional ways have not been successful. Such tasks are designed to permit each child to execute them successfully by him/herself or with minimum help.

Many of these tasks have been adapted from commercially marketed puzzles and perceptual-motor games. The author developed some and others originated from observing children with learning problems. The tasks are not particularly unusual but have worked for the author and children with whom he works. Any interested leader can adapt some of these suggestions or design new ones to meet the needs of an individual or group. Keys to effectiveness for this approach are:

. Specific, sequential steps to accomplish the task.

. Immediate high interest in tasks by students.

. Positive rewarding feelings upon completion of each task.

Obviously, time and effort are necessary for this as in any worthwhile under-taking. Students of all ages, however, not only like the approach but learn from the experiences.

The Program in Action

Regardless of specific methods to implement this program, a circuit approach or station techniques are used. Among endless ways of putting this program into action are:

. Make and place instruction cards for each activity in a specific area. Students who can--read and follow instructions. Others have someone else read instructions to them. If possible, instructions should be in picture or graphic form so everyone can follow them easily. Consider use of audio-cassettes as another possible way to provide instructions.

. Devise stations or areas so students move in a prescribed order, stay at each for a specific time, then rotate at a signal. Use contact paper, tempera paint, or other means to show movement patterns among stations. Use music for background during the action phase of activity; stop the music as a signal to move to the next station. Aides, peer tutors, and volunteers can be used to work with students who need extra help or at especially difficult stations.

. Devise a check-off list so each child can maintain a record of what has been accomplished, how long it has taken, and other information to show achievement.

. Include sufficient stations and activities so each youngster has a chance to become more proficient and meet new challenges through active participation. Obtain ideas and suggestions from children on new ways tasks can be used at each station.

. Incorporate appropriate commercial activities, e.g., Perfection, Beat-the-Clock, Tug-Boat, puzzles, dominoes, Twister, and Toss-Across, as activity stations. Visit toy stores for additional games and ideas for this approach.

Perceptual—Motor Task	PAGE	VISUAL TRACKING	VISUAL DISCRIMINATION AND COPYING OF FORMS	SPATIAL BODY PERCEPTION	FINE MOTOR COORDINATION: HAND—EYE/EYE—FINGERS	TACTILE DISCRIMINATION	DEPTH PERCEPTION
COUNT THE BEANS	5				X	X	
COUNTRY STORE	5				X	X	
HOMEMADE PEG BOARD	6	X			X	X	X
NUTS AND BOLTS FOR YOUNG CARPENTERS	6	X			X	X	X
ONE FINGERED TYPING	7	X			X	X	
WHICH KEY?	7	X			X	X	X
CATTLE RUSTLERS	8			X	X	X	
SHARPEN THREE PENCILS	8				X	X	
FINE TOUCH	9	X			X	X	
BLINDFOLD FISHING	9				X	X	X
WORK THE COMBINATIONS	10	X			X	X	
SANDPAPER FIGURES	11	X			X	X	
HOMEMADE SOFTBALLS	11	X	X		X	X	
BATHROOM TILE MOSAICS	12	X			X	X	X
MAIL A PAPER HOME	13	X	X		X	X	
PENNY PACKAGING	13				X	X	
COUNTING MONEY	14	X			X	X	
BOMB SITE PRACTICE	14	X			X	X	X
LACE UP THE BOOTS	15	X				X	
LIGHT THE LIGHTS	15	X			X	X	

COUNT THE BEANS

Objectives: Develop finger dexterity, tactile sensitivity, and visual tracking.

Materials: Pint sized jar filled with dried lima beans; tin can in which beans can be placed; counting board or space.

Procedure:
1. Use the right hand, count fifty beans and place them in the tin can.
2. Re-spread beans on the counting board.
3. Count beans again, use the left hand, and place beans in the can again.
4. Pick up fifty more beans alternating with right and left hands.
5. Return beans to the jar for the next classmate to count.

   Note: Repeat the activity using different numbers of beans to count.

COUNTRY STORE

Objectives: Manipulate materials and acquaint pupil with the experience of a small store keeper...academic learning in using weights and measures is a secondary objective.

Materials: An old, used store or baby scales; paper bags of various sizes and weight capacities; several boxes/cans/containers of dried peach seeds, acorns, golf balls, bottle caps, glass marbles, discarded checkers, or homemade wooden blocks...cleaned pebbles will do.

Procedure:
1. Weigh ½ pound of peach seeds into a bag.
2. Weigh 1 pound of acorns into a bag.
3. Weigh 2 pounds of bottle caps into a bag.
4. Weigh 2½ pounds of wooden blocks into a bag.
5. Weigh 1 pound, 12 ounces of discarded checkers.
6. Weigh 3 pounds, 2 ounces of cleaned pebbles into a bag.
7. Empty materials into correct tin cans or containers.
8. Smooth out and replace bags for other classmates to use.

HOMEMADE PEG BOARD

Objectives: Place varied colored milk container tops over upright dowels to form different shapes and forms.

Materials: Homemade peg board 14 inches x 14 inches with 144 ¼-inch dowels placed one inch apart; 144 dowels, 1 inch high by ¼-inch diameter mounted in ¼-inch diameter holes recessed ½-inch deep; 144 (or more) gallon milk container screw-on metal tops painted in a variety of colors and with a ¼-inch hole drilled into the center of each; number 10 tin can to hold tops. Soda pop bottle tops can be used, but sharp edges can scratch some floors.

Procedure:
1. Place dowels in the holes so that all holes are filled.
2. Arrange blue tops on the periphery of the board to form a square frame.
3. Use red tops to form an equilateral triangle.
4. Place yellow tops in positions to form a rectangle of any color; (a) make as large a rectangle as possible; (b) use exactly 18 tops of any color to form a rectangle; (c) make two other sized rectangles.
5. Pick out black tops to form a pentagon shape.
6. Use as many green tops as you like to form an octagon.
7. Select any tops with commercial labels and make the outline of a house.
8. Make any shape or design which you choose...i.e., outline of a church, boat, star, monument.

NUT AND BOLTS FOR YOUNG CARPENTERS

Objectives: Use finger manipulation in fixing nuts and bolts into correct holes; recognize correct sizes and spaces.

Materials: Homemade wooden upright with holes for fifteen varying sized nuts and bolts; tin can to hold dismantled parts; red bandanna.

Procedure:
1. Remove all nuts and bolts from the wood block.
2. Place nuts and bolts in the can and shake.
3. Replace nuts and bolts in proper slots.
4. Put on the blindfold and repeat 1, 2, and 3 above.
5. Remove the blindfold and replace all parts for the next classmate.

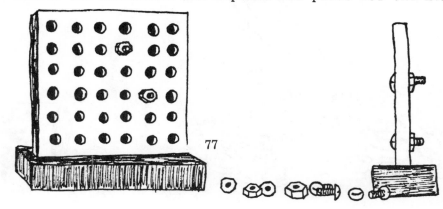

77

ONE FINGERED TYPING

Objectives: Recognize letters; develop elementary finger dexterity and eye-hand coordination.

Materials: Used, old typewriter; supply of 8½ inch x 11 inch--preferably used--typing or ditto paper.

Procedure:
1. Type the alphabet using lower case (small) letters.
2. Set "shift lock" and type alphabet with capital letters.
3. Type your name and address.
4. Type a short poem or copy one of the following:

   Little Bo Peep has lost her sheep,
   And can't tell where to find them.
   Leave them alone and they'll come home
   Wagging their tails behind them.

   and/or--The quick, little, brown fox jumped over the lazy,
         sleeping dog.

5. Type a short letter to your mother, father, or to a friend.

WHICH KEY?

Objectives: Locate from a large collection of keys ones that unlock the four locks.

Materials: Four padlocks (can be more or less); four keys that fit locks; fifteen or twenty dummy keys; tin can.

Procedure:
1. Empty keys onto a work area.
2. Continue experimenting with all keys until all four locks have been successfully unlocked.

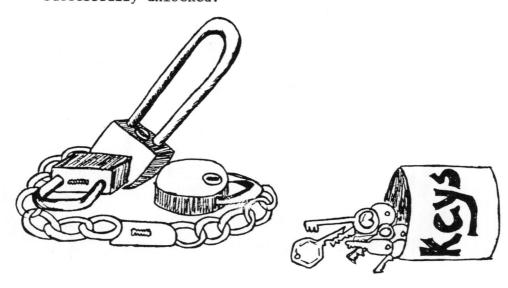

CATTLE RUSTLERS

Objectives: Tie-up your classmate, Big Buddy or leader four times using four different length ropes.

Materials: Four ropes with painted (marked) tips to distinguish between different lengths--red tipped, six feet; black tipped, nine feet; white tipped, twelve feet; and yellow tipped, fifteen feet; box; chair.

Procedure:
1. Use the red tipped rope to tie the Rustler's wrists (i.e., your partner) so that he/she cannot untie him/herself. Now untie him/her.
2. Tie the Rustler's ankles with the black tipped rope. Can he/she untie him/herself. If not, release him/her.
3. Use the white tipped rope to tie the Rustler's ankles and wrists. Can he/she untie him/herself? Untie him/her.
4. Use the yellow-tipped rope to tie your partner completely to a chair.
5. Replace ropes in the box for your next classmate.

SHARPEN THREE PENCILS

Objectives: Develop finger dexterity by manipulation and control of pencils and varying types of pencil sharpeners; improve eye-hand coordination.

Materials: Snoopy or similarly battery operated pencil sharpener; two hand operated sharpeners; supply of new or unsharpened wooden pencils; two number 10 tin cans.

Procedure:
1. Sharpen one pencil with the Snoopy sharpener.
2. Sharpen the second and third pencils by hand manipulation.
3. Place sharpened pencils in the number 10 tin can.

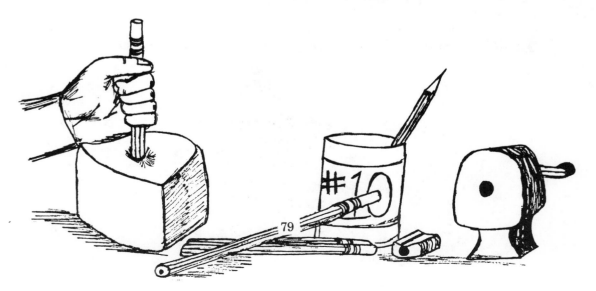

FINE TOUCH

Objectives: Develop fine motor skills and eye-hand coordination.

Materials: Five each of fourteen different sized small tacks and nails...in a glass jar container; pair of medical tweezers (for splinter removal!); cooking pan; ice cube tray with standard fourteen cube sections.

Procedure:
1. Pour tacks and nails into the cooking pan.
2. Pick up each item one at a time with the tweezers and place it into a separate compartment of the ice cube tray--use one compartment for each type item.
3. Replace tacks and nails in the jar for your next classmate.

Note: . If you wish to establish a time for accomplishing this task, set a kitchen timer...or use the sweep second hand of a wrist watch or wall clock.
. Reset the kitchen timer for a faster speed and try again.
. To experience an awkward variation, attempt these tasks using fingers only!

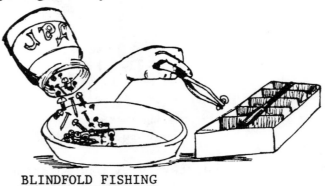

BLINDFOLD FISHING

Objectives: Develop tactile and kinesthetic perception by eliminating vis perception; heighten eye-hand coordination by eliminating vis acuity and affording only perceptual awareness.

Materials: Red bandanna/handkerchief; items for fishing--hammer, screwdriver, dust pan, boot, brush.

Procedure:
1. Have your partner or leader place a blindfold on you.
2. Fish in the box for each of the following items--hammer, screwdriver, dust pan, boot, brush.
3. Untie your own blindfold and replace items in the box.

80

WORK THE COMBINATION

Objectives: Develop finger manipulation and eye-hand coordination; acquaint the child with a practice which may be used frequently...now and in later life.

Materials: Two inexpensive combination locks, one red, the other blue-faced; card with ten sets of combinations.

Procedure:
1. Try as many of the ten combinations as necessary to open the red lock...leave it open and remember the combination, or make a note of it.
2. Try as many combinations as needed to open the blue lock; leave it open and make a note of the combination.
3. Practice re-locking and opening the red lock four times.
4. Practice re-locking and opening the blue lock three or four times.
5. Leave both locks closed for your next classmate to practice this task.

   Note: Examples of listing of combinations for trial and error that should be posted.

Right	Left	Right
6	10	3
4	25	13
7	29	10
8	16	4
27	4	30
8	2	5
7	10	2
3	12	36
24	36	24
13	31	3

SANDPAPER FIGURES

Objectives: Select correct numbers, letters, shapes to form words; develop tactile and visual perception through eye-finger coordination and in a blind-fold condition.

Materials: Sufficient numbers of letters, numbers, shapes from which to select; all forms to be constructed with sandpaper surfaces to permit tactile discrimination while blindfolded; working board.

Procedure:
1. Spell such words as cat, mouse, house, barn, door, boat, horse, cheese. Note: Difficulty of words is set to competency level of the children.
2. Form numbers to represent two million, three hundred ninety thousand, five hundred and sixteen. Note: Set number tasks to competency level of the group.
3. Use square pieces to form the outline of an igloo.
4. Repeat the above tasks with a blindfold.

HOMEMADE SOFTBALLS

Objectives: Use hands and fingers in tearing tape and crumbling newspapers to shape a spheroid.

Materials: Newspapers; masking tape; target barrel or trash can.

Procedure:
1. Crumple a large page of newspaper into a ball the size of a softball.
2. Wrap it with strips of masking tape.
3. Practice catching and tossing the paper ball with your partner, Big Buddy, classmate, or leader.
4. Compete with yourself or a partner in tossing the paper ball into a Clown Barrel, trash can, or some target; toss from lines 1, 2, and 3 marked with masking tape at different distances on the floor.

BATHROOM TILE MOSAICS

Objectives: Use the variety of tile pieces to make shapes and forms to provide visual perception experiences in forming simple mosaics; develop form perception skills.

Materials: As many bath room tile pieces as needed to provide a variety of colors and sufficient to fill up a square framed working board; some models and patterns for reference.

Procedure:
1. Form a blue frame around the periphery of the working board frame.
2. Create a right triangle within the working board area.
3. Make an equilateral triangle using another color.
4. Make a perfect square. Use a third color of tile pieces.
5. What is a rhomboid? If you know or can find out from a classmate, leader, or teacher, then make one in a variety of colors.
6. Make a basic design which is the same as the Pentagon Building.
7. Make the outline of some object--i.e., boat, church, monument, star, house.

   Note: Other materials which may be used include:

   • Wall-to-wall carpeting.
   • Wallpaper.
   • Cardboards of varying sizes and colors/designs.

MAIL A PAPER HOME

Objectives: Practice finger manipulation through coloring a picture, placing a stamp and sealing an envelope; afford practice in a practical experience in life.

Materials: Dittoed forms of pictures and figures; box of white, small sized envelopes; supply of crayons or coloring pencils; Easter or Epilepsy Foundation seals as imitation stamps; ball point or regular pencils for addressing envelopes.

Procedure:
1. Color various sections of the dittoed form using a variety of colors.
2. Address the envelope to your parents or to a friend.
3. Place a stamp in the upper right hand corner of the envelope.
4. Take the letter home for your parents to see or for delivery to a friend.

> Note: In lieu of a dittoed form with pictures or designs for lower grade children...the child can elect/be directed to write a note to parents, relatives, or friends.

PENNY PACKAGING

Objectives: Practice fine motor manipulation using both pennies and wrappers.

Materials: Pint sized glass jar containing two or three hundred pennies; regular bank paper penny wrappers--real pennies are recommended for this task.

Procedure:
1. Remove a handful of pennies from the jar.
2. Set pennies in five stacks of ten each.
3. Place each stack in a penny wrapper.
4. Place rolls of pennies in the second container.

BOMB SITE PRACTICE

Objectives: Concentrate on eye-hand coordination and <u>sighting-in</u> as a visual acuity
               and perception practice; develop balance and accommodation to height.

Materials: Four foot step ladder; three bean bags; one number 10 tin can...use of
               a higher ladder is optional if deemed practical and safe.

Procedure: 1. Stand at floor level and drop three bean bags into the can--repeat
                   until successful.
               2. Stand on the first step of the ladder and drop the three bean bags
                   into the tin can--repeat until successful.
               3. Stand on the second step and <u>fire</u> three bean bags into the tin
                   can--until successful with all three.
               4. Continue dropping the three bags from the top of the ladder until
                   all are in the can.

               <u>Note</u>: Adaptations can be developed for five, six, eight, ten, or
                      twelve foot ladders.

COUNTING MONEY

Objectives: Recognize sizes and shapes of coins; manipulate coins.

Materials: Jar; several metal discs of varied sizes; bottle caps; gallon milk
               tops; flat metal and rubber washers; ten pennies, five dimes, seven
               nickels, three quarters; additional play coins if available; tin can
               or other receptical. <u>Note</u>: Use of real money is recommended.

Procedure: 1. Empty all real and play coins onto a counting board.
               2. Pick up three quarters and place them in the tin can.
               3. Find ten pennies and place them in the can.
               4. Find five dimes and deposit them.
               5. Locate seven nickels and put them in the can.
               6. Gather all coins, both real and play, and replace them in the jar
                   for other classmates.

LACE UP THE BOOTS

Objectives: Develop hand and finger manipulation; develop eye-hand coordination; provide pupil with a functional and developmental experience.

Materials: Pair of large sized boots, preferably high topped; small chair; two balance beams--4 inches x 5 feet and 2 inches x 12 feet.

Procedure:
1. Remove your own shoes--if your foot and shoe are small enough, complete this task without removing shoes.
2. Put on both boots.
3. Lace boots to the top and tie laces in bow.
4. Stand up and walk around.
5. Walk forward and backward on the 4 inches x 5 feet balance beam.
6. Walk forward and backward on the 2 inches x 12 feet balance beam.

LIGHT THE LIGHTS

Objectives: Recognize sizes and shapes; see interrelationships of the parts; manipulate parts into a working project; get more acquainted with a practical and useful instrument.

Materials: Five flashlights (or more) in varied sizes from lantern type to pocket pen light; box to contain all disassembled parts; cushioning materials to prevent breakage.

Procedure:
1. Assemble correct casings, batteries, reflectors, bulbs, and shields to complete five flashlights. See if all five light-up-- if not, assembling is wrong!!!
2. Dismantle all five flashlights for your next classmate.
3. Replace all parts in the box as carefully as possible.

PRACTICAL POINTERS

*The mind of man is capable of anything
because everything is in it ...
all the past as well as the future.*

Joseph Conrad

INNOVATIVE PERCEPTUAL-MOTOR ACTIVITIES: PROGRAMING TECHNIQUES THAT WORK--PART II

Howard M. Sorrell

This _Practical Pointer_, sequel to Volume 2, Number 5, is geared to high interest activities with strong promise of immediate success for participants. Fun and success are important in learning tasks and situations for _everyone_ regardless of age or ability. However, these are crucial ingredients in learning for children with various general or specific learning difficulties. Activities and approaches presented in this _Practical Pointer_ provide opportunities for _fun_, enjoyment, pleasure, and laughter while at the same time challenging children into learning.

The following tasks are broken into specific progressive steps which permit each child to know that he/she is succeeding. With this inner awareness of growth, the learning phenomenon may trigger further involvement and perseverence by the child; these are qualities often lacking among children experiencing learning difficulties.

SUGGESTIONS FOR IMPLEMENTATION

Specific steps for each activity should be spelled out for the child; use pictures, drawings, and/or stick figures for children with reading difficulties. This can also be done in a check list with itemized steps for each task. If a child is unable to determine what to do, a peer or adult leader can work along with him/her. Repetition of individual tasks for as many times as interest is high is recommended; always end an individual task and a session of these activities in positive ways.

Parallel or similar perceptual-motor tasks developed by teacher or instructor are encouraged--these activites can spring from any base. Primary springboards in creating the following tasks have been responses to such basic questions as "What does the child need?" "How and/or where does the child need to develop?" "What perceptual-motor deficiencies does the child have?" These questions are easily answered by lay-persons by simply observing a child in normal activities, or by assigning simple manipulative tasks, puzzles, or craft designs.

Opportunities for development in the perceptual-motor realm are unlimited. This is an ever-expanding growth horizon that continues throughout life. Certainly, in early youth, as many experiences in these areas as possible should be afforded young children. The following are types of inexpensive, high interest tasks that give promise of high development of each youngster's perceptual and motor skills.

THE PROGRAM IN ACTION

Regardless of specific methods to implement this program, a circuit approach or station techniques are used. Among endless ways of putting this program into action are:

. Make and place instruction cards for each activity in a specific area. Students who can, read and follow instructions; others have someone else read instructions to them. If possible, instructions should be in picture or graphic form so everyone can follow them easily. Consider use of audio-cassettes as another way to provide instructions.

. Devise stations or areas so students move in a prescribed order; stay at each station for a specific time, then rotate at a signal. Use contact paper, tempera paint, or other means to show movement patterns among stations. Use music for background during the action phase of activity; stop the music as a signal to move to the next station. Aides, peer tutors, and volunteers can work with students who need extra help or at especially difficult stations.

. Devise a check-off list so each child can maintain a record of what has been accomplished, how long it has taken, and other information to show achievement.

. Include sufficient stations and activities so each youngster has a chance to become more proficient and meet new challenges through active participation. Obtain ideas and suggestions from children on new ways tasks can be used at each station.

. Incorporate appropriate commercial games--e.g., Perfection, Beat-the-Clock, Tug-Boat, puzzles, dominoes, Twister, and Toss-Across--as activity stations. Visit toy stores for additional games and ideas for this approach. Developmental Purposes of Commercial Games (Practical Pointer Volume 1, Number 1) provides information about games which can have positive effects on associative learning, auditory memory, eye-hand coordination, fine and gross motor control, fine and gross motor skills, laterality, tactile discrimination, visual motor integration, visual discrimination, visual imagery, visual tracking, social skills, expressive skills, and sports skills.

- Devise stations or areas so students move in a prescribed order; stay at each station for a specific time, then rotate at a signal. Use contact paper, tempera paint, or other means to show movement patterns among stations. Use music for background during the action phase of activity; stop the music as a signal to move to the next station. Aides, peer tutors, and volunteers can work with students who need extra help or at especially difficult stations.

- Devise a check-off list so each child can maintain a record of what has been accomplished, how long it has taken, and other information to show achievement.

- Include sufficient stations and activities so each youngster has a chance to become more proficient and meet new challenges through active participation. Obtain ideas and suggestions from children on new ways tasks can be used at each station.

- Incorporate appropriate commercial games--e.g., Perfection, Beat-the-Clock, Tug-Boat, puzzles, dominoes, Twister, and Toss-Across--as activity stations. Visit toy stores for additional games and ideas for this approach. Developmental Purposes of Commercial Games (Practical Pointer Volume 1, Number 1) provides information about games which can have positive effects on associative learning, auditory memory, eye-hand coordination, fine and gross motor control, fine and gross motor skills, laterality, tactile discrimination, visual motor integration, visual discrimination, visual imagery, visual tracking, social skills, expressive skills, and sports skills.

Perceptual-Motor Task	PAGE.	VISUAL TRACKING.	VISUAL DISCRIMINATION AND/OR COPYING OF FORMS.	SPATIAL BODY PERCEPTION. SPATIAL PERCEPTION/AWARENESS.	FINE MOTOR COORDINATION: MIND-EYE/EYE-FINGERS.	TACTILE DISCRIMINATION.	DEPTH PERCEPTION.
CHOPSTICKS FOR A GOOD TIME.	5	X		X	X		
HANG IT ON THE LINE.	6	X	X	X	X	X	X
RING THOSE KEYS.	7	X			X	X	X
PUMP UP A BALL.	8			X	X		
DARN THOSE SOCKS.	7	X			X	X	X
GIFT PACKAGING.	9	X			X	X	X
TOP THE JAR.	9	X			X	X	X
METAL SMITH.	10	X	X		X	X	X
COAT HANGER FIGURENES.	5		X		X	X	
MARKETING PRODUCE.	6	X			X	X	X
EGG BOX TARGET.	10	X			X		X
INDOOR PLAY BIRDHOUSE.	11		X	X	X		
BURLAP BOOK MARKERS.	11		X		X	X	
BUTTON BEADS.	12	X			X		X
BE THE BIG MAN.	12	X		X	X	X	X
PIE PAN PUZZLES.	13		X	X			
STAPLING SHAPES.	8	X	X		X		
RACKETS FOR PLAY.	13		X		X		
HUMPTY-DUMPTY DOMINOES.	14	X		X			
BLACKBOARD SHAPES.	14	X		X		X	

CHOPSTICKS FOR A GOOD TIME

Objectives   Develop fine motor and manipulative skills with the fingers; improve eye-hand coordination skills, eye-tracking, and spatial perception.

Materials   Several sets of inexpensive chopsticks; rug mats 12 inches x 12 inches, or table placemats; dried peas, glass marbles, dried lima beans, and small pebbles; orange juice cans or containers; two chop sticks for each participating child.

Procedure

1. Empty from the small container five of each of the listed materials--i.e., dried peas, glass marbles, dried lima beans, small pebbles, navy beans--onto the rug mat or placemat.

2. Hold chopsticks with ring, middle, forefinger, and thumb... pick up one item at a time and place it in the tin can.

3. Practice as much as possible.

4. Set a kitchen timer to see how fast all twenty or twenty-five items can be picked up and placed in the tin can; see how many items can be picked up in a designated time--ten, twenty, sixty seconds.

5. Compete against a classmate.

6. Try the task with one eye shut or a blindfold over both eyes.

COAT HANGER FIGURENES

Objectives   Develop eye-hand coordination, muscular, and manipulative skills, concepts of forms and shapes by bending coat hangers into various shapes, letters, figures, and forms.

Materials   Supply of low-gauge, light weight wire coat hangers; plyers of various sizes and strengths, most with wire cutting capacities; sample figures, letters, shapes, and forms for patterns; <u>optionally</u>, various sizes of wire cutters for children unable to cut with selected plyers.

Procedure

1. Select a figure, shape, letter, or form.

2. Bend, twist, cut, manipulate, and form the shape, figure, form, or letter.

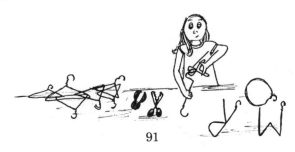

91

HANG IT ON THE LINE

Objectives   Develop eye-hand coordination, spatial awareness, and manipulative skills in practicing a life-long functional activity--hanging clothing items on a line to dry.

Materials   Two upright standards or two places to anchor a clothesline; clothes pins in generous supply; variety of boys', girls', men's, and women's clothes to hang out; stool or two-foot ladder.

Procedure

1. Select items to be hung on the line.

2. Compete with a classmate in a race to get the most items hung-up.

3. Hang clothes against a timing device--how long it takes to hang a given number of items or how many can be hung in a specific time.

4. Use one/two/three clothes pins per item regardless of its size, shape, color, or texture.

5. Use one clothes pin for one/two/three/more items regardless of their sizes, shapes, or textures.

6. Select only items of a specified type, size, shape, color, or texture to hang on the line.

7. Perform these and similar tasks while blindfolded.

MARKETING PRODUCE

Objectives   Develop concepts of sizes, forms, and shapes by using a miniature separation technique similar to that used in industrial food sorting and packaging plants.

Materials   Large number of various sized spherical objects--tennis balls, golf balls, marbles, ping pong balls, circular steel ball bearings, incline plane with dropthrough holes varying in sizes to accommodate various sized balls (spherical objects) representing oranges, apples, plums, cherries, berries, potatoes; bags and fasteners.

Procedure

1. Roll ball(s)--imitation vegetables and fruits--down the separator incline plane permitting various sized balls to drop through into recepticals.

2. Package various types of imitation produce into bags and fasten them.

92

RING THOSE KEYS

Objectives   Develop finger dexterity by inserting and removing a variety of car and house keys onto an equally wide variety of key rings from advertising agencies, locksmiths, and key makers; acquaint the child with a life-long functional activity.

Materials   Generous number of keys from various sources....the number that can be gathered is unlimited; large number of different types of key rings; containers for each; kitchen timer or sweep second hand wrist watch.

Procedure

1. <u>Ring</u> as many keys as possible onto one/two/three selected rings.

2. Separate different types of key rings and place one key on each ring.

3. Test yourself with twenty-five keys and a timing device--see how long it takes to ring all keys; see how many keys can be placed on rings in five, ten, fifteen seconds.

4. Divide keys in different ways--size, shape, color--and place in different ways on rings--alternate from ring to ring; alternate types of keys on each ring; keep all keys the same on each ring.

5. Use one hand only, both hands, alternate hands as keys are placed on rings.

6. Perform tasks with one eye shut or a blindfold over both eyes.

DARN THOSE SOCKS

Objectives   Develop eye-finger coordination, visual acuity, and visual perception by practicing the old repair craft of mending socks with holes in them.

Materials   Supply of clean, old socks with holes in toes and/or heels; needles and thread; light bulbs, golf balls, croquet balls, or similar objects to use in darning process.

Procedure

1. Select a pair of socks which needs to be darned.

2. Thread the needle.

3. Use a light bulb--or other base--inside the sock and mend the hole.

4. Secure the final threads.

Note   If Goodwill Industries or some charity can use or dispense repaired socks to needy people, this adds to purpose and motivation of the activity.

PUMP UP A BALL

Objectives   Develop finger dexterity; build control in wrists and hand muscles; acquaint the student with a functional skill for future play.

Materials   Supply of deflated balls in a large box; two hand pumps; needle valves; vaseline.

Procedure
1. Select a needle that fits the pump.

2. Lubricate the needle with vaseline.

3. Pump-up the ball until it is full and firm.

4. Remove the needle from the pump and replace it in a container.

5. Place the inflated ball in a second box so that it can be used.

6. See how many balls can be pumped up in a specified time--ten, twenty, sixty seconds.

7. Perform the entire task blindfolded.

STAPLING SHAPES

Objectives   Manipulate a frequently used instrument while forming shapes, designs, letters, or numbers to develop eye-hand coordination and spatial awareness.

Materials   Used paper; stapler; staples; ruler; pencil; templates for constructing preferred designs; 3 inch x 5 inch x 8 inch file cards.

Procedure
1. Select design to be constructed.

2. Outline with pencil borders of the design.

3. Use a loaded stapler and align staples on card or paper where lines are marked.

4. Select a second design for stapling shapes or designs.

94

GIFT PACKAGING

Objectives   Develop finger-hand manipulative skills in practicing a life-long functional activity.

Materials   Boxes of various sizes--shoe boxes, small jewelry containers; newspapers; used brown paper bags; scissors; Scotch tape; varied types of string.

Procedure
1.   Select the box which will be wrapped and tied.

2.   Judge amount of paper needed to wrap the box correctly and choose between newspapers and brown bag paper.

3.   Cut paper to preferred size.

4.   Wrap the box using Scotch tape to secure folds.

5.   Tie the package so as to be fit to send through the U. S. Mail.

6.   Dismantle the wrapped box, discard paper, and leave the box for the next classmate.

TOP THE JAR

Objectives   Manipulate tops onto correct jars; recognize sizes and shapes.

Materials   Box or container; seven glass jars of varied sizes--more may be used as preferred; seven corresponding tops to the jars plus several dummies that won't fit; red bandanna for a blindfold; kitchen timer may be used to speed the task effort.

Procedure
1.   Scatter tops and jars over a work area.

2.   Fit jar tops onto jars until all jars are topped.

3.   Remove all tops.

4.   Put on the blindfold and assemble jars and tops again.

5.   Try task with kitchen timer--see how long it takes to complete the task or how many jars can be topped in a specified time.

6.   Remove tops once more and scatter for classmate.

95

METAL SMITH

Objectives   Experience basic skill of a <u>Metal Smith</u>; develop eye-hand coordination skills by manipulating a punch and mallet in forming shapes, letters, and designs.

Materials   Liberal collection of old automobile license plates; masking tape; metal punches of various sizes; strong, solid metal plate thick enough to accommodate persistent pounding--wood of hard consistency will do; mallet or hammer; patterns of letters and/or numbers; outlines of shapes, forms, houses, boats, airplanes, or whatever else is desired.

Procedure   1.   Select any old, used auto license plates....motorcycle plates or even bicycle plates will do.

               2.   Place--fasten with tape or string--a plate onto the <u>pounding</u> plate.

               3.   Pick a design to copy or <u>pound-out</u> into a letter, figure, or shape.

               4.   <u>Punch</u>/<u>pound out</u> the figure, shape or letter of choice.

EGG BOX TARGET

Objectives   Develop eye-hand coordination by <u>targeting</u> marbles into openings in the top of an egg carton leading into the twelve spaces reserved for the corresponding twelve eggs.

Materials   Empty egg box with holes in the top just above each space for an inserted egg; twelve or more large or assorted size marbles; marble container.

Procedure   1.   Drop from a standing position twelve marbles into twelve different holes. How many tries does it take to drop twelve marbles into twelve different sections of the carton?

               2.   Open the carton and replace marbles in the tin can for the next classmate.

INDOOR PLAY BIRDHOUSE

Objectives   Develop hand-finger skill and control by assembling seven cardboard ready-cut pieces to form an indoor birdhouse for indoor play or display.

Materials   Seven ready-cut parts already outlined or with cardboard and templates with which to accomplish preliminary steps; seven parts to the birdhouse--two sides, front, back, base/floor, two panels to form a slanting roof; ice pick or punch; paper fasteners, scissors, pencil or ball point; cardboard.

Procedure   1.   Draw from templates the seven parts--sides, floor, roof, front, and back--to the birdhouse.

              2.   Cut out parts.

              3.   Punch holes with ice pick or punch.

              4.   Assemble parts with paper fasteners.

Note   This project could be BUILD A BIRDHOUSE but might require adults to cut-out the seven parts from quarter inch thick wood....in this project the result would be a real birdhouse usable for year round outdoor use. Small nails and a tack hammer would be added materials.

BURLAP BOOK MARKER

Objectives   Develop manipulative skills; motivate capacity for creative design.

Materials   Burlap bag cloth; scissors; magic markers; ruler; ball point pen or lead pencil.

Procedure   1.   Outline the book marker to size and shape desired.

              2.   Cut burlap to preferred strip and size.

              3.   Mark strip with insignias or designs of preference.

BUTTON BEADS

Objectives   Assemble any combination of sizes and colors of buttons to form a homemade string of beads; develop eye-hand coordination, form perception, and manipulative skills.

Materials   Nylon--or heavy fiber thread; collection of various sizes and colors of buttons; needle; bead end-fasteners.

Procedure
1. Sort buttons in desired stringing arrangement.
2. String needle with selected thread/fiber.
3. Secure one part of bead fastener on opposite end of the thread...from the needle.
4. Place buttons onto the thread per desired arrangement and length.
5. Secure second part of the fastener onto needle end of the thread.

BE THE BIG MAN

Objectives   Enhance overall body management through donning oversized, adult apparel.

Materials   Various items of adult clothing--man's shirt with buttons, trousers with zipper, jacket with zipper, belt with buckle or hook, other selected items; one suitcase.

Procedure
1. Put on each item of clothing by yourself...only ask for assistance if needed.
2. Put on clothing against a timing device.
3. Dress a friend with the same clothing.
4. Pack all items into a suitcase...then see how fast task can be done or how much can be done in a specified time.
5. Perform task blindfolded.

Note   Activity can and should include girls with women's items, if convenient. However, use of men's clothing is primarily recommended.

PIE PAN PUZZLES

Objectives   Enhance spatial awareness by fitting parts into three varied shaped pie pans.

Materials   Regular circular pie pan; rectangular pie pan; square pie pan; wood or cardboard pieces of exact shape and dimensions of each pie pan--cut into pieces/sections that will fit together within the three pie pans.

Procedure   1.   Spread three differently shaped pie pans onto work area.

2.   Spread pieces/parts to the complete shaped pie pans over work area.

3.   Assemble/fit pieces into the three differently shaped pans until all three pie pan puzzles are complete.

RACKETS FOR PLAY

Objectives   Develop skills in constructing a racket for play while developing hand and finger dexterity by using basic tools and dispensable supplies.

Materials   Wire coat hangers, preferably low-gauge; plyers of various sizes and strengths; wire cutters; used nylon stockings for webbing the face of the racket; two or three patterns of various sized rackets-- tennis, badminton, table tennis.

Procedure   1.   Select type and size racket which is to be constructed; use samples as guides.

2.   Shape wire to form the frame of the racket.

3.   Cut nylon stocking to fit over the face of the racket.

4.   Tie or tape nylon covering at the neck of the racket.

5.   Use a whiffle type ball or badminton bird for play.

HUMPTY-DUMPTY DOMINOES

Objectives
: Manipulate dominoes--or similar wooden blocks--to form shapes, forms, letters, or designs to emphasize spatial relations.

Materials
: As many dominoes or similar rectangular blocks as can be assembled; reasonably large working area.

Procedure
: 1. Decide what shape, letter, word, or design is to be constructed.

2. Place dominoes on their edges so they are standing upright.

3. Space dominoes so that upon <u>toppling</u> one it topples the next and so on until the constructed design has now the same design, but more pronounced with the dominoes lying flat.

4. Shuffle dominoes and construct another design.

5. See how many dominoes can be properly placed in a design and then caused to topple when the first one is pushed.

BLACKBOARD SHAPES

Objectives
: Develop spatial awareness, hand-finger manipulative skills, ambidexterity, and capacity to form shapes and figures.

Materials
: Blackboard; upright or small desk size; chalk; selected patterns and/or templates; eraser.

Procedure
: 1. Select templates and/or design patterns with which to practice.

2. Draw designs with templates and/or patterns.

3. Make shapes, figures, and designs without aid of templates and patterns.

Child is directed to use the non-dominant hand at judgment and discretion of the instructor.

PRACTICAL POINTERS

INNOVATIVE DEVELOPMENTAL PHYSICAL ACTIVITIES FOR
EARLY CHILDHOOD AND SPECIAL EDUCATION STUDENTS

Michael Marsallo

Children who learn early in life the positive benefits and pleasurable
effects of activity are more likely to remain active into adolescence and throughout adulthood than individuals who do not get this feel in their earliest years.
This important foundation for an active life beginning in the earliest years
is as important for children with handicapping conditions as for individuals
without such conditions. Young children are attracted and respond to the basic
and simple, the unsophisticated and uncomplicated, the pleasurable and enjoyable,
the relevant and challenging. Tried and true activities and approaches transcend
generations and different cultures.

FOREWARD

The following activities are samples of tasks and games students participate
in at Holly Park Early Childhood Center (Prince George's County, Maryland). These
activities include those of individual, small group, and large group types which
can be adapted according to abilities, interests, experiences, and disabilities
of individuals making up group or class. Skills required are necessary for every
participating child so that no age ranges have been suggested for any activity.
In choosing activities, focus on student's abilities, rather than what they should
be able to do based on ages. Each activity includes areas of concern for motor,
perceptual-motor, and physical characteristics or skills necessary for successful
participation. While these are important, always keep in mind a primary factor
in any successful activity--FUN--fun for the student, and fun for the teacher.

101

Name	Monster Box
Equipment	Bean bags; 2 boxes taped or tied together with <u>Monsters</u> drawn on all sides; bells or other noise makers tied onto the boxes; carpet squares.
Areas of Concern	Visual-motor coordination--throwing at a moving target; spatial awareness; control; throwing skills.

Activities

. Arrange carpet squares in a large circle--size of circle varies according to throwing abilities of students.

. Be sure each student has five bean bags.

. Stand the <u>Monster</u> in the middle of the the circle.*

. On a signal, the student inside the box begins to walk around and push the <u>Monster</u> along with the hands and feet. If the <u>Monster</u> gets too close to the edge of the circle, verbally direct it back toward the center. Students on the circle try to <u>kill</u> the <u>Monster</u> by throwing bean bags at it. When the <u>Monster</u> falls over, it is <u>officially dead</u> and all throwing stops.

Rules of the Game

. Students must remain on carpet squares at all times, even when all bean bags have been thrown.

. If a bean bag lands near a carpet square, it may be picked up and thrown again.

. When the <u>Monster</u> falls, <u>all</u> throwing <u>stops</u> immediately.

. After the <u>Monster</u> falls, each student gathers five bean bags and returns to a carpet square.

. Student in the boxes (<u>Monster</u>) returns to circle and is replaced by another student.

Hints

. Boxes may be interlocked by sliding the leaves together, or they may be tied together.

. If the <u>Monster</u> fails to fall, a slight <u>push</u> usually topples it.

. If you are not an artist, use an overhead projecter and trace favorite cartoon characters on the boxes.

Additional Games

When boxes become too worn to be effective, stand the <u>Monster</u> in the middle of the circle. Place a tire or two on flattened leaves on the floor to steady it. Students toss bean bags or ball <u>into</u> the <u>Monster</u> box. An additional task is to have students throw from various positions. Setting equipment up around the circle can add exciting dimensions to the game--i.e., balance beams, tires, steps, or any equipment which can be used to alter the child's normal throwing position; throw from sitting, kneeling, or lying positions.

* With one student inside the box (<u>Monster</u>).

Name	Box Races

Equipment   3 small boxes (large enough to step into) per child; sizes may vary.

Areas of Concern   Motor planning; static and dynamic balance.

Actitivties

. Place boxes on the floor in this pattern -

. Have child stand with one foot in box #1 and and the other in box #2.

. Pick up box #3 and place it in front of box #1.

. Place the foot from box #1 into box #3.

. Pick up empty box #1 and place it in front of box #2.

. Remove foot from box #2 and place it into empty box #1.

. Continue this sequence across the room.

. Place the empty box in front of one foot, then the other to move across the floor.

. Do not be concerned if students come up with interesting combinations--often students end up with all three boxes in a straight line, or they try to pull the empty box between their legs.

. Some children may need assistance getting started-- assist by verbally instructing what box to move, where to place it, and which foot to place into it.

Variation

. Use four boxes and have children move up two at a time as they move across the room.

<u>Name</u>	Newspaper Games
<u>Equipment</u>	One page of newspaper per child.
<u>Areas of Concern</u>	Fine motor manipulation; tactile awareness.
<u>Activities</u>	<u>Scrubbing</u>

. Have each child tear newspaper into two pieces.

. Kneel down and place a piece of newspaper under each hand.

. Move the hands around randomly, as if scrubbing the floor.

. Make **different** <u>shapes</u>--i.e., circles, rectangles, squares, triangle**s, names,** letters, numbers, words; initially move the hands **in the s**ame direction--

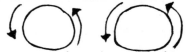

then move them in opposite directions---

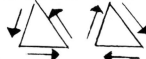

<u>Flick Ball</u>

. Keep each piece of paper on the floor.

. Use one hand only and crumple paper into two small balls.

. Place each ball in front of the hand that crumpled it.

. Use thumb and forefinger of each hand to <u>flick</u> each ball as far as possible.

. Do the same using thumb and middle finger, thumb and ring finger, and finally, thumb and <u>pinky</u>.

. Have races using specific fingers.

<u>Snow</u>

. Uncrumple each ball and flatten out the paper

. Tear each piece of paper into as many small pieces as possible.

. Pick up all pieces of paper.

. Gather everyone into a group close together.

. On a signal, everyone throws the <u>snow</u> into the air!!!

. Pick up all snow and dispose it properly.

Name	Bomb the Ball
Equipment	Bean bags; 1 large ball (large lebon ball or beach ball at least 12 inches); 2 long carpet tubes.
Areas of Concern	Throwing from sitting position; control.
Activities	. Place tubes on the floor, parallel and about five feet apart.
	. Place the ball in the center.
	. Have one child sit cross-legged at either end with bean bags in front of each child.
	. Tape tubes to floor to prevent rolling.

. On a signal, each child throws bean bags at the ball trying to knock it past the other child.

Hints	. Be sure students remain seated at all times.
	. Place additional students along tubes to keep ball inside in case it should get knocked over the tubes.
	. Use students on sides to push bean bags to throwers to keep game active.
	. Place students at distances closer to or further from ball depending on throwing abilities. If students are too close, they will continually knock the ball over the tubes.
Variation	Place tubes farther apart and have teams throw at ball. All other rules remain the same.

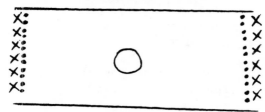

Name	IBM Tube Activities

Equipment

IBM tubes--small cardboard tubes obtained from businesses which use machines that need rolls of paper, i.e., xerox reproducing businesses.

Areas of Concern

Tactile stimulation; motor planning; risk taking; visual-motor coordination; number recognition and sequencing.

Activities

. Place twelve tubes on their sides next to each other on the floor.

. Perform the following tasks--

1. Lie on top of the tubes and roll over them by placing the hands on the floor and pushing as on a gym scooter. At the start, have the chest on the tubes and the rest of the body on the floor. As the student rolls over the tubes and nears the end, stop, reverse hand push, and roll back over tubes to starting position. Repeat sequence three times.

2. Place tubes about twelve inches from a wall. Have child lie on tubes as above. Bend legs and place feet against wall. Raise hands and arms off floor and push off wall with the feet and roll over the tubes. Encourage child to push hard enough to roll completely over and off tubes.

3. Place seven tubes between a wall and another barrier-- i.e., desk turned over or table which must be supported by a person when child pushes off it. Student lies on tubes and pushes off wall using the feet as above. As student approaches barrier, the hands and arms are extended to absorb the body weight. Then, student pushes with hands until feet make contact with wall. Continue sequence for five pushes with hands and feet. The distance between barriers is determined by size of child. Child should be able to roll back and forth and always remain on the tubes.

4. Sit on tubes with legs on top. Use hands to push back and forth over the tubes.

. Stack tubes as high as possible, using desks or a step-ladder to reach higher levels.

. Number tubes and stack them sequentially. To vary this, have two or three sets of tubes, each set numbered in a different color. Divide into teams and have each team stack tubes of their color.

. Stack tubes as high as possible, but, place a piece of paper between each pair of tubes. Next time, put a piece of cardboard between each pair of tubes.

INDIVIDUALIZING MOTOR SKILLS

The system and procedures presented have been developed to <u>individualize</u> the motor development program for students at Holly Park Early Childhood Center. Skills are those most often described in developmental scales. They are presented sequentially and with instructional suggestions for various steps leading to mature levels of performance in each area. No mention of age is made in the various areas. This program is based on <u>functional</u> abilities of students who are given tasks appropriate to their abilities.

This system can also be used as basis for individualized educational programs (IEPs). Each area is evaluated in an initial screening and the student's level of proficiency obtained. In preparing an IEP all that is necessary to include is the step at which the child is currently functioning and then add the next one or two steps as short term instructional objectives. This is a task analyzed system easily integrated into a motor development program.

At Holly Park, each area is printed on a large piece of poster board and displayed on the walls around the room. Each area has necessary equipment for the various taks. At each station is a list of students requiring work in that area. Numbers of tasks are listed for that area. As a child completes a step, an X is placed under that task number. The next number is the new short term objective which can then be transferred to an IEP.

When a class arrives, the teacher or aide remains throughout the period. The group may than be split with the motor specialist taking a group to an area and the teacher or aide going to another area. All assistants need to do is look at the list of names, locate appropriate task numbers on the cards, and proceed. As students become accustomed to the program, the group may be further divided for more stations; after an explanation of tasks, individual students may work independently. This depends largely on the nature of tasks and abilities of students. Certain tasks require supervision and assistance while others do not.

This system can be used for any type of skill. All that is necessary is analysis of skills so they can be presented sequentially to students beginning at the level at which each student is performing. By listing students' names on a large card, they are able to see individual growth as they progress to final stages of a skill. The most important aspect of this system is to set up progressions in ways that <u>success</u> can be obtained and each child be aware of his/her success. If increments are spaced too far apart, the student becomes frustrated and soon learns how to fail rather than succeed.

STATIC BALANCE

. Bears weight on extended arms and hands while lying prone for 1-3-5-8-10 or more seconds...

   ... place pillow or jouster under child's arms; encourage child to bear weight on arms; assist physically if needed.

   ... extend child's arms physically to assist in maintaining position.

   ... lie on stomach facing child; assume position--ask child to imitate.

. Lies still while prone (supine) with (without) support...

   ... touch body part if child moves it and remind him/her to remain still.

   ... place IBM tubes (small cardboard tubes) close enough so that any movement upsets them.

   ... place objects (tubes, balloons) on child.

. Sits on floor with (without) support for 30 seconds, 1-3-5-10 or more minutes...

   ... sits with legs extended in V position.

   ... sits between adults legs and may (may not) use adult's chest for support.

   ... sits with back erect against some support--i.e., wall, table, chair, side horse, parallel bars, partner.

   ... sits in cardboard box with one (two) side(s) removed.

. Supported around the trunk, bears all weight on the legs...

   ... hold both hands of child gradually releasing support and encouraging child to bear weight.

   ... stand behind child with rope or towel around his/her waist or under the arms; provide as little support as necessary.

. Stands supported under arms and bears all weight.

. Stands with support...

   ... place child holding onto chair or rail in standing position.

   ... allow child to begin with wide base gradually reducing until standing with heels together.

. Assumes and maintains a kneeling balance for 1-3-5-10-30 or more seconds...

   ... kneel and face child--do not sit on heels; ask child to imitate.

   ... uses wall or other support if necessary--do not allow child to support self for the entire time; encourage child to release hands from support.

- Stands without support for 1-3-5-10-30 or more seconds...

    ... if necessary allow child to use wall for support; removes hands for increasing periods of time.

    ... stand facing child maintaining correct position; ask child to imitate.

- Stands without support, heels together for 1-3-5-10-30 or more seconds; adds variations as above.

- Stands on one foot and with (without) support and raises the other foot off floor; adds variations as above.

- Stands on one foot with (without) support and eyes open for 1-3-5-10 or more seconds...

    ... stand on one foot facing child; ask child to imitate.

    ... hold child's hands; make sure child supports self on one leg and not on your hands.

    ... places both hands on back of chair or against wall; removes hands momentarily then replace them; increases non-support gradually

    ... stand about three feet from child; hold an object at child's eye level and have child focus on object while attempting balance.

- Stands on one foot with (without) support and eyes covered for 1-3-5-10 seconds or more...

    ... increase verbal reinforcement throughout.

    ... adds variations as above.

- Stands on tiptoes for 1-3-5-10 or more seconds with arms extended over head...

    ... place small blocks under child's heels.

    ... hold ball over child's head and ask child to reach and touch it with both hands.

    ... raise ball, forcing child to stand on tiptoes allowing child to touch ball when on tiptoes.

- Imitate and maintain various body poses, for 5-10 seconds...

    ... 4 points--hands and knees balance.

    ... 2 points--right hand, left knee.

    ... 2 points--left hand, right knee.

    ... 2 points--left hand, right foot.

... 2 points--right hand, left foot.

... any other body balances.

. Perform various balances with child--maintain each position for 5-10 seconds;
   if necessary, touch body part to be raised by child.

. Stands, feet together on a line.

. Maintains heel-to-toe standing position...

   ... have child stand on a line with the heel of one foot touching the toes
        of the other; if necessary, move the feet apart far enough so the child
        can maintain a comfortable balance; gradually bring feet closer to heel-
        to-toe position; switch lead foot periodically.

   ... have child stand next to wall and use it for support; do not allow child
        to use wall for entire balance; releases hands for longer periods of
        time.

   ... stand about three feet from child; hold an object at child's eye level;
        have child focus on object during balance; keep object stationary.

110

DYNAMIC BALANCE

. **Walks alone without difficulty.**

. **Walks backward 3 to 10 steps...**

   ... face the child, hold a ball with the child, and walk--provide enough force to make the child walk backward; use large ball.

   ... hold rope or towel around the child's waist or under his/her arms; stand behind the child and gently pull him/her backward so as not to force the child to make unnecessary balance adjustments.

   ... have the child pull a toy on string while walking backward.

   ... crawl or walk toward the child, making no contact; force the child to walk backward; be a <u>monster</u> making sure the child maintains eye contact throughout so as to ensure true backward movement.

. **Walks sideways several steps...**

   ... kneel or stand facing child; both hold a ball and move to the side forcing the child to move sideways.

   ... stand next to the child--move sideways forcing the child to move; <u>bump</u> the child along if necessary.

   ... have the child pull a toy while moving sideways.

   ... have the child move sideways between a wall and a continuous barrier set about 9 to 12 inches from the wall--size of the child determines distance between wall and barrier; barriers may be chairs, desks, tubes, or other objects.

   ... stand facing child--move to the side exaggerating movements; have child imitate; hold child's hands, then just one; perform from about 3 feet away without touching child.

. **Walks 2-4-6-8 feet between or on 2 lines--10"-8"-6"-4"-2" apart...**

   ... face child, holding ball with child--walk backward so the child walks forward; guide the child between lines by manipulating ball and controlling the child's movements.

   ... place barriers along edges and have child walk between lines without upsetting barriers.

   ... direct child verbally between lines; use occasional tactile cues.

   ... have child walk heel-to-toe the entire length; use footprints to guide child or touch (point to) the foot to be moved then touch (point to) the spot on which the foot is to be placed.

. Walks between curved lines 10"-8"-6"-4"-2" apart.

. Walks 1 to 3 steps on 1" x 10' line...

    ... touch (point to) foot to be moved, then touch (point to) area on line where foot is to be placed.

    ... place footprints on line for child to follow.

. Alternates feet full length of 6' board...

    ... demonstrate correct method emphasizing placement of feet.

    ... guide child tactilly by placing hands on the backs of the child's hands-- do not hold child's hands; release assistance gradually.

    ... stand behind the child; hold rope or towel around child's waist or support him/her under the arms if necessary--pull child slightly.

    ... face child; touch (point to) foot to be moved then touch (point to) spot on board where foot is to be placed.

. Walks sideways full length of 6' board...

    ... face child; hold ball and guide child sideways along board.

    ... face child and touch backs of hands as child moves along board.

    ... stand next to child and move sideways, forcing child to move; if necessary, <u>bump</u> child to force side movement.

    ... stand facing child and move sideways, verbally directing child to do same on the board.

. Walks backward full length of 6' board...

    ... stand on board and face child; hold ball and walk forward forcing child to walk backward.

    ... hold towel or rope around waist or support him/her under arms; pull slightly forcing child to walk backward.

    ... touch foot to be moved, then area on board where it is to be placed.

    ... stand on board and face child; walk toward child making no contact forcing child to walk backward; be a <u>monster</u>.

. Walks forward (backward) sliding feet on 4" board.

. Walks forward, alternates feet part way on 4" board keeping eyes focused on board.

. Walks on 1" x 10' line without stepping off.

. Walks circle 1" x 4' without stepping off.

. Walks on curved lines.

. Walks forward, alternating feet full length of 4" board.

. Walks forward, alternating feet on 4" board while keeping eyes on a stationary target held at eye level at the end of the board...

   ... straddle board about 6' from child and hold ball or other object at eye level; slowly walk backward as child moves forward; stop child as soon as his/her eyes look away from ball.

   ... same as above but slowly move ball up and down (side to side; in a circle, diagonally) as child moves.

. Walks forward, alternating feet over objects (rope, bean bags, tires and other objects on board) on 4" board; if necessary, give touch support to back of child's hands when stepping over objects.

. Walks forward heel-to-toe on 4" board; touch foot to be moved, then touch board where it is to be placed; emphasize the heel touching the toes of the other foot on each step.

. Walks forward on 4" board with eyes covered...

   ... hold ball with child; walk backward forcing child to walk forward; encourage child to see with the feet.

   ... assist by touching back of child's hands; do not hold child's hands.

. Walks sideways on 4" board with eyes on target...

   ... stand facing child; hold attractive object at child's eye level and move sideways--hold ball steady; stop child if eye contact is lost.

   ... same as in above but move ball slowly up and down (side to side, in a circle, diagonally).

. Walks backward on 4" board with eyes on target...

   ... walks entire length of board heel-to-toe.

   ... touch foot to be moved then the spot where it is to be placed.

. Walks sideways (backward) on 4" board with eyes covered...

   ... assist by touching back of child's hands; do not hold hands--gradually release assistance.

   ... encourage child verbally across board.

STAIR ACTIVITIES

. Crawls up stairs.

. Creeps backward down stairs.

. Ascends stairs with assistance...

  ... hold both (one) hand(s) (2 feet per step).

  ... grasp clothing from back, near waist.

. Descends stairs with assistance (2 feet per step)

  ... hold both (one) hand(s).

  ... grasp clothing from rear near waist.

. Ascends stairs unsupported (2 feet per step).

. Descends stairs unsupported (2 feet per step).

. Ascends stairs, one foot per step with assistance...

  ... hold both (one) hand(s).

  ... indicate by touch which foot goes to which step--touch child's foot, then touch step on which it belongs.

. Descends stairs with assistance (one foot per step).

. Ascends stairs without assistance alternating feet; verbally direct and encourage child up stairs.

. Descends stairs without assistance alternating feet...

  ... verbally direct child up steps indicating where to step.

  ... touch foot and show child where to place it on next step.

JUMPING

- Jumps in place; does not raise both feet off floor at the same time.

- Jumps in place raising both feet off the floor at same time...

  ... stand facing child; jump 2-3 times--ask child to imitate.

  ... hold child's hands and jump together; if necessary, lift child off the floor--demonstrate and emphasize bend of knees and forceful extension.

- Jumps off 7" step (12"box), one foot ahead

- Jumps off 7" step (12" box); two foot take off and landing with/without) assistance...

  ... demonstrate--ask child to imitate.

  ... hold both hands and assist in take off as necessary.

  ... hold one hand during jump.

  ... have child jump; catch child or the hands upon landing.

- Jumps over tape line on floor, one foot ahead.

- Jumps over rope on floor, two foot take off and landing...

  ... demonstrate--ask child to imitate.

  ... hold child's hands; as jump begins, pull forward a bit over tape or rope.

- Jumps over 2" high rope, one foot ahead

- Jumps over 2" high rope, two foot take off and landing; exaggerate height during demonstration by emphasizing crouch, arm action, leg action, extension, and landing forward.

- Jumps off 18" box, one foot ahead.

- Jumps off 18" box, onto mat, two foot take off and landing.

- Jumps over rope 8" high, one foot ahead.

- Jumps over rope 8" high, two foot take off and landing.

- Jumps off 28" box, one foot ahead.

- Jumps off 28" box, two foot take off and landing.

- Jumps over rope 12" high, two foot take off and landing.

DISTANCE JUMPING

. Jumps forward, one foot leads (leap).

. Jumps forward, two foot take off and landing...

   ... demonstrate jump--ask child to imitate.

   ... face child, hold both hands--as child begins to jump, pull forward slightly.

. Jumps forward 8" to 10" (two foot take off and landing).

. Jumps forward 14" to 18" (two foot take off and landing).

. Jumps forward 19" to 24" (two foot take off and landing)...

   ... demonstrate jump; exaggerate movement--crouch, forward lean, arm swing, leg bend, extension, and forward landing--ask child to imitate.

   ... have child jump over obstacles--rope, tubes; add to the number of obstacles to increase distance.

   ... jump onto or into targets--hoops, tires, tape marks.

Although this young boy has only one leg, he shows
good form and effort in the standing long jump.

116

HOPPING

- **Imitates one foot stand with assistance**--face child; stand on one foot-- **ask child to imitate;** if necessary, hold child's hand and touch or lift the **foot to be raised.**

- Stands on preferred (non-preferred) foot 1-3-5-10 seconds...

  ... stand on one foot facing child--ask child to imitate.

- Jumps on both feet 4 to 6 steps...

  ... face child; hop on both feet--ask child to imitate.

  ... hold child's hands and hop together; if necessary, have child try to do one two-foot jump, then two.

  ... hold child's hands--have child bend at the knees; as child extends legs, lift slightly off the floor.

  ... hops on 2 feet for a distance of 10 feet.

  ... hops on 2 feet while inside a 2 foot square.

- Hops on one foot 4 to 6 (7 to 9, 10 to 12) steps...

  ... have child hold onto back of chair or rail and hop on one foot.

  ... hold child's hands and hop together; it may be necessary to perform one hop at a time, rest, and then try another; then two-three........

  ... have child hop over a distance (a specified number).

  ... have child stand in same spot while hopping.

  ... when child is hopping for a distance, and non-hopping foot touches the floor, have the child <u>stop</u>, take a breath, begin again.

- Hops inside 2 foot square at least 5 continuous hops.

- Hops 50 feet on preferred foot in 11-seconds...

  ... set up two rows of chairs back to back, about 2 feet apart; set each row side by side--hops on one foot between the rows, holding onto the chairs when necessary; remove chairs gradually from each side until the child no longer needs added support.

  ... ask child to hop as far as possible--as soon as non-hopping foot touches the floor stop, relax and then continue; if necessary, count the number of hops out loud; then encourage the child to hop one more the next time.

Performs additional tasks...

... stands in front of steps with one foot on bottom step the other on the floor; lift off floor but do not place foot on step; hold one foot balance for as long as child can up to 10 seconds; reverses feet and repeat.

... place two rows of various sized boxes on floor--child must walk the entire distance, lifting each foot and placing it into the next box.

KICKING

. Kicks large stationary ball...

   ... place ball in front of kicking foot; ask child to kick it; if necessary, demonstrate proper method; kick with each foot.

   ... physically move child's leg through the proper kicking method.

. Kicks slowly moving ball...

   ... kneel about 3 feet from child and roll ball very slowly at each foot; ask child to kick it when it arrives.

   ... if necessary, demonstrate proper method.

   ... say kick when child should be beginning to prepare the leg to kick; experiment to discover correct timing for child.

. Move to kick ball rolled to left...

   ... demonstrate how to move to the left and be ready to kick ball when it arrives.

   ... stand about 3 to 4 feet from child; slowly roll ball just a bit to child's left forcing child to move about one step before kicking ball.

   ... gradually increase distance to the left.

   ... gradually increase speed of rolled ball.

   ... increase distance ball is rolled to child.

. Moves to kick ball rolled to right...

   ... use two balls; as child kicks one, roll the other one to the opposite side; continue, forcing child to change directions.

20

THROWING

- Throws ball with forward fling.

- Throws ball with forward fling without falling...

    ... put ball in child's hand, preferred hand if possible; kneel behind child and raise hand into throwing position near the ear; physically move child's arm through throwing motion.

    ... kneel facing child, 3 to 4 feet away; have child pick up object and throw to you; if necessary, position your arm correctly and have child imitate, then throw.

    ... use verbal cues regarding arm position.

    ... have child place foot opposite throwing arm slightly forward before throwing.

    ... gradually increase distance until child begins to move feet when throwing.

- Throws 3" ball overhand at least 3 feet and within arms length of tester, between knees and face.

- Throws 3" ball 7, 11, 13, 18 or more feet...

    ... have child place foot opposite throwing arm slightly forward before throwing.

    ... have child stand in small boxes (on footprints) correctly positioned for the feet.

    ... have child step forward with opposite foot while throwing.

    ... stand on footprints, then step and throw.

    ... have child throw from different bases of support--standing, kneeling, sitting.

    ... have child throw at targets.

    ... have child throw all different types and sizes of balls--yarn, nerf, tennis, utility, bean bags.

PRACTICAL POINTERS

Together we can do it......

MOVEMENT DISCOVERY
LINKING THE IMPOSSIBLE TO THE POSSIBLE
Donald G. Bornell Ed.D.

"The importance of activity as a positive learning experience for all children cannot be overemphasized. All children in their formative years must identify with their humanness and, through awareness of the mental and physical self, be able to say and/or feel 'I AM!' Thus, an inner balance contributes to sound emotional development and understanding of similarities and differences in human beings."*

"In the process of growth and development, all children should experience movement success within each of their capabilities and limitations and in an atmosphere which allows for optimum enjoyment through appropriate and well planned activities."*

It's that little bit of difference in planning activities or creating new activities and equipment in the adapted or regular physical education program that links the impossible to the possible for many children. Through this linkage, each individual has the opportunity to experience movement success, so necessary for participating in pleasurable physical recreational activities throughout life.

"Children need to be challenged and stimulated in a constructive way, and they need time to develop the appropriate skills necessary to feel a part of and not threatened by physical recreational activities or sport activities programs. Children should also be given the opportunity to make choices under appropriate conditions between competitive and noncompetitive sports, and nonvigorous and vigorous activities."*

"As we look into the future, it appears that humankind will pursue the physical activity through recreation that work once partially fulfilled, for the body is an energy system. Adults of tomorrow will seek physical recreation that involves the whole self in the way children are involved in play."*

The activities on the proceeding pages are representative of many ways in which a teacher can help pupils in physical education, regular or adapted, link the impossible to that which eventually becomes possible. Each of these activities evolved as a result of perceiving specific needs and interests of individuals in my adapted physical education program. And, keeping formost in mind that many children can learn to participate in at least a few of the many lifetime sports now available in our society, if given the opportunity to progress in a less obvious way from that which has been so commonly used in physical activities programs. HOWEVER, THE SUCCESS OF ANY ADAPTED PHYSICAL EDUCATION PROGRAM LIES IN THE TRUST LEVEL BETWEEN TEACHER AND PUPIL. ONLY WHEN THE TRUST LEVEL IS REACHED CAN SELF-CONFIDENCE EVOLVE. THE TEACHER HAS TO REALLY CARE!

*MOVEMENT IS INDIVIDUALITY, Donald G. and Cecil Jean Bornell, 1978,
   Publisher, G.S.C. Athletic Equipment, San Pedro, California.

AERIAL SHUFFLEBOARD, AERIAL GOLF, AND BOTTLES AND EGGS

Aerial shuffleboard, aerial golf, and plastic bottle and styrofoam eggs were created to improve eye-hand coordination and throwing ability while maintaining a high level of interest and enthusiasm. These activities evolved out of the need for dimensionalizing the program in inexpensive ways. The activities are ideal for pre-school, primary and adapted physical education classes. Furthermore, all three activities can be played from a standing or sitting position, thus allowing for pupils in wheelchairs to be as involved as other children.

CREATING THE AERIAL SHUFFLEBOARD

The shuffleboard targets can be made from 1/2" or 3/4" plastic water pipe, jump ropes, or drawn with chalk on blacktop or concrete. Hula hoops can also be used. If the targets are made from the plastic pipe, the following steps should be taken:
1. Using a hack saw, cut the flexible black plastic pipe into 9' lengths.
2. For each 9' length, cut a piece 3" long and each 3" length cut lengthwise.
3. If the 9' lengths are too stiff to form a circle, soften in hot water.
4. Use the 3" pieces as holding dowels by gluing them into the ends of the 9' loops, thus creating approximately 34" diameter plastic hoops.

The shuffleboard discs are made from bottoms of one gallon bleach bottles or other similar plastic bottles. The following steps should be taken for cutting the bottoms off of the plastic bottles:
1. Insert a sharp pointed scissors into the bottle about 1" from the bottom of the bottle and parallel to the bottom.
2. Keeping the scissors parallel to the bottom, cut around the bottle until the bottom is free. The bottom should resemble a mini frisbee.

CREATING THE AERIAL GOLF

The same hoops that are used for aerial shuffleboard can be used for aerial golf. Bean bags, nerf balls, tennis balls or small playground balls can be used as the throwing object. Bean bags can be made as a parent or P.T.A. project and old tennis balls can usually be obtained from high school, college, or tennis club coaches.

CREATING THE BOTTLE AND THE EGG

The one gallon plastic bottles that have had the bottoms cut off, become the catching device. The styrofoam eggs can usually be purchased at a hobby or craft shop and are very reasonable. Plastic eggs can also be used, however are more expensive.

PROCESS

For the game of aerial shuffleboard, each pupil should be given one hoop and at least two mini frisbees (the bottoms of one gallon plastic bottles). The game should be played on a smooth surface such as a wooden floor or on a blacktop surface. Sufficient space should be provided for each pupil to practice without interfering with another. The mini frisbee is thrown the same way as a regular frisbee. It will probably be necessary to demonstrate both throwing and positioning of the mini frisbee in the hand. It may even be necessary to move the arm through the motion.

For the game of aerial golf, have each pupil practice throwing whichever object is going to be used in the game. In practicing throwing, make sure that when throwing with the right hand the left foot is forward, and vice versa when throwing left-handed. Some children will throw equally well with either hand and should be given that opportunity.

For the game of the bottle and the egg, each pupil should be given a one gallon plastic bottle with the bottom cut out and one styrofoam or plastic egg. For right-handed children, the bottle should be held in the left hand by the handle, with the open bottom up, and in the right hand for left-handed children. The egg is held in the free hand. If the child has only one hand, the egg should be placed in the bottle, and the one hand is used for both tossing and catching.

AERIAL SHUFFLEBOARD ACTIVITIES

1. Each pupil should have one hoop and two to four mini frisbees. The hoop should be laid flat on a smooth surface and, from a distance of five feet away, the pupil should try to sail the mini frisbee so that it lands in the hoop.

2. After 3 out of 4 mini frisbees land and stay in the hoop, extend the throwing distance to 10 feet and continue as in step 1.

3. When sufficient skill in throwing is developed, pupils can pair off and create their own game of aerial shuffleboard by placing the hoops an agreed upon distance apart. They then take turns tossing the mini frisbees and can record on paper the number that stay within the hoop. Pupils can also decide if they want a pre-agreed upon number of tosses or points scored for a game.

AERIAL GOLF ACTIVITIES

1. Place a series of three to nine hoops far enough apart so that it takes more than one throw with whichever object will be used to get from one hoop to the next.

2. If a bean bag is used, each shot should be tossed. If a ball is used, all except the last or approach shot should be thrown towards each hoop. The approach shot should be rolled into the hoop area.

3. Practice throwing the bean bag or ball at just one of the hoops. Several pupils can practice at a time by being spread out over the course.

123

4. As accuracy improves, move further away from the hoop until it takes more than one toss to reach the hoop.

5. If sufficient hoops are available, several courses can be set up so that pupils do not have to stand in line waiting for a turn. It may also be advisable to set up three 3-hoop courses rather than one 9-hoop course.

6. After practicing going through the course, pupils can begin to keep track of the number of throws it takes to complete the course, and class and/or individual records can be established.

7. The above steps can be repeated using a nerf ball, tennis ball, or small playground ball. Remember, when using a ball, the last shot or attempted last shot for each hoop should be rolled.

BOTTLE AND EGG ACTIVITIES

1. The one gallon plastic bottles with the bottoms cut off are held by the handle with bottoms up, in the left hand for a right-handed pupil, and the right hand for a left-handed pupil.

2. The plastic or styrofoam egg is held in the dominant hand and with an underhand toss thrown straight up into the air. The egg should then be caught in the bottle. Tell the pupils that the eggs are very fragile and should not fall to the ground. This helps the child to focus in on the task. Emphasize throwing the egg a very short distance into the air so that it will not be missed.

3. After the pupil catches 3 out of 5, reverse hands using the catching hand as the throwing hand. Practice until some skill is achieved. The advantage in using a plastic or styrofoam egg not only allows for the child to focus on the task, it also will not roll very far if missed, which keeps frustration at a minimum.

4. Have the pupils pair off and practice throwing one egg back and forth, trying to see how many times they can catch it without missing.

5. Substitute small bean bags for the plastic eggs and repeat the above steps.

6. Substitute a tennis ball for the bean bag and repeat steps 1 through 3.

124

DIMENSIONS

Allow children to try using the bottles and eggs or balls in different ways. For example, placing the throwing object in the bottle and tossing it in the air with an upward movement of the bottle; then catching it in the bottle. Another example would be throwing a ball against a handball wall and catching it in the bottle. As a class project, the eggs can be decorated and the plastic bottles can be painted for individuality and personal identification. For aerial shuffleboard, children can create scoring zones drawn directly on the blacktop. A higher level of throwing skill is needed to toss the mini frisbee into the scoring zone without it sliding out. The scoring zones can be painted in bright colors as a class project. Aerial golf can also be painted on the playground, with hoops added behind obstacles such as benches, trees, handball courts, and tables.

MOVEMENT RELATIONSHIPS

Ball throwing
Frisbee tossing
Ball catching
Juggling

ENVIRONMENTAL RELATIONSHIPS

Casting in fishing
Tossing a boat line
Catching hot rivets in construction
Carnival midway

EVALUATION

The following three levels of evaluation are offered as guidelines for pupil entry into the activity, and for the learner to establish short and long-term objectives with teacher assistance.

LEVEL I

	YES	NO	COMMENTS
1. Toss mini frisbee into hoop 3 of 5 tries from five feet away.			
2. From a distance 1½ times maximum throw, get the nerf ball into hoop in three tries.			
3. Toss styrofoam egg into the air and catch it in plastic bottle 3 of 5 tries.			

LEVEL II

1. Toss mini frisbee into hoop 3 of 5 tries from ten feet away.			
2. Set up a three-hoop course, with hoops set further than one throw apart from each other. Complete course in 9 or fewer turns.			
3. Toss tennis ball into the air and catch it in plastic bottle 3 of 5 tries.			

LEVEL III

1. Repeat Level II #1 using opposite hand.			
2. Create an obstacle aerial golf course using 5 hoops and 3 obstacles.			
3. Throw a tennis ball against the wall and catch it in the plastic bottle 3 of 5 tries.			

Catalyst for Movement Discovery .....

CARDBOARD WALKING STILTS   (with elastic and non-elastic cords)

The cardboard walking stilts are used to improve kinesthesis and gross motor planning through movement patterns designed to stimulate positive perceptual awareness. Some of the recommended activities also bring about vestibular stimulation. The class set of blocks are strung in two different ways. Half of the set is strung with elastic cord, and the other half is strung with non-stretch cord. In working with children who exhibit motor coordination problems, or who are slow learners, the elastic cord strung cardboard stilts are ideal. Because these cords can be held with slight tension, it is not necessary to raise the arm and hand each time the foot is raised in order to keep the foot on the stilt, thus allowing the pupil to focus on only one motor task at a time instead of the usual two. Most children, whether in the regular or the adapted physical education class, can experience success in walking on these stilts with the elastic cords.

After the child experiences success with the elastic cord stilts, the non-elastic cord stilts can be tried. These stilts add another motor task by requiring the child to raise the arm and hand in unison with the foot to keep the stilts in contact with the sole of the foot.

Cardboard walking stilts are ideal for use in the preschool through primary grades physical education and adapted physical education programs.

CREATING THE STILTS

The cardboard walking stilts are made from centers of carpet rolls, which are long cardboard tubes approximately four inches in diameter. The handles are made from any durable round elastic and non-elastic cord.

1. Cut the cardboard into 4" lengths using a fine tooth saw or a band saw.
2. Drill two holes in each 4" section opposite each other and 1" in from the edge.
3. Cut the cords into 5' lengths.
4. Thread the cord through the two holes and tie.
5. If used as a class project, give each child two 4" long pieces of pre-drilled cardboard tubing, two 5' long cords, and a set of paints.
6. Allow each child to create his or her own designs on the tubes before threading the cords through.

PROCESS

Before using the cardboard walking stilts, it would be helpful if the child had the opportunity to practice walking on the mini metric beams and balancing on the walk 'n balance disc.* After learning to walk on the stilts, the child will be ready to participate in group activities using the stilts.

The stilts with the elastic cords, although designed for lower level entrance performance than the non-elastic cord stilts, still require some balance skill and eye-foot coordination. When first working with a child, it may be necessary to help the child properly locate the foot on the stilt. Always make certain that the foot is far enough on the stilt for a secure feeling.

*Beams and balance platforms can be made or purchased through equipment supply companies.

CARDBOARD WALKING STILTS ACTIVITIES

1. When the child first begins to use
    the stilts, the teacher should
    stand next to or in back of the
    child to lend assistance. The
    teacher may even have to demon-
    strate using the stilts. Place
    the stilt in front of the child's
    foot and have the child step on
    to it. Hand the cord to the
    child. Have the child take a
    step with the stilt. Have the
    child practice using one stilt.

2. Practice using the stilt on the
    opposite foot.

3. Now have the child step onto both
    stilts. If the child has dif-
    ficulty walking with the stilts,
    replace with stilts strung with
    elastic bands. Have child anchor
    bands on knees or thighs by holding
    the band so that it is slightly
    stretched. Have the child try
    walking without moving the hands
    and concentrate on the feet only.

4. Practice walking forward and
    backward.

5. Practice a side step to the right
    and to the left.

6. Now exchange the elastic band
    stilts for non-elastic band
    stilts and repeat steps 4 and 5.

7. If the child has difficulty co-
    ordinating the hand-foot movement,
    walk behind the child holding on
    to each hand, lifting it with each
    step of the stilt.

8. After the children experience walking
    success on the stilts, a mini ob-
    stacle course can be created out
    of small boxes, cones, hoops,
    plastic bottles, and bicycle tires
    for the children to move around,
    over, and into.

127

9. Make sufficient obstacles available for the children to create their own mini courses and practice at an individual pace.

10. After sufficient skill is attained on the stilts, a child can be given a six inch playground ball to practice kicking while on the stilts.

11. Once skill is attained in kicking the ball, children can be paired up and practice kicking the ball back and forth to each other.

12. As soon as a group of children learn to control the ball, they can be grouped into a game of zone soccer or other modified ball kicking games which can be played in a limited area.

13. When a child attains a high level of skill on the stilts, he or she can be further challenged by crossing the cords and having the right hand control the left foot and the left hand control the right foot.

14. Using the pattern in step 13, have the child try walking backward.

15. Using the same holding pattern, try moving through an obstacle course.

16. Competitive activites may include:
    a. Kicking a ball for distance while on the stilts.
    b. Kicking a ball for accuracy at a plastic bottle or between two cones.
    c. Backward walking relay on the stilts.
    d. Ball kicking relay on the stilts.
    e. Obstacle relay on the stilts.

DIMENSIONS

Allow children to try different ways of using the stilts. For example, a modified bowling game can be created by using pint or quart size plastic bottles and the 6" rubber playground ball. Create a new relay such as holding a tennis ball between chin and chest while walking on the stilts. Try some of the above activities on higher cardboard stilts cut up to 12" long. Create a dance to music while on the stilts.

MOVEMENT RELATIONSHIPS

Walking the balance beam
Pedaling a bicycle
Using a pogo stick
Walking on wooden stilts

ENVIRONMENTAL RELATIONSHIPS

Walking in elevator shoes, or high heels
Working in high construction
Performing in a circus
Climbing a ladder

EVALUATION

The following three levels of evaluation are offered as guidelines for pupil entry into the activity, and for the learner to establish short and long-term objectives with teacher assistance.

LEVEL I

1. Pupil walks on one stilt using elastic cord.

2. Pupil walks on both stilts using elastic cords.

LEVEL II

1. Pupil walks forward on two stilts using non-elastic cords.

2. Pupil walks backward on stilts using non-elastic cords.

3. Pupil can kick a 6" playground ball while on the stilts.

LEVEL III

1. Pupil walks through obstacle course on the stilts.

2. Pupil can kick a ball between two cones from a specified distance while on the stilts.

3. Pupil can create a new activity with the stilts.

YES	NO	COMMENTS

CHARLESTON TO "ME AND MY SHADOW"

Because the basic steps of the "Charleston" are fun to do, the dance has a built-in motivational factor not always present in many of the dances taught in school. Furthermore, the primary step is a simple forward and backward walking movement and can be learned by many exceptional children. When children have difficulty coordinating the steps to slow music such as "Me and My Shadow," DISCO TAP® * taps can be used on the shoes so as to feel and hear the body rhythm in relationship to the music. When hearing the taps and the music, it is often easier to synchronize the two sounds as opposed to hearing the music without the tap sound. After the pupil begins to feel the rhythm, he or she may have the choice of removing the taps or continuing with them on. Taps are especially helpful for children with hearing impairments and for those who are blind. If the pupil had difficulty coordinating the foot pattern to the music, the teacher may need to walk the child through the movement, demonstrating each step while slowly increasing the speed.

PROCESS

The pupils should be given the opportunity to listen to slow 4/4 music such as "Me and My Shadow." After listening to the music for awhile, the teacher can tap or clap the beat and the children can then join in. The teacher can recite with the beat, "get/the/rhy/thm." If DISCO TAP® taps are available, they can be placed on the hands and tapped on the desk, tapped against each other, or on a lap tap board made from masonite. By using this approach, the feeling of rhythm can begin to evolve prior to actually trying to move the feet to the music.

BASIC STEPS FOR THE CHARLESTON

1. From a natural standing position, step forward on the left foot, step forward on the right foot; step back on the right foot, step back on the left foot.

2. Take four steps forward, starting on the left foot and ending on the right foot.

3. Take four steps backward, starting on the right foot and ending on the left foot.

4. Do a complete circle to the left, starting on the left foot by taking four steps and finishing on the right foot in the original position.

5. Do a complete circle to the right, starting on the right foot by taking four steps and finishing on the left foot in the original position.

*DISCO TAP® taps are portable taps held in place with elastic straps and velcro and can be used on the shoes or hands for tap dancing or lap tapping. They are manufactured by E. B. Smith Tap Co. and are available at most tap dancing supply stores or through G.S.C. Athletic Equipment of San Pedro, California.

6. With feet in line parallel and about 6" apart, bend knees slightly and place hands on knees. Bring knees together and slip the right hand over the left and the left under the right simultaneously finishing with the right hand on the left knee and the left hand on the right knee as the knees move apart. The arms are now crossed. Bring knees together again and exchange location of hands so that they are again right hand on right knee and left hand on left knee as knees move apart. Arms are now uncrossed. <u>Some may find it easier to slide the left hand over the right hand and the right hand under the left hand.</u>

7. Taking the same starting position as in # 6, point the toes of the shoes in by pivoting on both heels. Point the toes out by pivoting on both heels. Repeat, toes in, toes out.

8. Again taking the same starting position as in # 6 with hands on knees, move to the right by pivoting on the right heel and left toe, heels come together; left heel right toe, toes come together; right heel, left toe, left heel, right toe (this is a very difficult movement and some children may not be able to learn it).

9. Take four steps forward starting on the left foot and finishing on the right foot with feet parallel to each other and in line. Place hands on knees and take four jump steps backward (like a hopping rabbit).

10. Again take four steps forward starting on the left foot. With hands on knees take four jump steps backward, slapping the knees between each jump step, which becomes a hop, slap, hop, slap (this is also a difficult movement and may not be learned by all children).

11. Step forward on the left foot and swing the right leg in front of the left leg. Step back on the right foot and bring the left leg back so that the toe of the left foot touches the floor behind the right foot and to the rear.

12. Repeat # 11 adding arm movement. As the left foot moves forward, both arms swing simultaneously to the left; as the right foot swings forward, both arms swing simultaneously to the right; as the right foot comes back, both arms swing simultaneously to the left; as the left foot comes back, both arms swing simultaneously to the right.

131

CHARLESTON TO ME AND MY SHADOW
(Eric Rogers and his Orchestra)
(The Percussive Twenties)

MEASURES	LYRICS	STEPS
1	No music (four beats of tapping)	No steps (listen to the beat)
2	No music (four beats of soft shoe)	No steps (listen to the beat)
3	No music (two beats of tapping, two beats of soft shoe)	No steps (listen to the beat)
4	No music (one beat of tapping, one beat of soft shoe, one beat of tapping, one beat of soft shoe)	No steps (listen to the beat)
5	Me and My	Step forward on left foot, step forward on right foot, step back on right foot, step back on left foot (basic step # 1)
6	Shadow	Repeat measure 5
7	Music	Take four steps forward starting on the left foot (basic step # 2)
8	Music	Take four steps backward starting on the right foot (basic step # 3)
9	Me and My	Step forward on left foot, step forward on right foot, step back on right foot, step back on left foot (basic step # 1)
10	Shadow	Repeat measure 9
11	Music	Do a complete circle to the left starting on the left foot by taking four steps and finishing on the right foot in the original position (basic step # 4)
12	Music	Do a complete circle to the right starting on the right foot by taking four steps and finishing on the left foot in the original position (basic step # 5)
13	Music	Step forward on left foot, step forward on right foot, step back on right foot, step back on left foot (basic step # 1)
14	Music	Repeat measure 13

MEASURE	LYRICS	STEPS
15	Music	Place hands on knees, bring knees together and slip the right hand over the left hand and the left hand under the right hand, finishing with right hand on left knee and left hand on right knee as knees move apart; bring knees together again and exchange location of hands so that they are in starting position, right hand on right knee, and left hand on left as knees move apart (basic step # 6)
16	Music	Repeat measure 15
17	Me and My	Step forward on the left foot and swing the right leg in front of the left leg. Step back on the right foot and bring the left leg back so that the toe of the left foot touches the floor behind the right foot and to the rear (basic step # 11)
18	Shadow	Repeat measure 17
19	Music	Hands on knees, move to the right by pivoting on the right heel and the left toe, left heel and right toe, right heel and left toe, left heel and right toe (basic step # 8)
20	Music	Repeat measure 19 moving to the left
21	Music	Rest with hands on hips
22	Music	Step forward on the left foot and swing the right leg in front of the left leg. Step back on the right foot and bring the left leg back so that the toe of the left foot touches the floor behind the right foot and the rear (arm movements can be added as in basic step # 12)
23	Music	Repeat measure 22 using arm movements
24	Music	Take four steps forward starting on the left foot (basic step # 2)
25	Music	Take four jump steps backward, slapping the knees between each jump step (basic step # 10)
26-47	Music	Use any steps that have been learned

DIMENSIONS

Ask the class to talk to their grandparents or other senior citizens to obtain more information about the era of the 1920's and about the Charleston Dance, and what the world was like then. Ask each pupil to work out a dance routine using at least four of the steps they have learned. Practice the steps until they can be danced to the music "Charleston." Try making up new steps and new arm movements.

MOVEMENT RELATIONSHIPS

Folk dancing
Square dancing
Disco dancing
Tap dancing

ENVIRONMENTAL RELATIONSHIPS

Waves against rocks
Rhythmic walking
Rain drops
Assembly line movement patterns
Grandfather clock

EVALUATION

The following three levels of evaluation are offered as guidelines for pupil entry into the activity, and for the learner to establish short and long-term objectives with teacher assistance.

LEVEL I   (with or without DISCO TAP® taps)

1. Take four steps forward starting on left foot and finishing on right foot.

2. Take four steps backward starting on left foot and finishing on right foot.

3. Take two steps forward starting on left foot and two steps backward starting on right foot.

LEVEL II   (with slow 4/4 music)

1. Take four steps forward keeping in time with the music.

2. Take four steps backward keeping in time with the music.

3. Take two steps forward starting on left foot and two steps backward starting on right foot, keeping in time with the music.

LEVEL III   (without taps)

1. Perform three different "Charleston" steps to the music of "Me and My Shadow."

2. Perform three different steps to any "Charleston" type music, feet synchronized to the music.

3. Create a new step to previously used music.

	YES	NO	COMMENTS

134

MODIFIED SKATEBOARD

The modified skateboard was designed to allow students who show signs of poor motor coordination or have CNS (central nervous system) impairment to learn the rudiments of skateboarding. The skateboard is substantially heavier than standard boards to give greater stability. The rear of the board is flat, and the handle is placed behind the front wheels in order to keep the board from tipping up if the foot is placed too far to the rear, or tipping forward if the foot is placed too close to the front. The handle can be removed without the use of tools, thus eliminating the problem of misplacing nuts, bolts, or wrench. The quick removable handle allows for greater continuity in progression and for working with pupils of varying stages of ability.

CREATING THE MODIFIED SKATEBOARD

1. Cut the skateboard base from 3/4" plywood 26" by 6".
2. Using a 3" radius, mark semicircles at both ends of the board and cut along the line with a portable jigsaw or band saw.
3. From the scrap plywood cut a 3" square.
4. Glue the 3" square 4½" on center from the end of the board (since both ends of the board were cut the same, either end will do). For added strength, secure the 3" square in all four corners with four 1¼" flat head wood screws.
5. Using a 1¼" bit and electric drill, drill a hole through the center of the 3" square and skateboard base.
6. Cut a 1½" dowel 30" long and make a pencil mark 1½" in from one end completely around the dowel.
7. On that same end make a circle 1¼" in diameter, and using a sharp knife or wood rasp, trim that end down to the pencil marks until it fits snugly into the 1¼" hole drilled through the skateboard base. It may be necessary to sand the trimmed end for a better fit.
8. Drill a 3/16" hole about 1" deep into the same end and screw a 2½" long ¼" two-way wood/machine thread screw into the hole. Wrap the machine threads with masking tape to protect the threads while screwing it into the hole with a pair of plyers.
9. Drill a 7/8" hole about 1½" on center from the other end of the 1½" dowel. The handle grip will be slid through this hole.
10. Cut a 10" piece from a 7/8" dowel and slip through the hole, leaving 6¼" protruding from both sides. Drill a small hole in the 1½" dowel at right angles to the 3/4" dowel, and insert 1½" flathead screw to secure the handle grip.
11. Mount the skateboard wheels ½" in from the two ends on the same side as the 3" square is mounted. The front wheels should be between the 3" square and the front edge. The rubber mountings of the two sets of wheels should face each other.
12. Insert handle through the hole, place two 1½" washers and ¼" wing nut on the end of the screw and secure, making sure the handle grip is at right angles to the skateboard.

PROCESS

In the process of learning to use the modified skateboard, the pupil should first practice on a low balance beam, being able to walk to the center, turn around, and walk back. The pupil should also be able to perform a scale on the low balance beam. To perform a scale, the arms are extended out from the side, the upper part of the body is bent at the waist, either foot is extended to the rear and raised about waist high. A pupil can practice the above on a chalk line marked on the floor or blacktop. Protect the severely handicapped with helmet and knee and elbow pads.

MODIFIED SKATEBOARD ACTIVITIES

1. Hold handle grip with both hands and place the right foot on skateboard with toe against handle. Push with left foot propelling the skateboard. Begin slowly. It may be necessary to demonstrate the movement. It may also be necessary to hold onto the handle while pupil is practicing. Keep practice area clear of debris.

2. Have pupil practice step 1 using the left foot on skateboard.

3. Go through steps 1 and 2 increasing the speed. Move along with pupil staying on side opposite push foot in order to lend assistance.

4. After pupil begins to feel balance while in motion, suggest holding push foot up while coasting.

5. Repeat step 4 using opposite foot.

6. After steps 4 and 5 are learned, have pupil push off three times and place push foot behind foot on board. This movement may have to be demonstrated. Some children can balance better using only one side of the board for pushing. To lend assistance with this movement, move along with the pupil staying on the side opposite the push foot.

7. Observe the location of the feet on the board and make sure they are lined up along the center for better balance.

8. Repeat step 6 reversing the foot position.

9. After pupil is able to coast with both feet on the board, ask the pupil to release the left hand while continuing to coast. Again, this movement may have to be shown.

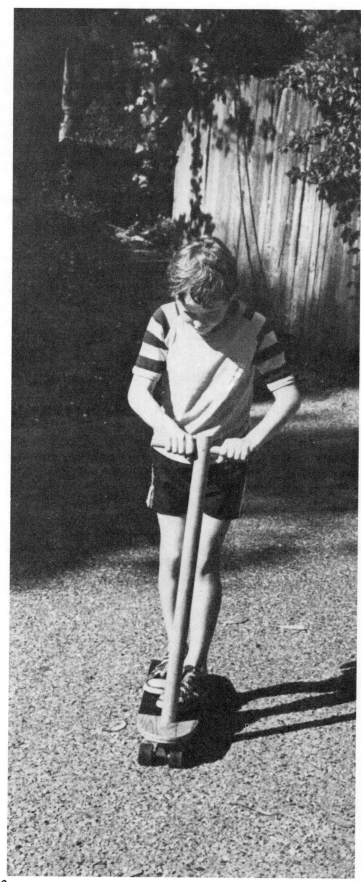

10. While holding the handle with one hand, push off three times and coast. While coasting, release the handle with holding hand. Move along with the pupil to lend assistance if necessary.

11. When the pupil is capable of releasing both hands while coasting, ask the pupil to try pushing off three times and placing the push foot on the board without the hands touching the handle grip.

12. When the pupil feels balance in motion without holding on to the handle grip, remove the handle and repeat step 11. Again move along with the pupil to lend a helping hand if necessary.

13. Ask the pupil to reverse the foot position and try it from the opposite side. Demonstrate if necessary. Then allow the pupil to work from the side that seems most natural.

14. Replace the handle and practice turning. To turn to the right, lean slightly to the right with knees bent slightly towards the right. Hold onto the handle grip through the turn.

15. To turn to the left, lean slightly to the left with knees bent slightly towards the left. Hold onto the handle grip through the turn.

16. Practice steps 13 and 14 while releasing the handle.

17. After sufficient skill has been attained, remove the handle and practice the turns in either direction.

18. To develop skill and confidence, have pupil move around plastic bottles or cones placed about twenty feet apart.

DIMENSIONS

The pupils who have mastered the above steps can then go on to participating in community skateboard activities. Some pupils will always need to use the handle, however, can still enjoy the feeling of free movement on wheels. Allow pupils to set up their own skateboard course using plastic bottles. They can also time themselves to find out how long it takes to move through the course and then try to improve on their own times.

MOVEMENT RELATIONSHIPS	ENVIRONMENTAL RELATIONSHIPS
Riding a bicycle	Controlling a vehicle in traffic
Roller skating	Balancing on a ladder
Surf boarding	Driving a moped
Skiing	Conveyer belts

EVALUATION

The following three levels of evaluation are offered as guidelines for pupil entry into the activity, and for the learner to establish short and long-term objectives with teacher assistance.

	YES	NO	COMMENTS
LEVEL I			
1. Holding handle grip, with right foot on skateboard, pupil pushes off with left foot and coasts.			
2. Holding handle grip, pupil pushes off and coasts, placing push foot on skateboard.			
LEVEL II			
1. Holding handle grip with one hand, pupil pushes off and coasts.			
2. Holding handle grip with one hand, pupil pushes off and coasts, placing push foot on skateboard.			
3. While holding handle, pupil can turn skateboard by leaning in appropriate direction.			
LEVEL III			
1. Without holding handle grip, pupil can push off and coast.			
2. Without holding handle grip, pupil can coast with both feet on the skateboard.			
3. Without holding handle grip, pupil can turn skateboard while coasting with both feet on the board.			

PRACTICAL POINTERS

MOTOR DEVELOPMENT RELAYS

Bruce Thiele
Psychomotor Specialist

Sally Warner
Recreation Therapist

Tom Marsh
Physical Education Instructor

The Devereux Foundation in California
Santa Barbara, California

Study of neuromuscular and perceptual development of the human organism shows existence of an orderly sequence of developmental stages. Individual abilities develop from undifferentiated motor activities through a complex hierarchy which includes formation of both concepts and perceptions. Sensorimotor activities affect formation of concepts. These concepts influence formation of new perceptions which in turn direct motor activities.

Unfortunately, neurological impairments, environmental deprivations, illnesses, emotional disturbances, and physical handicapping conditions prevent some individuals from progressing smoothly through the sensorimotor perceptual development hierarchy. When this occurs an individual can be helped overcome or reduce deficits through participation in controlled activities that stimulate development of kinesthetic differentiation, body image, balance, agility, spatial organization, motor planning, fine motor control, and visual perception.

Obstacle course relays were devised to serve these purposes in structured, challenging, and enjoyable activities. Relays also promote development of communication skills and the concept of teamwork; leadership skills are also encouraged. An important characteristic of these relays is flexibility. They may be adjusted in simplicity or complexity to all ability levels. Students of various ages and skill levels can participate together. An obstacle course may be run individually, against one challenger, against the clock, or as a team activity. In most cases younger or more severely involved students respond best to races against the clock or one challenger; older or more capable students are more motivated by competitive team relays.

MANAGEMENT OF RELAYS

Layout of Obstacle Courses

Two courses are set up, each with three to twelve different stations which lead students down the sides of the area to the end of the field or gymnasium and then back to the center of the area to the starting point. Courses are identical except that a station or activity approached from the right by one team is approached from the left by the other team. Students alternate courses from one race to the next. Each course includes stations with activities designed to develop both gross and fine motor skills. Three or four relay races are conducted per class period. Relays increase in difficulty when new tasks are added after each race. The variety of tasks is limited only by one's imagination and can include any task thought to promote sensorimotor development.

The following instructions should be adapted to meet intellectual, social, and skill levels of participants.

Choosing Teams

The instructor chooses two captains; captains then choose teams which must have equal numbers of students. Alternate Method--class elects captains who choose teams so that order in which students are chosen is known only to team captains

Instructing Teams

Instructions are given by the instructor to team captains before the start of each race. Captains in turn convey instructions to their teams. If a participant has a question, he/she must ask the captian who must consult the instructor. Limit time captains are allowed for giving directions to their teams before starting a relay. Points may be given to the first team ready to begin.

Starting Relays

Teams line up at the starting line so that each participant is in a straddle poisiton--legs apart--and one student is behind another. After the instructor signals start of the race, an object--ball, scooterboard, bean bag--is passed between the legs of the players to the end of the

140

line. The last player in line negotiates the obstacle course first. After completing assigned tasks on the obstacle course, each participant returns to the front of his/her team and passes the object to teammates until it reaches the individual now at the end of the line. Teams must keep their lines straight and be ready for returning players since this procedure is followed until all participants have completed the obstacle course.

Finishing Relays

Before starting a relay, the participant on each team assigned to go first is instructed to perform a special finishing task after all team members--including him/herself have competed. The finishing task should be exacting, conclusive, and have a high degree of difficulty within the range of each student's abilities. This makes the race more exciting for students, often allows a team which is behind to catch up, and makes it easy to determine the team finishing first.

Scoring

Participant motivation usually increases when points are scored and the winning team determined by a cumulative score at the end of class. Point values are assigned each race and doubled for following relays--first relay, 5 points; second, 10; third, 20; fourth, 40.

A team's score may be increased by players earning points for successfully completing individual tasks on the obstacle course. For example, if the task is to throw four bean bags into a pail, score one point for each bean bag making the target; two targets, one more difficult to hit than the other, maybe set up so that greater point values are assigned the more difficult target. Another method to score points is by giving students three opportunities to complete a task successfully--ring toss, shoot a basket. If successful on the first attempt, score 15; on second attempt, 10; third, 5. Running scores are kept for the two teams, not for individual students.

141

LEG POWER

Levels   Elementary and Junior High

Objectives   Develops balance, ability to change
                directions, figure-ground discrim-
                ination, spatial organization, and
                fine motor control.

Equipment   2 9" utility balls; 1 incline
                mat; 12 24" cones; 2 image ball
                boards; 2 card tables.

Sequence   Line up, pass ball through legs--

                1. While holding ball, run in
                    and out of the cones, down
                    and back.

                2. Begin as in #1. On the way
                    back do a somersault on the
                    mat while holding onto the
                    ball.

                3. Same as #2. After the
                    somersault, run to the card
                    table. Hold the utility ball
                    between knees. Take the ball
                    out of the board and replace
                    in the same design.

                4. Same as #3. Before doing the
                    somersault, go to basketball
                    net and shoot until a basket
                    is made.

Finishing Task Run straight to the basket with
                ball and shoot--first basket
                made wins race.

142

BASIC BASKETBALL

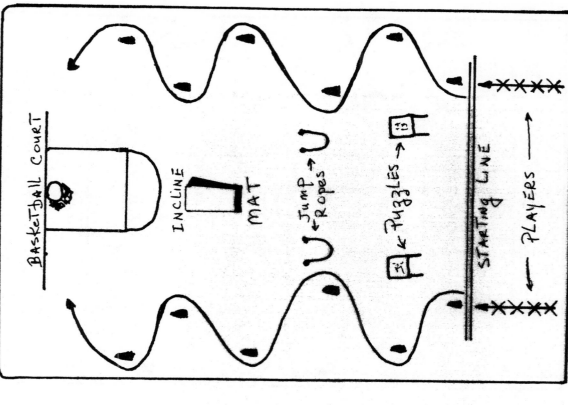

Levels

Junior and Senior High

Objectives

Develops balance, ability to change directions, figure-ground discrimination, spatial organization.

Equipment

12 24" cones; 2 volleyballs; 1 incline mat; 10 nuts and bolts; 2 jump ropes; 2 card tables.

Sequence

1. While holding ball, run in and out of the cones down and back. (5 points)

2. Run down holding ball (as in #1), run to incline mat and do a somersault. (10 points).

3. Same as #2. After somersault, run to jump rope, put volleyball between knees and jump 5 times. (20 points)

4. Same as #3. After jumping rope go to table. First player takes nuts and washers off bolts; second player puts them on, continuing to alternate in this manner. (40 points)

5. Begin as in #1. Go to basket, shoot 3 times (1 point for each successful basket). Run back to line.

Finishing Task

Run straight to the basket with ball and shoot.

DOWN ON THE FARM—GATHERING EGGS

Levels

Elementary, Junior and Senior High

Objectives

Develops eye-hand control, balance, spatial orientation, visual memory, grasping, fine motor control, form perception.

Equipment

12 24" cones; 12 12" softballs; 2 plastic garbage pails; 2 image ball boards; 1 walking board; 1 incline mat; 2 climbing ropes; 2 card tables.

Sequence

Line up, pass pail containing balls through legs.

1. With pail, run up and set softballs on cones. Run back, take softballs off, and return them to pail.

2. Run up setting balls on cones. With empty pail, walk across balance beam (walking board) and run back to line. Next person puts balls in pail, next sets them on cones, continuing to alternate in this manner.

3. Same as #2. Add somersault on incline mat. Go to card-table, take image balls out of the board and replace in the same design.

Finishing Task

Climb rope to top and touch ceiling.

144

PUSHING THE PUCK

Levels

Junior and Senior High

Objectives

Develops spatial relationships, visual depth perception, temporal rhythm, arm-leg coordination, fine motor dexterity.

Equipment

12 24" cones; 2 shuffle board cues; 2 shuffle board discs; 2 individual jump ropes; 2 pegboard puzzles; 2 basketballs; 2 card tables.

Sequence

Have discs at the starting line. Line up; pass cue through legs.

1. Push disc with cue in and out of the cones, up and back.

2. Push disc in and out of cones to the end, then go to the jump rope, set down cue and jump 5 times.

3. Same as #2. After jumping rope, go to the table and take pegs out of board and replace in the same design.

4. Push disc in and out of cones. Go to basket, set cue down and pick up basketball; shoot until a basket is made. Return straight to line pushing disc.

Finishing Task

Run up without cue, pick up basketball and make a basket.

BASKETBALL COURT

JUMP ROPE

PUZZLES

START

PLAYERS

145

HALLOWEEN SPECIAL

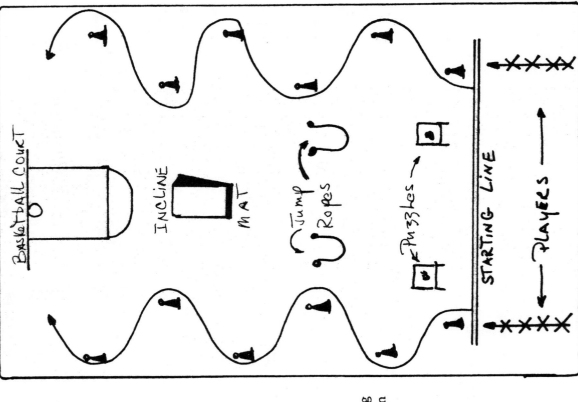

Levels   Elementary and Senior High

Objectives   Develops fine motor ability, visual
                memory, spatial orientation, rhythm,
                motor integration, form perception.

Equipment   2 funny hats; 12 24" cones; 12 12"
                softballs; 1 incline mat; 2 jump
                ropes; 2 image ball boards; 2
                plastic garbage pails; 2 card
                tables.

Sequence   Line up. Pass hat between legs of
                players. Last person puts on hat
                for relay.

                1. Pick up pail containing soft-
                    balls. Run up setting balls
                    on cones. Run back, taking
                    softballs off and returning
                    them to pail. Go to line, set
                    pail down, pass hat.

                2. Begin as in #1. Before returning
                    to line, go to mat, set pail down
                    and do somersault. Go to jump
                    rope, jump 5 times. Pick up
                    pail and return to line. Next
                    person takes balls off cones,
                    next puts them on, continuing
                    to alternate in this manner.

                3. Same as #2. Before returning
                    to cone, go to card table, take
                    image balls out of board.
                    Replace in same design.

Finishing Task Run without pail to basket. Pick
                up ball, make basket.

146

OUTSIDE OBSTACLE COURSE

Levels

Elementary and Junior High

Objectives

Develops right and left integration, agility, visual memory, balance, and strengthens arms and legs.

Equipment

1 outdoor field; 15 24" cones; 10 tires; 1 rope ladder; 1 36" concrete conduit; 2 24" playground balls; 2 image boards; 2 card tables.

Sequence

1. Dribble playground ball in and out of cones, and return to line.

2. Same as #1, plus climb over rope ladder, and hop through tires.

3. Same as #2, plus take puzzle apart, crawl through conduit, and assemble puzzle.

Finishing Task

Roll ball through conduit and knock over cone.

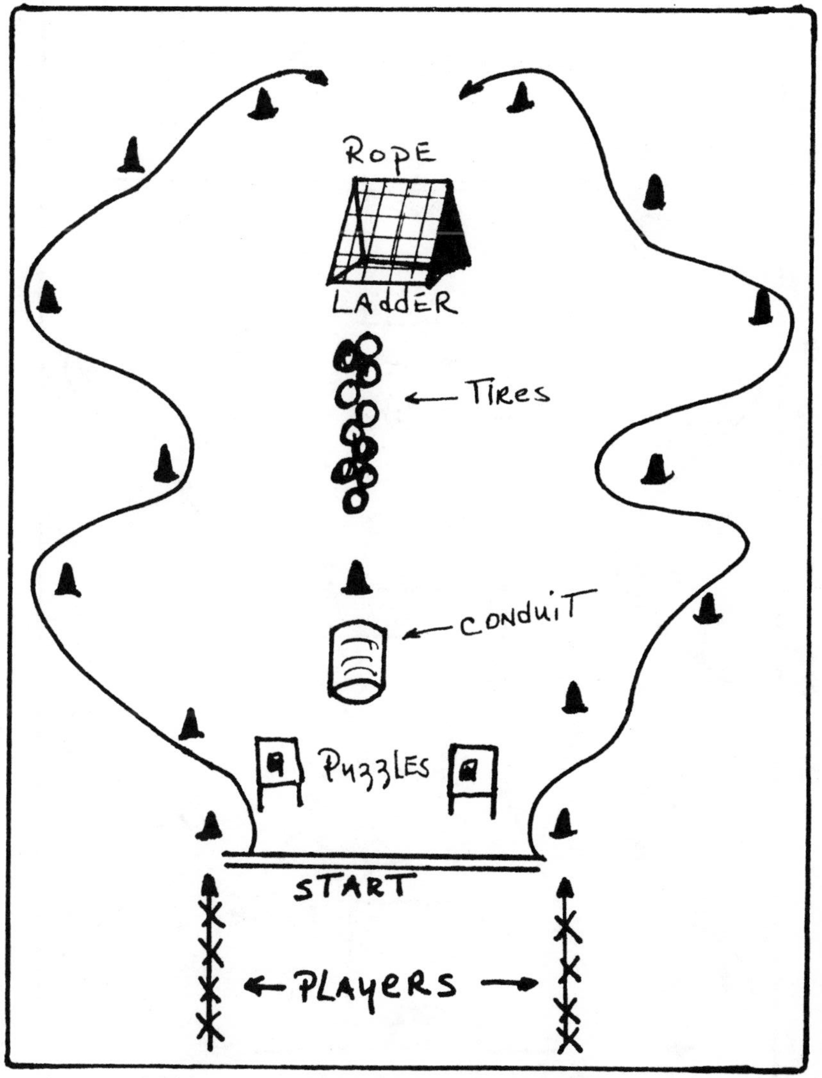

147

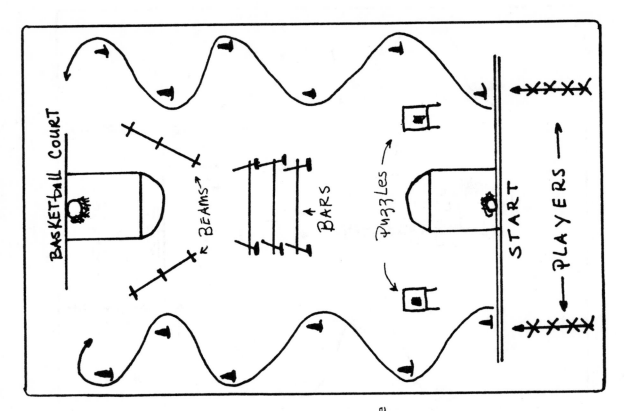

SCOOTING ALONG

Levels

Junior and Senior High

Objectives

Develops spatial awareness, motor integration, balance, arm and shoulder strength, form perception, sequential memory.

Equipment

12 24" cones; 2 scooter boards; 2 3½" x 12' balance beams; 3 high jump bars; 2 card tables; 2 image ballboards; 2 playground balls.

Sequence

Line up, pass scooter board through legs of players.

1. Sit on scooter board and scoot in and out of cones (forward or backward) up and back.

2. Kneel on scooter board. Push with arms in and out of cones (balance up. Go to walking board, (balance beam) straddle it with scooter board and scoot across. Pick up scooter board, go under, over, under 3 times on high jump bars.

3. Same as #2. Go to card table. Kneel on scooter board and take balls out of board; replace in same design.

4. Same as #3. Go to basket, kneel on scooter board, shoot for basket with playground ball.

Finishing Task

Run to basket, set scooter board down, pick up ball and make a basket from the free throw line.

148

CHRISTMAS SPECIAL

Levels

Junior and Senior High

Objectives

Develops balance, leg and ankle strength, agility, spatial awareness, motor integration, form perception, memory.

Equipment

12 24" cones; 2 utility balls; 1 incline mat; 2 jump ropes; 2 2" x 4" x 10' walking beams; 2 scooter boards; 2 card tables; 2 image ball boards; 2 elastic bands with Christmas balls attached.

Sequence

Line up, pass ball and bells through legs of players. Put band around ankle.

1. Holding the ball, hop in and out of the cones down and back. Pass ball and bells through legs to each player.

2. Same as #1. Before returning to line go to incline mat and do forward roll. Go to jump rope and jump 5 times with ball between knees.

3. Same as #2. Go to card table and take balls out of image board and replace in same design.

4. Same as #3. Before going to puzzle, scoot across beam on scooter board.

Finishing Task

Shoot basket from free throw line.

149

DRIBBLE, WRITE AND ASSEMBLE

Levels

Elementary, Junior and Senior High

Objectives

Develops agility, fine motor ability, directionality, visualization, sequential memory, body image, balance, depth perception.

Equipment

22 24" cones; 2 basketballs; 1 large chalkboard; 2 high jump bars and standards; 2 balance beams; 10 rope rings; 10 nuts and bolts; 2 card tables; 2 boxes.

Sequence

Line up. Pass ball over the head of first player and through legs of second player, continuing in this alternate manner.

1. Dribble in and out of cones with right hand, touch wall, dribble back with left hand.

2. Dribble in and out of cones to stage. Put ball in box. Go to chalkboard and make a word out of letters in PHYSICAL EDUCATION. Pick up ball and run back.

3. Dribble up, touch wall. Go over first high jump bar and under second. Go to balance beam. Toss rope rings on cones while side-stepping across beam (point each). Take nuts and washers off bolts and put back together.

Finishing Task

Make basket from free throw line.

150

WORD PUZZLES

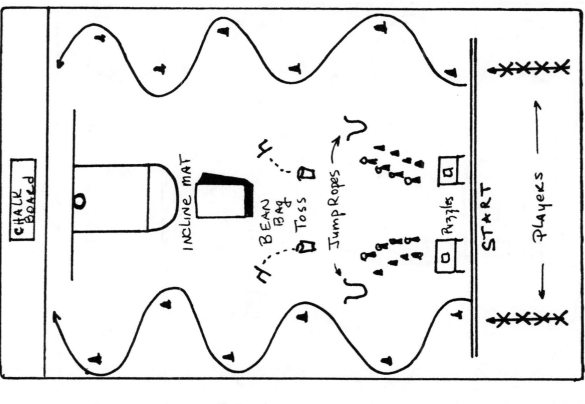

Levels

Junior and Senior High

Objectives

Develops body image, agility, orientation in space, visualization, rhythm, motor integration, form perception, memory, fine motor ability.

Equipment

28 24" cones; 2 utility balls; 1 large chalkboard; 8 12" softballs; 1 incline mat; 8 bean bags; 2 plastic pails; 2 jump ropes; 2 image ball boards; 2 card tables; 2 burlap bags.

Sequence

Line up, pass utility ball through legs of players.

1. Run in and out of cones. Shoot 3 times at basket (5 points each). Go to chalkboard. Each player makes a word (4 or more letters) beginning with one of the letters in current music. (Examples, BLACK SABBATH or DEEP PURPLE.)

2. Same as #1. Add forward roll on mat. Sit on chair and toss bean bags into pail (5 points each).

3. Same as #2. Go to jump rope and jump 5 times holding ball between knees. Go to cones and transfer balls from one side to the other.

4. Same as #3. Go to puzzle. Take image balls out, put in box. Shoot 3 times at near basket (5 points each). Return to puzzle and replace balls in original design.

Finishing Task

Three legged race to basket; each player makes basket.

151

SOCCER STYLE

Levels

Elementary, Junior and Senior High

Objectives

Develops agility, foot-eye co-ordination, left-right integration, leg and arm strength, space structure, balance, visual memory, fine motor control, body image.

Equipment

2 waste baskets; 1 outdoor field; 16 24" cones; 1 rope ladder net; 8 tires; 2 kickballs; 1 concrete conduit; 2 balance beams; 2 image ball boards; 2 chairs; 12 rope rings; 2 card table.

Sequence

1. Kick ball in and out of cones, down and back.

2. Kick ball down. While holding ball, climb rope ladder, jump with both feet through tires. Walk backward across walking board (balance beam).

3. Same as #2. Crawl through conduit. Go to puzzle, take balls out of puzzle. Sit on chairs, toss bean bags until one lands in waste basket. Return to puzzle and replace in original design.

Finishing Task

Sit on top of rope ladder frame. Throw rope ring on cone placed 6' from base of frame.

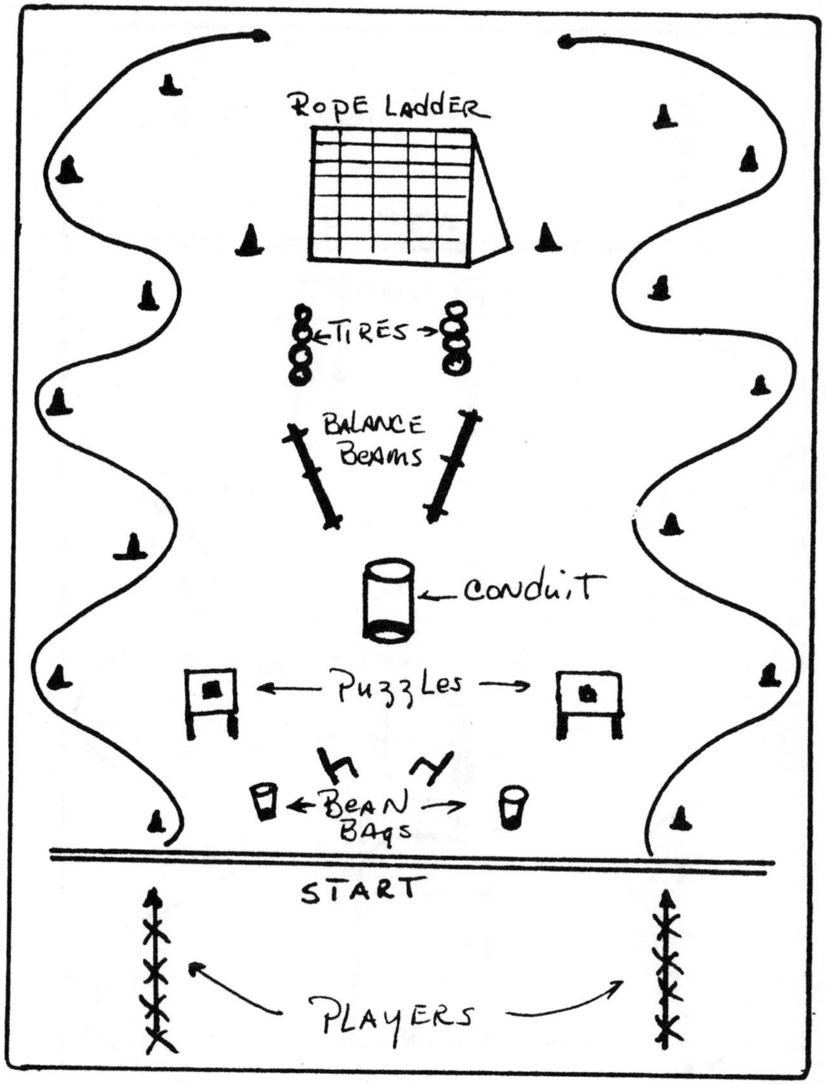

152

THE CARNIVAL SPECIAL

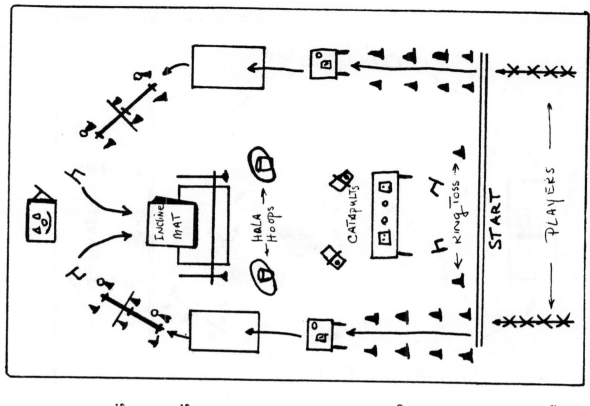

Levels

Junior and Senior High

Objectives

Develops body image, dynamic balance, spatial orientation, hand-eye coordination, integration of two halves, sequential motor planning.

Equipment

2 3" stocks; 2 12" softballs; 22 24" cones; 7 4' x 8' tumbling mats; 1 incline mat; 2 4' balance beams; 1 clown face bean bag target; 2 hula hoops; 2 5 gallon pails; 1 high jump bar with standards; 2 card tables; 1 3' x 6' table; 6 rope rings; 8 bean bags; 2 wooden catapults; 4 image board puzzles; 2 12" playground balls.

Sequence

Line up and pass ball through legs of players.

1. Run through cones to table and disassemble puzzle. Do three log rolls on mat. Mount balance beam. Transfer soft balls to opposite cones and step over hurdle while walking beam. Run back to line (second player assembles puzzle).

2. Same as #1. Straddle chair and throw bean bags at clown target. Do somersault on incline mat and crawl under high jump bar. Put ball in pail and jump through hula hoop 5 times. Run back to line.

3. Same as #2. Stomp catapult board and catch bean bag in each hand. Take apart puzzle. Straddle chair and throw rings on cones (5 points each). Return to table and assemble puzzle. Return to line.

Finishing Task

Move cones 2 feet further away from chair--first player to ring cone with rope ring wins.

153

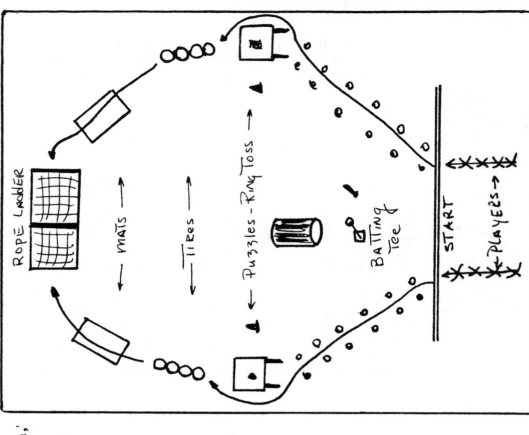

BATTER UP

Levels

Elementary, Junior, and Senior High

Objectives

Develops body image, fine motor ability, laterality, depth perception, arm and leg strength, visual memory, form perception, agility.

Equipment

26 24" cones; 12 12" softballs; 8 rope rings; 2 card tables; 2 tumbling mats; 8 tires; 1 concrete conduit; 1 batting tee; 2 water polo balls; 1 6" utility ball; 2 image ball boards; 1 baseball bat; 1 rope ladder.

Sequence

Line up behind starting cones, pass water polo ball over, under, over.... to last player.

1. With ball, go to cones, transfer row of softballs setting on top of cones from one side to the other. Go to card table. Pick up rope rings, toss across table until one lands on cone. Put rope rings back on table and return to line.

2. Same as #1. Do a forward roll on mat, run through the tires, climb up and over rope ladder.

3. Same as #2. Before doing somersault, take image balls out of the board. After climbing rope ladder, return to card table and replace balls in original design.

Finishing Task

Hit 6" utility ball off of batting tee through the concrete conduit.

154

PRACTICAL POINTERS

DANCE FOR STUDENTS WITH ORTHOPEDIC CONDITIONS--Popular/Square/Folk/Modern/Ballet

Cordelia Graves Harris

All children love to dance. Dance can easily be adapted for individuals with various orthopedic conditions. In addition to being entertaining, dance activities provide children with opportunities to improve posture and coordination while at the same time acquiring better self-images.

Many boys need special pushes to get them involved in modern dance. To accomplish this, provide boys with masculine themes for modern dance--Indian war dances, karate related dances, search and rescue dances, and football related dances. Ballet may have little appeal for some boys. However, all other dance materials contained in this <u>Practical Pointer</u> are appropriate for boys as well as girls.

When working in dance, students with orthopedic conditions can substitute swinging, walking, sliding, wheeling, or use of arm movements for regular dance steps. Planning ahead is critical to the success of these activities. A teacher might have to practice dancing on crutches or in a wheelchair to lean types of movement patterns germane to these modes of ambulation.

GETTING READY

Activities which can be used to prepare students with orthopedic conditions for dancing include:

. Place big <u>left</u> and <u>right</u> posters in the front and back of the room.

. Have students raise their right and/or left hands on cue.

. Instruct students to raise their right and/or left feet on cue--if able.

. Have students in wheelchairs practice turning with control.

. Have students on crutches or with braces practice turning with control.

. Select walkers with good balance to push students in wheelchairs who are unable to push themselves; always be careful when turning wheelchairs.

. Demonstrate correct ways to push wheelchairs--do not touch anyone with a wheelchair or rush to the center of a circle with a wheelchair.

. Ask students to explain proper ways to push a wheelchair before being allowed to push for any type of dancing.

. Instruct walkers with poor balance to be careful when stepping backwards.

. Explain proper ways to fall.

. Allow walkers with extremely poor balance to use wheelchairs if they are available.

. Instruct students to practice walking around in a circle without touching individuals in front or in back of them.

. Have students make a small circle by turning left to the count of four; repeat this same activity to the right.

. Instruct students to take a scattered formation. Use a drum beat with a loud accent on the first beat; play second, third and fourth beats softly. Each time the first loud beat is played, students must change directions. Caution students not to bump into anyone.

. Conduct slow motion races to music.

. Have students compile a list of things to remember when starting and stopping.

. Have students volunteer safety tips to remember when walking backwards.

. Do a short dance to music using the following sequence...

...forward eight steps, backward eight steps.

...forward four steps, backward four steps.

...forward one step, backward one step.

. Have students in wheelchairs complete these dances by equating one or part of a wheel turn to one step.

. Caution students with crutches always to put them in safe places. If a student is dancing in a wheelchair or doing a stationary dance in a chair, crutches should be either on the top of a table or in the crutch rack provided in the back of a wheelchair.

. List on the chalk board ten things to do while participating in dance--i.e., push wheelchairs slowly and with control and only push if you are an assigned pusher; be patient with your partner if you can move a lot faster than he/she; hold the chair for a crutch walker if he/she is going to sit down or get up--crutch walkers are allowed to perform an entire dance from a chair in some circumstances; if you are not dancing, be a good audience.

. List on the chalk board ten things not to do while dancing--i.e., no running; no shoving another student off balance; no passing the person in front of you when traveling around in a circle; no dancing without a seat belt on if in a wheelchair.

. Show students how they can safely swing their partners. If two walkers are swinging and one has poor balance, the student with good balance might dance around the student with poor balance. Two students with good hand usage in wheelchairs can hold wheelchair arms and propel themselves around each other by using their other arms to push the wheels.

. Have a student unable to use a foot use a hand when words in Hokey Pokey specify, "Put your left foot in,"--have the student put his/her left hand into the circle.

. Have students unable to make full turns just turn a little to the left/right and then come back to starting positions in square dancing.

. Have an assigned pusher push a student in a wheelchair unable to push him/herself through a full turn.

. Have students with extremely poor balance--walker or crutch walker--sit in a regular chair or use a wheelchair in ballet dances.

. Assist students who are very weak and incapable of voluntarily moving their own body parts by moving their arms through simple dance patterns.

. Omit moves or just clap to music if a student finds any particular move too difficult.

POPULAR DANCE

Since popular dance is highly individualized, it is the easiest form of dance to be done by students with orthopedic conditions. Most crutch walkers who manifest an adequate amount of coordination and balance are able to dance without assistance from teachers, aides, or other students. Crutch walkers exhibiting poor balance can be given either a regular chair or wheelchair depending on the format of a particular dance. Students with strong upper extremities who are in wheelchairs can dance in any configuration without assistance from others. Students with marked weaknesses who are in wheelchairs may dance in stationary positions or have pushers assigned to them.

Pair students carefully--put a student with good balance with a student with poor balance; pair a walker with a student in a wheelchair; sometimes students must be given opportunities to pick their own partners! Just as students enjoy picking their own partners, they also enjoy making up their own moves to popular records.

After allowing students to complete their own variation of popular dancing, try Soul Train. Even though Soul Train has been around for a number of years, it is excellent for students with orthopedic conditions because only one couple is spotlighted at a time.

Soul Train

. Place students in two parallel lines--girls on one side and boys on the other side.

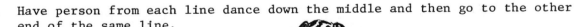

. Have each student dance in place until it is his/her turn to dance down the middle; be sure to assign pushers for students in wheelchairs who need this type of assistance.

. Have person from each line dance down the middle and then go to the other end of the same line.

. Continue in this way until everyone has had a chance to dance down the middle. Repeat the same procedure with the two students who danced down the aisle last now going first and proceeding in the opposite direction.

Bump

Another exciting popular dance enjoyed by youngsters with orthopedic conditions is the Bump. Instead of bumping hips in traditional fashion, students in wheelchairs bump elbows with partners. Many crutch walkers have sufficient balance to bump without any special aids. With the general populations dances last a short time. However, once individuals with orthopedic conditions find something good, they hold on to it. For example, the Bump has been a popular dance at Sunbeam School for six years. To get rhythm down pat many students bump walls with hips or forearms.

This dance is broken down into four beats. On . . .

...one, two students rock their hips or forearms towards each other.

...two, these students move their elbows or hips in opposite directions away from their partners.

...three, students again move their hips and forearms towards each other and actually bump into each other.

...four, they again move their hips or elbows in opposite directions away from their partners.

 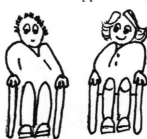

159

<u>Variations</u>

. Instead of hitting or bumping one time, <u>Bump</u> twice on each advance and once on each retreat.

. Change levels of bumps by bumping shoulders, feet, or fingers instead of hips or elbows.

. Complete this dance with three dancers rather than two. With three dancers the individual in the middle should be the most coordinated. First the person in the middle bumps with the person on the left, then proceeds by bumping with the person on the right; the center person then swings back and bumps with the person on the left and then again with the person on the right.

<u>Hand to Hand Disco Dancing</u>

. Encourage students with good balance to spin while students with less stable balance turn spinning students.

. Let students with good balance and flexibility be spun by individuals in wheelchairs.

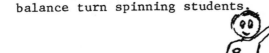

. Remember, double hand dancing is excellent for individuals with poor balance who are walkers; make sure strong partners are assigned to these students.

. Encourage students (girls) to lean against partners with good balance instead of leaping up on partners and extending legs to the side; after attaining a good balanced position, a leg may be extended to the side.

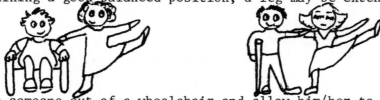

. Take someone out of a wheelchair and allow him/her to do disco dance on his/her knees.

The following is a sample basic foot pattern that can be used in disco dancing.

. Step forward with the left foot

. Step forward with the right foot

. Step backward with the right foot

. Step backward with the left foot. On this step the left foot travels in a backward direction until it is about one foot behind the right foot. At this time the body sways backwards to complete a dip.

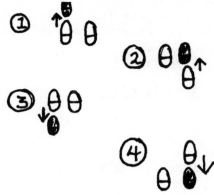

SQUARE DANCE

Square dances may also be adapted to accomodate dancers with handicapping conditions. A circle formation works well since it enables a teacher to keep an eye on all students. This is important because many students get caught up in excitement generated by the music, calls, and general square dance atmosphere. Furthermore, many students with orthopedic conditions need models to follow. For example, the command <u>Honor Your Partner</u> means little unless they see someone performing these movements.

It is important to keep manuevers simple when involving students with orthopedic conditions in square dance. If some students can perform complicated moves and patterns, just call them to the center of the circle to do them after which these students return to positions in the circle. In general, avoid using square dance records that have calls since these movements have been designed for dancers with normal mobility and movements. Students with orthopedic conditions, especially beginners, have difficulties in completing skills and patterns in time provided for calls. Some maneuvers may also be too difficult for some of these students.

    <u>Do-si-do</u>. <u>Walkers</u> move toward each other, pass right shoulders, go back around each other without turning, and walk backwards to place passing left shoulders. Each dancer always remains facing his/her starting direction. Students in <u>wheelchairs</u> wheel around each other and then return to place.

    <u>Honor your partner</u>. <u>Walkers</u>--<u>boys</u> place feet together and bend forward from the waist; <u>girls</u> extend one foot forward and curtsy. Students in wheelchairs--<u>girls</u> bow from the waist and extend both hands over an arm rest of the wheelchair; <u>boys</u> bend forward from the waist to bow. If some individuals are unable to move the trunk area, they may just bow heads.

    <u>Circle left</u>. Students in <u>wheelchairs</u> who need pushers should be assigned them before the dance begins. All students move in circular fashion to the left.

    <u>Circle right</u>. All students move in circular fashion to the right.

Play the fiddle. All students pretend they are playing fiddles.

Stamp your feet. All students who are able stamp their feet in time to the music; others move different parts of their bodies.

Country shout. All students let out a big country yell, Hew Haw!!!

I can't hear you. Students yell Hee Haw again but louder than the first time.

Clap your hands. All students clap hands in time to the music.

Ladies to the center. Girls walk or wheel to the middle of the circle.

Gentlemen to the center. Boys walk or wheel to the middle of the circle.

Gents go back home where you belong. Boys return to starting positions.

Give your partners five. Each student slaps hands with the person on his/her left and then with the person on the right.

Pat your knees. All students pat knees in time to the music.

Wash clothes. All students pretend they are washing clothes on a scrub board and say Scrub Ba-Dub-Ba five times.

Make a bridge. Students 5, 4, 3, and 2 follow student 1 under the bridge, turn to the left, and then go back to their original places. Next, students 6, 7, 8, and 9 follow student 10 under the bridge, turn to the right, and then go back to their original places. Reminder--assign pushers to students in wheelchairs who are unable to push themselves.

Allemande, grand right and left. All 1s face left and all 2s face right. On the cue go all 1s pass 2s on the outside and 2s pass 1s on the inside. Next 1s pass 2s on the inside and 2s pass 1s on the outside. Following this in-and-out weaving procedure students work their ways around the circle until they reach original starting positions. Students use the same floor pattern followed in a traditional Allemande grand right and left. However, students do not complete hand movements; they simply weave in-and-out passing shoulders. Timing is critical to this maneuver; make sure slow moving students in wheel-chairs are assigned pushers. If several students have difficulty ambulating, assign them number 2 and let 1s weave in-and-out around them. Instruct 1s to travel on the outside first and then the inside.

Sunbeam School Version of the Texas Star

Four couples form a set with each set positioned in the middle of one side of a twelve foot square; all dancers face the center. Make provisions for students who cannot keep up. For example, assign a pusher to any student in a wheelchair unable to push him/her self. Provide a wheelchair for any crutch walker who tires easily or is unable to keep up.

Honor your partner. Ladies curtsy and gentlemen bow.

Honor your neighbor. Boys turn to the left and girls turn to the right, bow or curtsy to neighbors.

Ladies to the center and back to the bar. Ladies walk or wheel four steps to the center of the circle; then step or wheel back four steps to original positions.

Gents to the center and form a star with the right hand cross. Walkers put right hands in; students in wheelchairs who are able also put right hand in. A person assisting a student in a wheelchair who is unable to put a hand in can substitute by putting his/her own hand into the circle.

Back with the left and don't get lost. Boys make the star in the opposite direction with the left hand in.

163

Pass your honey and go on to the next. Boys find new partners when they are one girl past original partners.

Clap your hands. All students clap hands eight times.

Stamp your feet. All students stamp feet eight times. Students in wheelchairs who are unable to stamp their feet may hit sides of wheelchairs.

Swing your partner. Walkers swing in usual fashion. If one partner is in a wheelchair and the other partner a walker, the walker may turn the wheelchair two complete times. A crutch walker who is unable to hook arms may just pivot around his/her partner. Two strong students in wheelchairs may swing each other using free arms with which to pivot.

Do-si-do your partner. Walker or crutch walker can do-si-do around a student in a wheelchair if the student in the wheelchair has trouble moving. If two students in wheelchairs are partners, one stays still and lets the other go around.

Now ladies swing in and gents swing out. Couples stay close together if they are unable to hook elbows. Each couple walks four steps out to the center of the circle. On fifth, sixth, seventh, and eight steps ladies swing in to the center and form a star; girls do not have to actually move around the star. Next, girls back out of the star and boys move into the star.

Go back home where you belong. All students return to the square figure with their partners.

Repeat calls as many times as desired.

Reminders

. Space students in wheelchairs and walkers evenly around the circle.

. Assign pushers to students in wheelchairs who are unable to push themselves.

. Have students leave enough space between themselves and their neighbors for an invisible person.

. Make a tape of calls to be used during the dance so you, the teacher, can be free to help.

. Turn volume up loud so the tape can be heard above noise of crutches and wheelchairs.

FOLK DANCE

Many folk dances require such vigorous movements and complicated steps that it is difficult for the majority of students with orthopedic conditions to participate successfully. However, after much experimentation, I have discovered that working with bamboo poles affords an excellent chance for students in wheelchairs as well as walkers to participate, be successful, and have fun in folk dance.

- Have two students with good hand usage move poles on the floor.

- Instruct students in wheelchairs to put a crutch or stick between moving poles.

- Have walkers with good balance put one foot between moving poles.

- Ask walkers with poor balance to sit on the floor and place their hands between moving poles.

- Have crutch walkers with good balance place one foot or one crutch between moving poles.

- Have a crutch walker with poor balance sit on the floor and place his/her hand between or sit in a chair and place a stick between moving poles.

- Have a student in a wheelchair who cannot hold a long stick play some type of musical instrument.

- Do not move poles so that students with more severe problems can participate successfully.

Mexican Hat Dance

The Mexican Hat Dance is another folk dance which is throughly enjoyed by students at Sunbeam School. Use a double circle formation and assign students who have trouble ambulating to the inside of the circle; assign students who are able to move independently to the outside of the circle.

. Kick in hopping fashion the left heel out, then the right, and then the left. After hops are completed, students clap their hands two times. Foot movements--left-right-left. Hand movements--clap-clap. Repeat this series four times. Adaptations for students unable to kick their heels out in a hopping fashion. Use the hands as follows--push out left hand-right hand-left hand and then clap twice.

. Have students who are able swing their partners eight beats.

. Have students take off and wave their hats in the air for eight beats. If students do not have hats, have them wave hands over heads like they are waving to someone far away.

. Have dancers on the outside of the circle walk or wheel around eight steps to the left; the person in which each is in front of is his/her new partner.

MODERN DANCE

Modern dance and movement techniques work extremely well with students possessing orthopedic conditions. Since no movements are wrong, students can feel free to explore with their bodies. Many students with doctor's approval can be taken out of wheelchairs for modern dance. Crutch walkers can be liberated from their crutches so they too can be free to express themselves physically. The potential and possibilities of modern dance are unlimited--not even the sky limits as is seen from the following approaches and suggestions.

. Dance out building a fire. Students who are able to move can build an imaginary fire around students who are unable to move a great deal. Students with limited amounts of movement can use arms to show flames flickering. Students unable to move arms can accomplish this by moving their heads.

. Dance out building a snowman. Students who are able to move can pack imaginary snow on students who cannot move.

. Do short dances pretending to be different animals. Students in wheelchairs can lean forward and swing one arm to imitate elephants. Crutch walkers can bounce a little to represent movement patterns of rabbits. Some students can crawl on the floor weaving in and out other students as they pretend to be snakes. Girls in wheelchairs can float arms like birds while boys in wheelchairs complete rough moves pretending to be lions or tigers. Soft drum beats can be used when girls move and harsh percussive beats direct boys to move.

. Instruct students who are walkers with good balance to push students unable to push themselves. They can also dance through or around wheelchairs to make interesting floor patterns.

. Discuss different means of traveling or moving from place to place in dances.

. Discuss types of movements that can be done in stationary space--vibrate, shiver, shake, quiver, tremble.

166

- Discuss different ways students can <u>turn</u>. Students in wheelchairs can <u>spin</u> slowly in their chairs. Crutch walkers can <u>twirl</u> slowly around on their crutches. Walkers can turn in standing positions or turn by <u>rolling</u> on the floor.

- Explain how <u>stops</u> or <u>pauses</u> in dances are important. For example, when students can freeze movements for a few seconds they have mastered a difficult dance technique.

- Have students participate in four percussive moves by dancing out words such as <u>stamp</u>, <u>punch</u>, <u>explode</u>.

- Show students how to <u>contract</u> and then have them show how <u>small</u> they can make themselves.

- Show students how to <u>expand</u> and then have them show how <u>big</u> they can make themselves.

- Demonstrate how it is possible to <u>change levels</u> in which dances are taking place and then have students practice <u>rising</u> and <u>falling</u>.

- Show how <u>advancing</u> and <u>retreating</u> are used in dances as effective techniques of getting messages across.

- Discuss the three main parts of a dance. The <u>beginning</u> starts in a definite place with a definite shape. In the <u>middle</u> of the dance or near the end should be a high point known as the <u>climax</u>, a point in which something outstanding is done. The dance should <u>end</u> in a special way with the last move being held for a few seconds so the audience knows the dance is completed.

- Discuss effects <u>tempo</u> has on dance. Explain how a dance can look serious if done <u>slowly</u> and comical if <u>speeded up</u>. Play a record at forty-five rmp and then play the same record at seventy-eight and/or thirty-three rpm.

- Have students dance out a <u>fly stuck in butter</u> or a <u>piece of chewing gum being chewed</u>.

- Have students dance out a <u>ping pong ball bouncing back and forth across a table</u> or a <u>rocket being launched</u>.

- Pretend to be in a room filled with jello so that students can give their own dance interpretations on how to get out of this <u>jellowish</u> situation.

- Pretend to <u>have a fight</u> (no contact) with a partner.

- Be a <u>seed growing into a flower</u>, <u>spaghetti cooking in a pot</u>, or <u>bacon frying in a pan</u>.

- Make a <u>tape</u> of appropriate <u>sounds</u> to go with each dance theme. Announce the theme on the tape and then have related music play for about twenty-five seconds.

- Have boys dance out a complete <u>Indian War Dance</u>. In <u>Part I</u> all students show that they are warming themselves by a fire. In <u>Part II</u> one of the braves goes off and returns with information about another tribe that has declared war against them. In <u>Part III</u> students make up their own war dances. In <u>Part IV</u> students show their audience through dance how the story ends. This dance should be twenty-five beats or more.

- Have girls dance out a complete <u>Indian Rain Dance</u>. In <u>Part I</u> students dance slowly looking towards the floor or earth. In <u>Part II</u> students take ten beats to raise their arms and heads slowly towards the ceiling or heavens. In <u>Part III</u> students compose a twenty-five beat dynamic rain dance.

- Allow both boys and girls fifteen minutes or more to <u>practice</u> and work out their ideas.

- Suggest different movements to students if they get stuck.

- Encourage students to use <u>props</u>. Boys might use <u>drums</u> or <u>tomahawks</u>. Girls can use <u>thin pieces of material</u> to wave for rain.

- Discuss different <u>levels</u> of movements and how they can make mirror dances more interesting.

- Explain how different <u>speeds</u> of music can make mirror dances more exciting.

- Have students work in a <u>circle</u> with one student as the leader. The leader initiates some type of movement; then the person to his/her left does the movement to the best of his/her ability. That movement travels around the circle until everyone has had a chance to try it. Then the first person to the left of the original leader becomes the new leader who initiates a completely different movement.

- Give students time to practice movements they might want to try in <u>mirror dances</u>.

- Place three mirrors safely around the room so students can study their own dance <u>reflections</u>.

- Explain how <u>reflections</u> are always opposite--students who pretend to be reflections of other students must lift right hands when the other students left their left hands.

- Pair students of similar abilities together.

- Mirror each other's <u>facial expressions</u> and <u>head motions</u> when partners are unable to lift their arms.

- Have students wave long thin pieces of colorful material to show a <u>tree blowing in the wind</u>, <u>thunder and lightening</u>, a <u>rain storm</u>.

- Supply students with newspapers, have them arrange these papers in patterns resembling <u>leaves</u> and then dance out <u>playing in leaves</u>.

. Have the class create a dance using balloons. Divide students into two
groups with half having yellow balloons and half having red balloons.
On cue all students with red balloons raise them in some fashion to the
music; all students with yellow balloons lower them. Have one group make
big movements and the other small ones with the balloons.

. Have students make up spider web dances using ropes.

. Assign each student a partner and then have each couple make up a dance
using a rope. Caution students to avoid wrapping the rope around his/her
body or the partner's body. Have students turn the rope or make waves.

. Discuss how different movements go with different feelings--happy, sad,
glad, mad, frightened, amazed.

. Play a game where students do five movements to show whether they are
happy or sad, hot or cold; the student who first guesses the action becomes
the new leader.

. Play a game of opposites with two lines facing each other. Line A is hate
and Line B is love. Next have Line A be sadness and Line B be happiness.
Have the lines invisibly pulling at each other.

BALLET

Many students with orthopedic conditions have the ability to ge graceful.
Many of these students can dance with their hands even when their legs cannot
move. Special considerations include providing chairs for walkers with balance
problems. Following is a dance called Bluebirds which was designed especially
for students with orthopedic conditions; it's major emphasis is on use of hands
and arms.

Bluebirds

. Start the dance with all students situated in a horizontal line, crutch
walkers seated in chairs and walkers equally distributed between students
in wheelchairs and in chairs.

. All students hold their arms in front of their bodies in rounded positions
with finger tips touching.

169

. Have students raise their arms simultaneously, make two complete circles, and return to starting positions with arms out in front forming circles with finger tips touching.

. Have students take their arms from position five, extend them out to the sides, and flap the arms gracefully like a bird's wings; flap the wings twice.

. Have students criss-cross arms four times, waving hands along with the arm movements.

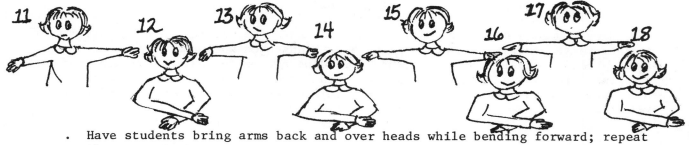

. Have students bring arms back and over heads while bending forward; repeat these movements.

. Have students in wheelchairs and in chairs repeat steps 6 to 10 twice. Walkers dance completely around students in wheelchairs and chairs and then kneel in front of students in wheelchairs and in chairs.

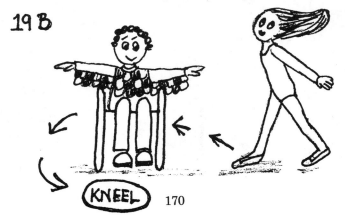

170

. Have all students move together again. Whether kneeling or sitting,
students take their left arms, sweep them across the fronts of their bodies,
and then place them over their heads on the right sides of their bodies.
This is done twice on left sides and twice on right sides.

. Have all students gracefully return to original starting positions at
which time they repeat 19A twice and hold four beats for the end of the
dance.

IN CONCLUSION

Most examples included in this <u>Practical Pointer</u> have been tested over a
period of six years. Many complicated skills have been purposely left out.
Students at Sunbeam School include children with both mild and severe handicapping
conditions. These activities have been designed exclusively for children with
orthopedic conditions.

It is often difficult to take a complicated dance such as the <u>Texas Star</u>
and incorporate every move into an adaptation. This can be compared to translating
a language. In some situations there is no exact translation. Or perhaps so much
is lost in translating that the original meaning is lost. My emphasis is more on
<u>accomodating</u> skill levels of children with orthopedic conditions than on making
an exact copy of what <u>able-bodied people</u> do.

In addition to affording children with orthopedic conditions chances to have
a lot of fun dancing, this approach gives students opportunities to have successful
experiences in physical education; in dance there is little emphasis on competition.
Dancing is an important part of our culture that might be a vehicle to help students
with orthopedic conditions be more accepted by their peers. It has been my experience
that many able-bodied people are afraid of individuals with handicapping conditions.
However, when most people see that those with orthopedic conditions can do activities
they associate with able-bodied people, this reality can help break the ice.

Dressing up in costumes and use of props are always infectious when attempting
to generate interest. The art teacher at Sunbeam School made lovely cartoon type
drawings of children with orthopedic conditions dancing. This is another important
way to provide role models for children with orthopedic conditions in dance to
be successful. It will be necessary for <u>you</u> to put your own personality and lots
of energy to make these recommendations and approaches come alive.

RECOMMENDED MUSIC

Popular Dance

- Soul Train--<u>The Soul Train Theme Music</u> or <u>Get Off</u> (Foxy-Dash Records, 1978).

- The Bump--<u>The Bump</u> or <u>You Got To Keep On Bumping</u>.

- Hand to Hand Dico Dancing--<u>Macho Man</u> (Village People Casablanco Records, 1978) or <u>La Freak</u> (Chic Atlantic Record Company, New York, 1978).

Square Dance

- Square Dance Activities--<u>Square Dance Party--Side Two</u> (The Rhythm Rangers, Tops Records).

- Texas Star--<u>Skate Away</u> (Folkcraft Records, 1159 Broad Street, New York, New York) or <u>Bingo</u> (Folkcraft Records).

Folk Dance

- Bamboo Pole Dance--<u>Meitschi Putz Di</u> (The Folk Dancers, Michael Herman's Orchestra, 1950).

- The Mexican Hat Dance--<u>La Raspa</u> (RCA Records or Kimbo Educational Activities Records, Side B).

Modern Dance

- Use a drum.

- Record appropriate sounds--i.e., water, footsteps, wind, traffic--to accompany a variety of dance situations.

Ballet

- Bluebirds--<u>The Swan Lake Ballet</u> by Tchaikovsky.

ADDITIONAL RESOURCES

1. <u>Write</u>: Improvement Instruction for Low Incidence Handicapped Children in Ohio 1150 Beatrice Drive, Dayton, Ohio, 45404

    Ask for: Dance Module of Instruction, written by Cordelia A. Harris, Cleveland Public Schools, May 15, 1976.

2. Mosston, Muska. <u>Developmental Movement</u>. Columbus, Ohio: Charles F. Merrill Books, Inc., 1964.

3. Nagel, Charles and Fredericka Moore. <u>Skill Development Through Games and Rhythmic Activities</u>. Palo Alto, California: The National Press, 1966.

4. Hackett, Layne C. and Robert G. Jenson. <u>A Guide to Movement Exploration</u>. Palo Alto, California: Peek Publications, 1975.

5. Hunt, Valerie V. <u>Recreation for the Handicapped</u>. Englewood Cliffs, New Jersey, Prentice-Hall, Inc., 1955.

Section III—
Practical Pointers for Activity Programs for the Severe and Profound, Multiply Handicapped

PRACTICAL POINTERS

PHYSICAL ACTIVITIES FOR CHILDREN WITH

SEVERE MULTIPLE IMPAIRMENTS

Susan J. Grosse

A trend from the mid-1970s that continues to intensity in the 1980s is greater attention to meeting needs of children with severe multiple impairments. Right to treatment, right to education, and zero-reject concepts emphasize responsibilities of providers of services for these populations in every setting--residential, clinical, educational, vocational, and community. Early childhood intervention and parental involvement can help bring out untapped developmental potential in these populations. Physical activities have been shown to be valuable and indispensible tools for reaching and teaching children with severe multiple impairments.

For several years there has been a steady cry and demand for information, materials--HELP--in the physical and motor areas for these populations. So often articles and publications dealing with activities for children with severe multiple impairments have actually been inappropriate for these populations. Little attention has been given to chronological age, maturity, experience, and untapped interests of these individuals. So often the myth of everlasting childhood has been perpetuated. So many times lack of growth and progress has been because of us; development and achievement in spite of us!

Contents of this Practical Pointer can be used directly, be modified according to child needs and teacher/leader comfort, and stimulate new and creative applications by each reader based on his/her background, philosophy, and experience. Publications of this type are valuable and important in the process of helping children with severe multiple impairments reach zeniths not even within perceptions of the most optimistic among us.

173

They do not move! If they do move it is probably to engage in some random, self-stimulating behaviors. They do not play. Left to themselves they would probably sit, lie, or recline--forever. These are children with severe multiple impairments. Their mental levels are so low as to be untestable. If they were, just retarded they would fall into the severe and/or profound categories. Their developmental lags are extreme. Physically they are impaired--by cerebral palsy, hydrocephalus, multiple congenital anomolies or rare syndrones.

Their behaviors are on extremely low functional levels. Some talk; most do not. Grunts, squeals, and random noises are all that is heard. A small percentage of this population can walk; most are in wheelchairs. Whether or not they are mobile when out of their chairs depends on motivation as well as ability. Left to themselves many self-stimulate, some destructively, others compulsively, tantruming when interrupted. These children have little, if any, age appropriate behaviors.

Educationally they are on the lowest rung of the ladder. They are not candidates for mainstreaming. They are served in self-contained classes, many still in residential facilities. The teacher-student ratio is extremely low. For any real education to take place, these children require one-to-one instruction. Part of that education by law has to include the physical domain; but what does a teacher do with students whose inherent characteristics all serve as deterrents to such activity?

This Practical Pointer is designed to serve as a place to start for teachers of children with severe multiple impairments. Though some sections are approached from points of view of particular age groups, readers should feel free to select activities from the entire content depending upon needs of individual children being taught. Contents are not meant to be all inclusive in terms of teaching techniques and materials used. As a teacher gains experience in providing physical activities for these children that teacher can add much to these starter suggestions because working with children possessing severe multiple impairments is highly specialized and individualistic. There are as many activities and techniques for teaching them as children to teach.

Why?
Roles of Physical Activities
In Lives of Children with Severe Multiple Impairments

When a baby is born the first learning that takes place is through physical activity--hold the head up, push the chest off the floor, get up on all fours and crawl. A very young child with severe multiple impairments in many cases cannot perform such simple tasks. Yet these are motor skills directly related to the ability to function with physical independence. They are necessary for learning how to sit, focus attention--by having control of neck muscles the position of the head is directed so that eyes can see around the environment-- stand, and walk.

As a non-involved child matures, he/she learns to use the body to accomplish physical tasks, wash and dress, manipulate toys, and interacts with instruments of learning as papers, crayons, and books are handled. Though a child with severe multiple impairments may never get to the stage of book learning, a great many self care tasks are within the sphere of capability.

As we become older we learn that physical activity is very important to our own health. Organically the body needs physical activity for optimum physiological functioning. Mentally we need releases provided by pleasurable participation as well as feelings of pride in accomplishing through taking part in physical activities. A child with severe physical impairments is no different. Left to sit, obesity soon becomes apparent and health problems occur. A vicious cycle starts--a person who doesn't feel well, who carries a lot of excess weight doesn't want to move; if one doesn't move, weight and health problems continue. Even though a physical condition may preclude normal movements, it seldom eliminates all movements.

The following represent direct objectives in providing physical activity programs for students with severe multiple impairments--

. Improve physiological functioning, including more efficient operation of systems of the body as well as increased muscular strength and endurance.

. Improve development of motor ability, including head control, trunk balance, and arm and leg support.

. Improve mobility, including options such as creeping, crawling, rolling, seat scooting, walking, and or pushing a wheelchair.

. Improve functional motor skills such as grasping and releasing, carrying, pushing, pulling, and kicking and hitting objects.

. Improve ability to follow simple directions such as come, go, stop, no, yes, bring, put, let go, carry.

. Reduce negative and interfering behaviors such as rocking, head banging, hand chewing, random self-stimulation.

. Improve social interactions by providing positive contacts with others.

. Increase more appropriate use of leisure time through learning play and/or recreation activity skills.

. Make the child easier to care for by increasing both tolerance of being handled as well as ability to assist in personal care processes.

A majority of learning possible for a child with severe multiple impairments is in the phsyical domain. A good physical education program can greatly enhance a child's capabilities for that learning. One word of caution however--

no physical activity program should be initiated without consulting medical personnel involved with the child. Ideally such consultation should be an ongoing process so that medical and educational staffs plan together for continued development of the child.

Who?
Different Ages Mean Different Abilities

Some severely impaired children remain at infant levels for their entire lives. However even infancy has its stages. As most children grow physically, changes take place and learning occurs that indicate progress--however slowly-- through various stages of growth and development. In discussing activities, three chronological age divisions are used--

Preschool --birth to 6 years

Elementary--6 to 12 years

Secondary --12 to 21 years

Obviously a student can be of secondary school chronological age while functioning on a preschool level. In selecting activities a teacher needs to consider both age and functional abilities of every child, meeting each where he/she is while helping increase abilities to a more age appropriate strata.

Let's Get Moving!
Anything Counts with a Non-Mobile Child

When working with a child with severe multiple impairments--a child with little large muscle movement--the primary goal is to get the child to move-- any part in any fashion, but move! We learn how to use our bodies through actual use. Muscular capabilities only improve through activity--something must happen physically.

Preschool

Very young severely multiple impaired children go through the same motor development stages as their non-involved peers. However, such development is much slower with many gaps in motor skill progressions occurring as progress in particular areas is blocked by physical impairment. The major goal of the preschool program is to assist the child move through these stages by teaching use of the body. Activities are performed with the child out of the transportation chair and on a mat or other soft surface.

. Gentle rubbing body parts lets the child know a body part is there.

. Gentle tickling body parts--soles of feet, backs of legs, insides of elbows--not only focuses attention on that part but also encourages random movements of that part.

176

- Passive bending and stretching--teacher does all movements--arms and legs provide feedback on locations of the child's body parts and information on how each moves. At this stage, as with any activity involving physical manipulation, the teacher needs to be sure that movement is not attempted past the point of firm resistance to avoid injury to the student. Do not force any joint movement.

- Passive range-of-motion exercises--moving a body part through all positions allowed by the controlling joint--help to tell the child what the body is supposed to do.

- Baby exercises are valuable aids in helping teach a child how to move and aiding in building muscular strength and endurance. Even though a child is five or six years of age, if motor development is that of an infant--still working on head control, chest elevation, and creeping--then infant exercises are appropriate activities. Such exercises are too numerous to recount here; however many resources are available (20, 21, 22, 23, 24, 27, 28) for teachers needing to initiate such programs.*

- Putting a child in various positions as he/she goes through daily activities encourages learning to balance the head and trunk as well as rely on different muscle groups for support. A child who sometimes lies on the stomach, sometimes on the back or side, sometimes sits supported, sometimes sits alone, and sometimes rests on hands and knees, develops much better than a child left in one place all day. (9, 17)

Elementary

Many elementary school age children may still need infant exercises to stimulate movements. If this is the case then infant exercises should be continued. However, many other children with severe multiple impairments do have some movement capabilities. Left to their own devices, most of these children just sit, or sit and randomly manipulate a toy. The major goal for these children is to develop voluntary large muscle activity. Children are again out of their wheelchairs for activities and work done on mats.

In addition, small padded obstacles are used. They can be purchased as in the case of foam shapes, or improvised by rolling up mats, stuffing blankets into pillow cases, or padding furniture. Other helpful pieces of equipment for this age group include climbing apparatus such as all purpose trainers, lind climbers, or stegels; each has horizontal poles, a height adjustable ladder, and a slide.

- Getting down to the mat--initially activity relies on the child's desire to remain down on a mat in one place or position. Place

---

*Bracketed numbers occurring throughout the text refer to resource listings in Selected References.

the child on an obstacle—any <u>softie</u> or shape—that is close to
the ground. Placement should be just <u>insecure</u> enough—due to
angle of the body or position of the shape—so the child moves
to assume his/her original place on the mat. Possible positions
include—

  —Inclined with head up
  —Inclined with head down
  —On the back
  —On the stomach
  —On the side
  —Draped over with <u>seat</u> up
  —Combinations of the above

Children who are comfortably immobile where ever they are placed
can be <u>encouraged</u> by gentle poking or tickling. Positions where
a child is slightly <u>off balance</u>-encourage movement as the body
is pulled in response to gravity.

. <u>Motoring through</u> a task means a teacher, leader, or aide moves
the child's arms and/or legs so as to accomplish a given movement, pattern, or task. As the child becomes accustomed to
getting off a small shape, difficulty of situations can be increased in several ways—

  —Vary sizes and shapes of obstacles.
  —<u>Motor</u> the child through alternative ways to get back
   to the mat—forward, backward, using arms, using
   legs, using arms and legs.
  —Block the child from using accustomed methods so that
   other approaches must be used.

. <u>Getting onto and off obstacles</u> present additional challenges.
A teacher, leader, or aide can—

  —<u>Motor</u> a child through the climb-on.
  —Entice a child onto the object with a favorite toy.
  —Place several small obstacles together so the child
   has to go over one or two to get back to the mat.

. <u>Free climbing</u> over, under, and around obstacles is a higher
level skill. As the child gains strength and learns to move
arms and legs, even though movements have limitations, he/
she should be able to crawl through a variety of obstacle
situtations.

Secondary

The older a child with severe multiple impairments, the harder it is to
initiate <u>any</u> program of physical activity. <u>Movement is a habit that needs to
be established early in life</u>. A child who has been <u>just sitting</u> for twelve
to fifteen years is much more difficult to work with than a child who has been

as active as his/her condition allows. Initial get moving activities take place with a child in his/her wheelchair; in the case of an ambulatory student, while remaining seated or standing in one place. Given the goal of any large muscle movement, such movements are easier to obtain if only one or two body parts are involved in the activity. In this case parts involved are arms and the activity is parachute play.*

Parachute activity may seem like an unusual place to start, but the parachute has many unique characteristics that make it ideal for introducing movements to children with severe multiple impairments.

. All children in a group can participate at the same time. Seated around the perimeter are those who can grasp and hold the edge of the 'chute; those who cannot can be attached be adding sewn loops to the edge of the 'chute through which each child can slip a hand.

. A 'chute is colorful and easily moved, thus aiding in the focus of attention while providing instant results for any arm movements.

. Adults interspersed around a 'chute can easily control and direct movements by controlling the 'chute. Some students can imitate actions of adults while others move because they are attached.

. Various movements can be done with a 'chute--

   --Shaking.
   --Lifting and lowering.
   --Actions that are alternately fast and slow.
   --Actions that are alternately vigorous or soft and easy.
   --More mobile students move under the 'chute while
     others manipulate it.
   --Balls can be rolled or bounced on the 'chute.
   --Musical accompaniment gives extra stimuli to movements.
   --If all students can grasp the 'chute it can be passed
     along the edge from person-to-person.

. The activity can be as calm or as vigorous as a teacher, leader, or aide desires.

. Direct hands on help can be given to students without inter-rupting group activity. The helping person moves from student to student and reaches around from behind to guide arm move-ments.

---

*If a regular parachute or one of desirable size is not available, any relatively sturdy piece of fabric will do--a print sheet, for example, is a fine substitute.

But It Isn't All That Easy
Problems of Motivation

Obesity, self-stimulating behaviors, low mental levels, severe physical impairments, and deprivation of experiences all work against student involvement in physical activities. Involved physical effort and great length of time between effort made and observable progress tend to inhibit teachers in implementing physical activity programs for children with severe multiple impairments. Given these negative factors, <u>motivation</u> becomes a prime concern. Activities are easy to start. However, maintaining these initial activities over time and structuring them for student progress are major undertakings. <u>Both student and teacher motivation</u> can be improved in a variety of ways--

- <u>Enjoy the activity yourself</u>. Make a conscious decision <u>before starting</u> that the activity is going to be pleasurable for the student and you.

- <u>Do activities right along with students</u>-having a model to imitate aids their learning!

- <u>Motor through</u> the student during initial learning stages. Hands-on guidance makes positive differences in what a child is able to accomplish.

- <u>Inhibit extraneous and self-stimulating behaviors</u> by replacing them with positive activities. Expecting a child to just <u>stop</u> such behaviors is unrealistic. More success can be obtained if objectionable behaviors are replaced by activities such as movement, appropriate play, or object manipulation.

- <u>Be colorful</u>. Activities need to be visually stimulating to aid a child in focusing attention.

- <u>Have a large variety of activities</u> to accomplish a single goal. Doing the same thing over and over again can be boring to both student and teacher--variety encourages everyone's interest.

- <u>Use the same piece of equipment in various ways</u>. Once a child becomes familiar with a piece of equipment, use that device as a <u>bridge</u> to further learning and explore new areas of movement.

- <u>Praise--appropriately and frequently</u>, including pats, hugs, and strokes for little children, and handshakes and applause for young adults.

- <u>Be repetitious</u>. Learning specific skills takes lots of time. Don't become discouraged if progress is not always evident-- think in terms of months and semesters rather than days and weeks! Many times one must make haste slow!

- <u>Use non-threatening equipment</u>. <u>Softies</u> make play much more fun because a child is not likely to be unintentionally hurt.

. Improvise. Try any and every idea that comes to mind. Reject
  nothing until it has been given a good try--then don't reject it
  but file it away for use with another child under different
  circumstances (if it doesn't work)!

. Use age-appropriate equipment and activities, even for children
  with severe multiple impairments.

. Vary settings for activities. Get out of the classroom and into
  the gym, onto the playground, on the lawn, or into any other
  available space. Staying in the same environment all the time
  leads to cabin fever--for everyone.

. Plan activities on regularly scheduled bases--stick to the
  schedule. Putting it off 'til tomorrow won't get the job done.

. Make a committment. When you are motivated, you motivate your
  students!

Although any number of activities can be described to aid in motivation,
several techniques and approaches are particularly useful for a child with
severe multiple impairments. Some methods dictate that the child be out of
the wheelchair while others are done with the child in place--each activity
listed is only one of several possibilities. Approach each as a place to
start when working with a child that has some movement and needs to have his/
her movement capabilities developed further.

Preschool

At this age level emphasis is placed on a multi-sensory approach to movement--
this means providing a variety of individual stimuli. Some people mistakenly
bombard all of a child's senses at once--loud music, bright lights, stuffy room,
objects hanging from the ceiling, and lots of movement. All that teaches a
child is to block out what is discomforting! For a stimulus to be effective it
should be the predominating factor in the environment with other stimuli reduced.
Rubbing body parts and range of motion activities listed earlier (page 5) are forms
of tactile stimuli; others include (11, 15, 16)--

. Activities with clothes off as well as on.

. Rub body parts with different textures and levels of force.

. Touch body parts with something cold and/or wet.

. Perform activities with room lights off as well as on. Off is
  particularly helpful when using visual stimuli such as flashlights to prompt focusing attention and in doing head and neck
  exercise.

. Use various visual stimuli to attract attention and encourage
  head control--blinking lights, colored lights, pin point flashlights.

. Use mechanical devices such as vibrators or small blow dryers to stimulate movements of body parts.

. Use various strong odors to encourage head control.

. Perform activities on various surfaces--carpet, mat, water bed--- to provide different kinesthetic feedbacks.

. Use various individual sounds to encourage focus of attention and improve neck mobility.

Elementary

Once a child acquires some movement a teacher has something to work with and build upon (10, 12, 13, 14, 18).

. Imitative Activities. The preschool child has been working on focusing attention and discovering that body parts move-- imitative activities provide opportunities to apply such skills. Begin with simple arm exercises. While initially a child may have to be motored through an activity, once he/she is able to imitate lessens the need for complicated verbal directions in future activities. Imitative exercises can be enhanced by attaching objects to body parts involved in exercises. A child can hold the item or it can be attached to him/her. The teacher should have the same item as the child--ribbons, bells, rattles or shakers, aluminum pie plates, scarves or just colorful pieces of fabric. Initial movements should be simple and easy to follow. Start by using only one body part and add parts as the child becomes better at imitating movements.

. Scooter Play. Children with severe multiple impairments have a great deal of difficulty moving under their own power from place to place; scooter boards can help reduce or even eliminate this problem. Initially place a child on the board in a prone posi- tion. If necessary strap the child in place so he/she doesn't fall off. Some children in this position may use their hands to push and move on their own; other children may need hands-on motoring through. If the teacher stretches the child's arms out as far as possible, places his/her hands on the floor, and holds them there, the child pulls forward as he/she tries to get the hands back; with lots of repetition a child learns to propel. More able students may also be able to sit on the scooter in positions in which they can use either hands or feet, though many need hands-on help to attempt the task initially.

Secondary

Secondary students are hardest to motivate. Time may have to be spent with this group doing imitative exercises to accustom individuals to moving various body parts. Motoring through is more difficult due to sizes and weights of individuals, but still may be the only way to obtain movements.

However, if a child is _moving_, several activities can increase the fun of the experience (25).

. _Rubber Band Activities_. These are not conventional rubber bands but bands cut from old automobile inner tubes--cut across the tube at three inch intervals.* Primary activities with these bands involve pulling using different body parts in various positions. A student can pull against him/herself--use hands-on help if necessary to teach the feel of pull--or the student can pull against the teacher which also gives the teacher a measure of force being exerted.

. _Balloon Play_. Either party balloons or large play balloons help students gain control over gross muscle movements as well as improve hand-eye coordination. Students can--

   --Hold the balloon carefully.
   --Hit a balloon someone holds.
   --Hit a balloon that is _tethered_ and returns to be hit again.
   --Learn to hit or push the balloon when it comes to them through the air.
   --Keep the balloon up in the air using different body parts.
   --Participate in a group _game_ of _Keep It Up_ or volley the balloon over a line or rope.

It's Function That Counts
Developing Specific Motor Skills

Although achieving movement responses from a severely multiple impaired child is an achievement in itself, it is not the end goal. Applying movements to accomplish _functional_ physical tasks is the next step. Once a child has started to move, such movements need to be developed into functional skills.

The Individualized Education Program (IEP) sets format and provides direction for work with a student. To be useful an IEP should--

. Reflect a child's current levels of function--i.e., "He moves from place to place to place by rolling."

. State specific skills to be learned--i.e., "He will learn to crawl."

. State criteria for successful performance of said skill--i.e., "He will crawl on all fours for a distance of ten feet."

_____

*For some individuals narrow bands are necessary; for other individuals wide bands are appropriate. If inner tube bands, regardless of width, provide too much resistance, make similar bands with waist-band elastic purchased at any notions store.

. State time line for accomplishing the task--i.e., "He will crawl on all fours for ten feet by November 1" or "...within two months."

All IEP goals dealing with the physical domain <u>must</u> reflect observable, measurable physical behaviors. <u>A skill is not learned until the child can perform that skill independently and at levels consistent with measurement criteria</u> (1, 5, 6).

Preschool

Preschool skills usually center around mobility with the general initial goal being to move the child further along through normal developmental progressions. A teacher structures movement environments by (13, 16)--

. Choosing specific skills for a child to use during mat activities--rolling, creeping, crawling, seat scooting, arm pulling, and pushing with the feet from a supine position.

. Seeing that each child performs particular movements selected even if that means <u>motoring</u> the child through the movements--<u>again</u>, and <u>again</u>, and <u>AGAIN</u>.

. Providing a variety of situations for using and practicing each specific skill--crawling on a flat mat, on a lumpy mat, over another person, over a pillow, up a small stairway, over a foam shape, across a water bed, through a small space, into a tunnel--even if initially the child has to be <u>motored through</u> each individual situation.

. Providing positive feedback to the child--verbal praise, pat on the back, stroking, favorite toy when an obstacle is overcome, hug for successful efforts, and <u>always</u> a big smile for trying even if trying took place with lots of hands-on help.

The only way most severely multiple impaired children make progress in mastering physical skills is if the teacher provides direct experiences for developing these skills. The nature of the conditions often preclude the child's own abilities and resources in normal explorative and developmental processes of childhood.

Elementary

Functional skill development for elementary school age children with severe multiple impairments means continued progress along standard developmental lines and movement skills in response to simple directions. Whereas in the past a teacher physically directed almost all movements with hands-on help, now movement experiences need to be raised to higher levels of mental processing, that of <u>direction following</u>. A direction can be--

. <u>Verbal</u>--spoken word.

. <u>Physical gestures or signs</u>--without contacting the child.

. _Physical cues or prompts_--touching the child.

. _Auditory cues_--starting and stopping music, for example.

Typical directions affecting a child's everyday life functioning as well as participation in movement experiences include--

come	over	open	get
stay	under	closed	bring
go	up	give	hurry
start	down	take	slower
stop	through	carry	push
look	sit	pull	stand up
move			

Each one of these words or concepts can be applied to movement. Initially it helps if directions are given in a combination of forms--say, "Come," while smiling and using a beckoning gesture.

An excellent format for beginning direction following is through relays. Though relays involve competition between people or teams, they can be used for task accomplishment. In a simple relay a child starts at point A, moves to point B, and then returns to point A. Specific skill activity can include how the person gets from A to B as well as what is done when getting to points A and/or B. After directions are given a child may still need help getting from place to place--help pushing the chair, help from someone holding the hand or arm as a lead in walking. Plenty of repetition and watching examples of others aid the learning process. Relay ideas are as endless as the creativity of the teacher.*

Secondary

Students on the secondary level need assistance in applying whatever movements they are capable to improve functional skills of daily living and develop leisure play skills. Though learning to follow directions carries over from elementary school years, application to skills that improve a child's capabilities to assist in his/her own care and mobility is the next step in the learning process.

A Function Hike is an excellent activity for developing motor skills relative to daily living. Basic format is a hike--movement through environments surrounding the classroom--both inside and out. Hikes can be taken with one student and one teacher, or with a group of students, teacher, and aides. Students do not need to be ambulatory. As a hike progresses various other activities take place. Possibilities include--

_____

*Readers are referred to Motor Development Relays (Practical Pointer, Volume 3, Number 10, February 1980) for different and innovative approaches to using relays in developmental learning of students with special or exceptional needs.

. <u>Moving in different fashions</u>.

    --Forward, backward, sideward.
    --Large steps, small steps--or big pushes and little pushes.
    --Fast, slow.
    --Loudly, softly.
    --Starting and stopping.

. <u>Moving with changes of level</u>.

    --Sitting and getting back up.
    --Lying down and getting back up.
    --Getting in and out of the chair.
    --Lying down, rolling over, and getting up.

. <u>Moving in relation to other objects</u>

    --Under something.
    --Over something.
    --Through doorways.

. <u>Movement involving object manipulation</u>.

    --Opening and closing a door.
    --Touching something--high or low.
    --Carry something.
    --Pick up something.
    --Push something.
    --Pull something.
    --Kick something.
    --Manipulate something big, little, heavy, light, easy to move, hard to
      move.

. <u>Walk stairs</u>.

. <u>Use an elevator</u>.

. <u>Walk and collect something</u>.

. <u>Move with a wiggle, bounce, stretch, bend</u>.

. <u>Move blindfolded</u>.

. <u>Move using a rope lead as a guide, or follow a line or crack in the
floor surface</u>.

<u>Use your imagination</u>!!! Even if students do not always understand a concept they can imitate or be <u>motored through</u> an activity.

    Play skills are also important for a student with severe multiple impairments. Play provides opportunities for large muscle activity and includes components of social interaction and enjoyment important for attaining and maintaining high quality in life. Easy play situations include (2, 3, 4, 7)--

. <u>Target games</u>. A target can be anything an individual moves to,
  puts into, throws into, throws at, kicks into, kicks at, or hits
  at. Students can participate just to see if they can <u>hit the</u>
  <u>target</u> or they can compete against others--not so much for points
  involved and <u>winning</u> as for social interactions and taking turns.
  Initially a student may have to be completely <u>motored through</u>
  the activity--led to the target, helped with release of the ob-
  ject--but continued repetition in time improves performances,
  independence, and enjoyment. Some individuals use feet, mouth,
  or assistive devices to propel objects in target games.

. <u>Group games</u>. Group games are as much social experiences as
  physical ones. While there are a large variety of games to
  choose from, it may be helpful to consider--

    --Games where children remain seated in one place are
      easier than games where children must move around.
    --A game where only one child moves at a time is easier
      than a game where several or all players move.
    --A game that always repeats the same pattern is easier
      than a randomly organized game.
    --Games involving imitations are easier than games where
      players must initiate movements.
    --Physical cues in addition to verbal directions help
      players learn.
    --Games involving stationary objects are easier than
      games involving moving objects.
    --Adults playing the game right along with students
      serve as good role models as well as ready helpers
      to <u>motor through</u> students who need help.

<u>Making Choices</u>
How Appropriate is the Activity?

   Because there is often such a gap between chronological age norms and
functional physical and mental levels of a child with severe multiple impairments it is difficult to apply the concept of age development appropriateness.
<u>However if these children are to show any growth at all--other than physical--</u>
<u>every attempt must be made to move them toward higher levels of development</u>
<u>rather than just play with them where they are</u>. As shown by the following
figure (page 17) different teaching techniques are needed for different children on different developmental levels.

   Teachers must select activities that are as <u>individually</u> appropriate as
possible to aid each child in moving toward higher levels of functional ability,
no matter how low present functional levels appear to be.

Development of Functional Skills

Broad Range of Functional Skills

Instructions: Verbal
Goals: Obtainable
Reinforcement: When appropriate
Prior Experience: Present but limited
Skills Taught: Regular progressions and
      sequences
Verbal Directions: Explicit
Aids: Techniques from lower levels
Equipment: Age appropriate

Instruction: Demonstration
Goals: Observable
Reinforcement: Soon
Prior Experience: Very little
Skills Taught: Fewer number at
      slower pace
Verbal Directions: Simple
Aids: Joint participation by teacher
Equipment: Nonthreatening, softies

Instruction: Motoring through
Goals: Tangible
Reinforcement: Immediate
Prior Experience: None
Skills Taught: Individual tasks
Verbal Directions: Few
Aids: Cue words, physical prompts
Equipment: Appropriate to develop-
      mental level.

Initial Point of Having No Functional Skills

	Chronological Age:	Physical Development:	Mental Level:
	12 years to adult	Below Average/Average	Mildly Retarded
	6 to 12 years	Inadequate	Moderately Retarded
	0 to 6 years	Poor	Severely & Profoundly Retarded

As indicated by this chart different teaching techniques are needed for different levels of child development and capabilities. Arrows indicate direction of flow as a child with severe multiple impairments learns and progresses.

Selected References

1. Ackerman, Jeanne V. Developmental Physcial Activity: An Individualized Approach. Washington, D.C.: Hawkins and Associates, 1978.

2. American Alliance for Health, Physical Education, Recreation, and Dance. Best of Challenge (Vol. I). Washington, D.C.: The Alliance, 1971.

3. _____. Best of Challenge (Vol. II). Washington, D.C.: The Alliance, 1974.

4. _____. Best of Challenge (Vol. III). Washington, D.C.: The Alliance, 1977.

5. _____. "Individualized Education Programs," Practical Pointers (Vol. 1 No. 6). Washington, D.C.: The Alliance, October, 1977.

6. _____. "Individualized Educational Programs: Methods for Individualizing Physical Education," Practical Pointers (Vol. 1, No. 7). Washington, D.C.: The Alliance, December, 1977.

7. _____. Physical Education and Recreation for Individuals with Multiple Handicapping Conditions. Washington, D.C.: The Alliance, 1974.

8. American Association for the Education of the Severely/Profoundly Handicapped. Annotated Bibliography -- Materials on and For the Severely/ Profoundly Handicapped. University of Washington: The Association, 1976.

9. Bobath B., K. Bobath, and A. Jean Ayres. Tumble Forms Methods Manual. New York: J.A. Preston Corporation, 1980.

10. Bucher, Charles H. and Nolan A. Thaxton. Physical Education for Children. New York: MacMillan and Company, 1979.

11. Cunningham, Cliff and Patricia Sloper. Helping Your Exceptional Baby. New York: Pantheon Press, 1978.

12. Dauer, Victor P. and Robert P. Pangrazi. Dynamic Physical Education for Elementary School Children. Minneapolis: Burgess, 1979.

13. Diem, Liselott. Children Learn Physical Skills (Vol. 1--Birth to 3 yrs.) Washington, D.C.: AAHPERD, 1974.

14. _____. Children Learn Physical Skills (Vol. 2--Age 4-6 yrs.) Washington, D.C.: AAHPERD, 1974.

15. Drouillard, Richard and Sherry Raynor. Get a Wiggle On. Washington, D.C.: AAHPERD, 1975.

16. _____. Move It. Washington, D.C.: AAHPERD, 1975.

17. Finnie, Nancie R. <u>Handling the Young Cerebral Palsied Child at Home</u>. New York: Dutton, 1968.

18. Glass, Henry and Jack Capon. <u>Streamer and Ribbon Activities</u> (Record and Guide). New York: Educational Activities, n.d.

19. Jensen, Robert G. and S. Halpern. <u>Pop Rock Parachute</u> (Record and Manual). New York: Educational Activities, n.d.

20. Kock, Jaroslav. <u>Total Baby Development</u>. New York: Pocket Books, 1978.

21. Lehane, Stephen. <u>Help Your Baby Learn</u>. New Jersey: Prentice Hall, 1976.

22. Levy, Janine. <u>The Baby Exercise Book</u>. New York: Pantheon Press, 1973.

23. Painter, Genevieve. <u>Teach Your Baby</u>. New York: Simon and Schuster, 1971.

24. Prudden, Bonnie. <u>How to Keep Your Child Fit from Birth to Six</u>. New York: Harper and Row, 1964.

25. Reynolds, Freddie. <u>Cherokee County Curriculum Guide for Teachers of the Severely Handicapped</u>. Centre Alabama: Cherokee County Board of Education, 1981.

26. Seker, Jo Ann and George Jones. <u>Rhythmic Parachute Play</u> (Record and Manual). New York: Educational Activities, n.d.

27. Skinner, Louise. <u>Motor Development in the Preschool Years</u>. Springfield, Illinois: Charles Thomas Publisher, 1979.

28. Sparling, Joseph and Isabelle Lewis. <u>Learning Games for the First Three Years</u>. New York: Berkley, 1981.

PRACTICAL POINTERS

GAMES AND ACTIVITIES FOR SEVERELY HANDICAPPED STUDENTS UTILIZING SMALL
SPACE AND MINIMAL EQUIPMENT
Hezkiah Aharoni

The following games and activities have been gathered from experience with
severely multi-handicapped students in adapted physical education classes of
the Columbus public schools, Ohio.

The instructor who works with severely handicapped individuals in physical education is often faced with a dilemma of what to do and how to do it.
He/she is often at a loss as to how to accommodate the students' special needs
in physical education. He/she must search for appropriate games and activities
that will give motivation for skill acquisition and while also providing enjoyment. While it is important to retain the traditional elements of sport games
as much as possible, there is a need for change from the traditional when working with severely impaired students. One is required to change, adapt, and
invent new games and activities. This departure from the customary sport
activities is appropriate since it is the only avenue to provide severely
handicapped individuals with meaningful activities geared to their level and
ability.

The following games and activities are geared for those students who are
limited in mobility and have minimal use of hands, fingers, or other body parts.
The games and activities may be used to provide physical education and recreation for the severely involved (cerebral palsied students; those with orthopedic problems, those with muscular dystrophy, juvenile rheumatoid arthritis
youths, etc.). The games are also appropriate for all other students and most
may be used within the space of the classroom.

The games and activities are not arranged according to chronological age
or developmental order because severely handicapped children of the same age
may be extremely varied in their cognitive and physical abilities. For organizational purposes games were placed in categories. Some games may apply to more
than one category. Therefore, the instructor selects those activities suitable
for the particular student situation. Additional modification might be required
by the instructor.

ORGANIZING GAMES AND ACTIVITIES

- Be sure to select activities appropriate for each individual/group so that
  the level of difficulty will be challenging and stimulating (avoid frustration or dull play).

- Games and activities should relate to the overall theme for a particular day or week of the adapted physical education unit.

- Prepare equipment in advance. Make sure that there are sufficient activities to permit flexibility when some games do not work.

- Attempt new ideas for activities and games. Whether or not they succeed will be learned by trial and error, and will enhance instructor expertise.

- Vary the same activity to maintain player interest and to facilitate organization. Familiarity with the games increases student understanding, and contributes to active participation.

- Always consider optimal "positioning" for each student during the game where he/she is most comfortable for efficiency of skill acquisition. Use of devices, modified equipment, moving closer to or further from the target, and approaching the target from either its left or right side are all examples which could improve student performance.

- Provide short rest periods when necessary for certain individuals or slow down the pace with a less physically demanding activity. Handicapped students might become over-excited during activities, forgetting fatigue or causing possible bodily injury.

- Ensure fullest possible participation for all students. Let them help in organization of the game or activity; involve them in selecting or suggesting a new game or variation. Give each individual a feeling of being part of the activity.

- Praise accomplishments, both small or large. Immediate reinforcement is best. It is always important that participation in the activity is rewarding.

- List and organize all modified games and activities which were attempted and succeeded. Add new ones. This will help increase the activity list, will aid in retrieval as needed, and enable sharing of ideas with other teachers.

- Provide games and activities which *do not eliminate players* or require them to wait. One may use the point system instead of eliminating players. If the nature of the game requires player elimination, make sure that such elimination is *very short*.

- Be clear, concise, and avoid lengthy explanations. Children learn faster by doing. "The child thinks with the arms and legs."

ADAPTATIONS OF GAMES AND ACTIVITIES

The following is offered for consideration when adaptation or modification of games and activities is required in order for the handicapped to profit from them.

- The size, length, or weight of the equipment used for the activities may be increased or reduced, made shorter or longer, etc.

- The size of the playing area may be reduced to decrease the amount of activity.

- The size of the team and number of players may be reduced or increased depending on the situation.

- The height of the equipment may be reduced, e.g., in basketball and volley-ball the hoop and nets may be lowered.

- Rules of the game may be modified or changed in order to decrease the com-plexity and demand of the activity.

- Additional adaptive devices may be used with the standard equipment or by the player. These devices may improve body control and enhance use of the equipment.

- Boundary lines of the target or playing area may be enhanced by adding line markers, such as cones, colored tape, etc. This will increase visibility and provide safety for the activity.

- A more able player could be paired with a less able in such activities as folk and square dancing where the walker might push one who is non-ambulatory.

- The time to play the game may be reduced.

- Increase the ratio of adults to players, or of non-handicapped students who may assist in the activities.

GAMES AND ACTIVITIES

WALKING, RUNNING, AND WHEELING

Catch Them All

This game is appropriate for all levels of handicaps and contributes to cardiovascular endurance and fun. Areas of play should be designated using traffic cones, according to number and movement ability of students. One or more students is "it" (catcher). At the instructor's signal, "it" tries to catch all students playing in the designated play area. Players who leave the area during the game are considered out. "It" may touch any part of the player or wheelchair of player; that player is then considered "caught." Caught stu-dents leave the designated area. When players have had a chance to be "it," the game is over. Ambulatory players, or others who run well, might have to hop as they try to catch others, or they might have to hop, pushing the wheel-chair of a student who cannot wheel himself/herself. The teacher could record the time taken by each player who is "it" to catch all players, and this could be compared for all "its." In this game it is important to limit the play area so that "it" will quickly tag all players. This eliminates non-participation for long periods.

A Corner Cage Ball

Two to four players on wheelchairs or walkers are each in a designated corner. A 24" cage ball is placed in the center circle. At a signal, each player attempts to control the ball and push it toward his/her own corner. The player wins when he/she brings the ball to the "home" corner.

Blind Move

Group or individuals are arranged in line parallel to the walk area on one side of the gym or field. The students should be far enough from each other. Each student is blindfolded. A leader (teacher or student) gives directions when to move. The leader might say: move forward; stop; turn around once; turn to the left; turn to the right; etc. The object is to see who could reach a designated corner or wall in the gym first, or be in close proximity to it. Non-ambulatory students may be pushed by another player, whose eyes are blindfolded. Safety should be stressed.

Variation: There may be competition between two groups. Partners might work together. The blindfolded may be given directions by a partner as to where to move. Also obstacles could be placed in the gym.

Variation: Young and severely handicapped players might be placed on a large area in the room or the gym floor covered with a number of mats attached together. The playing will take place only in this covered area.

Basket-target

An empty basket or carton box turned on its side is placed on the floor and secured with masking tape. Players should be standing or sitting at various distances from the basket (depending on ability). The objective is to roll a playground ball into the basket. The ball could be deflated slightly to prevent too much bouncing. Points may be higher for a ball that stays in the basket than for a ball which went in and out, or just touched it. Severely handicapped individuals may roll

Figure 1.

the ball from a plywood ramp (12" x 48") with molding on each side. The ramp may be placed on the player's lap or wheelchair tray. (See Figure 1.)

Individual Moving Basketball

This game is most appropriate for wheelchair players. Two groups of wheelchair students are equally divided. A small plastic basket is attached to each wheelchair on the back. Before the start each group is in its half side of the designated play area. One of the group is given the ball. The object is to try to pass this ball and shoot. (See Figure 2.)

Figure 2.

Figure 3.

PUSHING AND PULLING

Push Ball to a Target

On the edge of a large table (or two attached) a funball is pushed by the individual to a target at the other end of the table. The target could be a goal area such as between two cups or other objects placed apart. One to three individuals may play the game. The winner is the one who scores the most goals. A helper may assist in ball retrieval. (See Figure 3.)

Variation: A bowling pin or empty cup, etc., may be placed at the edge. The object would be to push the ball and make it touch the object or knock it down. For each time the ball touches the object or knocks it down the player scores a point.

Bounce Table Tennis

This game could be played by one or two individuals. Half of the tennis table is folded at a 90° angle or a regular table may be placed against the

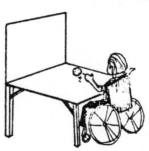

Figure 4.

wall. One individual may push a funball (wiffle ball) against the folded wing of the table and try to bounce it back and forth. Best score is the least times the ball falls on the ground. (Area may be restricted on both sides via placing wooden boards on each side of the table.) When two players play the game it could be played similar to handball. Player number one bounces the ball once only. The second time the ball has to be bounced by player number two, and vice versa. The winner is the player who missed the ball the least number of times. Hands or table tennis racquet may be used in this game. (See Figure 4.)

Adaptation: The table tennis racquet may be attached to the player's hand with velcro wide stretch band or masking tape if the student is unable to hold the racquet. The racquet should be attached loosely in order to avoid restricting the flow of blood.

Pendulum Bowling

Suspend a tetherball (soft one) from the ceiling, or basketball hoop, etc. On the floor, beneath the suspended ball, place one or more bowling pins (according to student ability). Position the students around the bowling pin and suspended ball. Student should try to push the ball or release it after holding it toward the bowling pin. The object is to see which student could knock the pin down. Teacher could give points for: number of pins knocked down;

who did it in the shortest time; number of trials allowed. (See Figure 5.)

Variations: (1) Place pin in front of or
beside each participant. Each player guards own
pin while trying to knock down the other player's
pin by striking or pushing the suspended ball.
(2) Suspend the ball to table height. The table
has bowling pins placed on the top of it and is
played as above.

Figure 5.

The Pull Games

A funball is tied to a heavy duty string or
thick rope (to permit better hold of the string).
The unattached end of the rope is given to a
player, with the end attached to the funball
stretched out 30' on the floor, away from the
player. Two or more students may each be given
a similar rope and ball tied to it. At the
teacher's signal the players are to pull it
all the way to the top of the wheelchair
tray or to their knees. The winner is the
first one to bring the funball all the way.

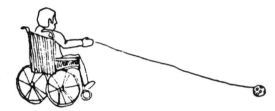

Variation: Objects or balls of varied
weights might be used to adapt the game for
different ability levels; different weights
and rope lengths could be used for each individual. (See Figure 6.)

Figure 6.

Pull It up and Release It down

A funball is tied to 30' heavy duty string or rope. The end with the
ball is placed through the hoop of the basketball
net, gymnastic ring, or any bar of appropriate
height found in the classroom. The ball has to
be suspended as each player has hold of the free
end to raise or lower the ball as they wish.
Players might compete to see who can raise the
ball all the way up and lower it all the way
down. One player may see how much he/she
could improve over trials. (See Figure 7.)

Variations: (1) A hook is attached to the
end of the string; the player tries to have the
hook in the hole of the funball or another object and tries to lift it up ("fish" it out).
(2) A box or coffee can could be placed on the
floor under the bar. The player tries to
place the ball within the box or can.

Put It in the Can

Figure 7.

A funball is tied to a heavy duty string or rope about 3' long. Each

196

wheelchair player is given the free end of the rope. A coffee can or small box is placed on the floor beside the wheelchair. The player tries to place the ball inside the coffee can. Two or more players may compete to see who does it first.

Box Push

Two teams playing relay games, or two or more individuals may play the following game. A paper box or other easily movable object is placed on the floor in front of each participant. Some distance from the wall at the opposite end of the gym a traffic cone is placed. The objective is to push the box (using a wheelchair all the way) around the traffic cone and returning to the starting position. This game is well-suited for electric wheelchair players. It teaches control and efficiency in wheeling the chair in a straight line and turning.

Variation: An obstacle course may be arranged with a number of cones. Player has to maneuver around the cones.

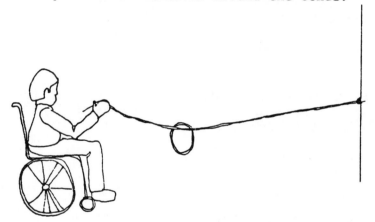

Figure 8.

Ring Sliding

Attach a rope or heavy duty string to a wall. Put the rope through a plastic, wooden, or rubber ring. Have the player move the ring from the free end of the rope (which is being held) to the opposite end attached to the wall. Hand or mouth movement may be used to move the ring. Two or more sets of players may compete against each other. (See Figure 8.)

Scooter Mat

Gym scooters usually are too small to give sufficient support to a severely orthopedically handicapped student. A mobile mat can be a large board of a scooter, usually padded. Commercial ones are expensive, but an excellent alternative is a mechanic's creeper used by auto mechanics to glide under cars, which costs $7.00 to $20.00. The original wheels do not move freely, but wheelbearing wheels could

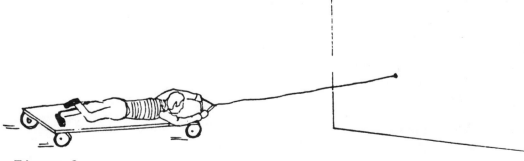

Figure 9.

be purchased for about $3.00 from Sears Stores, and could easily replace the original ones. The creeper could also be padded. The scooter mat could be used to increase usage of motion and reciprocal movement of severely handicapped individuals. When a rope is tied to a wall, a scooter mat rider lying on his/her stomach could pull himself/herself across the gym. Other students could push a student on a scooter or could pull a scooter tied to a rope. (See Figure 9.)

Rope Climbing/Pulling

A climbing rope is suspended from the ceiling. A wheelchair-bound student holds onto a knot in the rope or rubber rings may be attached to the rope at different heights, so that he/she can pull himself/herself up. A mat can be placed under the rope with the student on the mat being asked to pull himself/herself up to a standing position, or, if able, through a rocking motion. Spotting is necessary in this activity.

Rope Wheelchair

A 20' to 30' rope is secured to a wall bleacher or table stand. The wheelchair-bound player pulls himself/herself from the end to the beginning of the rope. Two or more students may compete to see who reaches the opposite end the fastest.

Variation: A more capable student could pull another wheelchair which is tied to the rope. In this case, a student who is pulling has to lock the wheelchair brakes. Emphasize safety rules in this game.

STRIKING WITH HANDS AND OBJECTS

Hand Ping-pong

Two individuals are sitting across from each other at a large table. A funball (wiffle ball), softball, or any other ball of the same size is used. The students have to place their arms on the table and push the ball or strike it toward their opponent. The object is to push the ball and cause it to fall at the opponent's edge of the table. Each player tries at the same time to keep the ball from falling or reaching his/her edge. Two wooden boards (2"-3" wide) could be placed on the left and right edges of the table to prevent the ball from falling off the side of the table. Only the opposite ends should be left open. The boards' distance could be adjusted to be narrower or wider. Scoring could be used to motivate students to improve performance. (See Figure 10.)

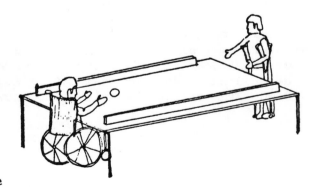

Figure 10.

Variations: (1) Same as above but using a tennis racquet. (2) A large number of students (3 to 12) could be placed around a tennis table or 2 to 6

198

tables attached together. The funball is thrown on the table and students try to push the ball or strike it across the table with the use of the hands or racquet. The winner is one who has the least number of times when the ball falls within his/her area of responsibility (usually 15" to 18", this could be marked on the table with masking tape according to each student's ability). *Rule:* Nobody is permitted to catch the ball. The ball must be pushed or struck continuously.

Balloon Activities

Punchball or heavy duty balloons may be used for the following activities. (Make sure an appropriate adjustment of suspended balloon height is provided according to individual ability.) Heavy duty balloons are available from K-Mart Stores, Children's Palace, and large toy stores. These balloons are easy to inflate, deflate, and last longer than ordinary balloons.

- Suspend a balloon from a ceiling near the wall area. Mark the wall height. The student strikes the balloon as far as he/she can, seeing how far or high (as shown on the wall) the balloon can go.

- Suspend a balloon. Strike. See if the student can make the balloon touch the ceiling (has to be suspended from a low ceiling).

- Suspend a balloon from a string. The string is suspended from another horizontal string. See if the student strikes the balloon and makes it go over a string or rope. Two students may play to push the balloon over the string from one side to another.

- Suspend the balloon. Two students face each other with a suspended balloon between them. Students have to strike the balloon to the opponent's face or shoulders. If it touches, then the student who achieved the strike to the opponent's body gets the point.

- As in above, but the student has to strike the balloon and cause it to go behind the opponent's head. If it does, then that player gets a point.

- As in above, but players try to prevent balloon contact to their faces.

- The balloon is suspended and two opponents face each other while the balloon is between them. When the teacher calls the name of one of the players, he/she has to strike or touch the balloon. If he/she succeeds, a point is scored.

- Players could strike the balloon using only their hands.

Group Balloon Volleyball

Two teams of students are arranged across from each other. Tables are placed in the middle between the two teams. A punchball is thrown in the center. The object is to strike the balloon beyond the other team. The balloon has to go beyond the opposite team at a level of the up-stretched hands of the opponents. The team which succeeds in striking the balloon beyond the opponent's team gets a point. Make sure to arrange the wheelchair

199

student who is less capable in front and the more able, standing student behind. (See Figure 11.)

Variations: (1) As above, removing
the tables. This is a more demanding
activity. (2) Team receives points only
when the opponents team lets the ball
fall on the floor. (3) A string or a
badminton net may be placed in the
center between the two teams at a low
height appropriate for wheelchair
players, etc.

Balloon Fight

A heavy duty balloon (punch ball   Figure 11.
available at all K-Mart's, Woolco's,
Children's Palace, and other toy stores) is used. Two players are sitting in
wheelchairs or standing facing each other. The balloon
is placed between their foreheads and faces. At
the given signal, both players try to push the balloon
toward the opponent without the use of hands. The
winner is the player who caused the ballon to go into
his/her opponent's territory (when the balloon falls
behind the opponent or at his/her side of shoulders,
etc.). The point system could be used as a motivational device. This game is appropriate for those
individuals with no upper limbs. (See Figure 12.)

Figure 12.

Variation: Have partners play against each other
to see which pair can hold the balloon the longest between the forehead and
face. See if they could move, sit, or turn while still holding the balloon.

Floor Shuffleboard

Each player holds a shuffleboard stick or
similar plastic tube, aluminum pipe, etc. A
disc is placed in front of each participant.
The object is to push the disc into the numbered triangle sections on the floor. Points
may accumulate to determine the winner. Students could be placed at varying distances
from the triangle, according to ability.
(See Figure 13.)

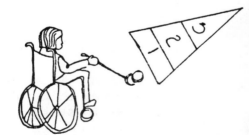

Figure 13.

Variation: Players shuffle the disc for distance. A light object such
as a plastic coffee can lid could be substituted for the heavier disc.

Tracking Object Target

Suspend two light tennis balls, etc., from a ceiling 3' to 5' away from

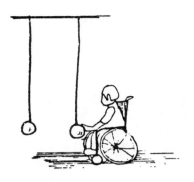

Figure 14.

each other. Let students try to strike one ball and make it touch the other ball. One may increase the distance between the two balls to provide a more challenging activity. (See Figure 14.)

Rope Bowling

A 20' rope is tied to the wall, table, or fixed object. The player holds on (with hands or mouth) to the free edge at the opposite direction. Two or six bowling pins are placed on the floor in a row under the rope. The object is to swing the rope from side to side or up and down and knock down the bowling pins. Two players could play the game and compete with speed. (See Figure 15.)

Figure 15.

Miniature Golf

A wooden box may be made with supporting 1" boards around the bottom. Holes could be made in any fashion to fit the size of a golf ball. Holes could be numbered according to difficulty, or in order. The player might use a light shuffleboard stick or plastic tube to push the ball from one hole to another according to the number. Players finish the game when they have moved the ball through all stations. Some sharp or uneven surfaces could be added for challenge.

Variation: This game could be played on the floor or on a table top, depending on the size of the box. Also, a student might use the mouth to hold the stick and play in this way.

Line Softball

Two groups of students line up facing each other about 20' apart. Wheelchair bound and walker players could be equally distributed on each team. The first team starts in order of player striking a funball (wiffle ball) from the top of a tall traffic cone or batting tee. The object is for the player to strike the ball across the opposite team who simultaneously tries to block it. Each time the ball crosses the line where the group stands, the team striking it gets a point. This continues until all players in each team have a turn. The winner is the team with the most points.

Adaptation: Varied weights, thicknesses, and lengths of softball bats could be used.

THROWING AND CATCHING

Target Throwing or Pushing

Every wheelchair player is given a beanbag. The object is to push the beanbag from the top of the wheelchair tray or throw it into a coffee can, box, or any container placed close to the wheelchair of each student. The distance that the container is placed from the wheelchair is dependent on each student's ability.

Variations: (1) Student may be given unlimited time to throw or push the beanbag. More capable students might have to try to get the beanbag into the container at the same time starting with the teacher's command "Go." (2) One big box could be placed in the center and the students could be placed at varying distances from it. (3) How far can the student throw the beanbag?

Circle Ball Passing

Form a circle of four or more wheelchair or walker-bound students. Students pass the ball around in any direction. At the teacher command of "change," the student passes the ball in opposite directions of the circle. The teacher should emphasize how to accurately pass the ball and how the student should approach the ball. Students with the use of only one arm can secure the ball to the lap or body. A more able student may help a less able one by reaching to him/her with the ball.

Variation: For young elementary students, the ball may be passed while singing: "The wonder ball goes 'round and 'round, To pass it quickly you are bound. And if you're the one to hold it last, Then the game for you is past ... and you are out!" When the song ends the person holding the ball will receive a "bad" point (in lieu of being eliminated from the game).

Fake Ball

The students are in a circle formation. The teacher stands in the center of the circle and passes the ball precisely to players at chest level in random order. The object is to remain still without moving the hands as the teacher attempts to confuse the players by faking or pretending to pass the ball to the player but actually not doing so. The player who gets confused receives one "bad" point. The player to whom the ball was actually passed, but who failed to catch it, receives one "bad" point for 3 misses. This game is fun to play and requires some practice and repetition for the players to be successful. It requires catching skills, attention, and concentration. The teacher might ask one of the students remaining last to direct or lead the next game as an award for winning the previous games. For the less able, or wheelchair-bound player the teacher could throw the ball right into his/her lap so that the student could press downward, securing it with the hand/s. Avoid throwing at face level as this might frighten the player.

Line Frisbee

Players are arranged in two teams facing each other. Each team receives 1 or 2 frisbees, depending on ability (best when each student has one). At the teacher's signal, the object is to see which team can throw the frisbee beyond the opposite team without being stopped by the opposing team who tries to block the frisbee. A point is awarded to the team succeeding in throwing the frisbee beyond the opposing team. In this game wheelchair-bound players should be placed in front, with players in walkers behind them. This game is most appropriate as part of a frisbee unit.

Ring Toss

Wheelchair-bound students may need some adaptation for a ring toss game, i.e., placing them closer to the target, or placing a long hollow tube on the ring stand. This extends the length and height of the ring stand and makes it attainable to the severely handicapped. (See Figure 16.)

Figure 16.

Target Frisbee

A group of players get in a line formation with cardboard boxes or containers placed in front of each player, at approximately 10' distance depending on ability. Each player attempts to toss a frisbee into the box. Players receive a point for each successful attempt. Indian clubs could be substituted for frisbees. A hula hoop may be placed on a mat and the student could throw the frisbee or Indian club into the hula hoop.

Variation: On a wall area marked with masking tape squares, arrange students in line. Have each student throw at least 5 successive trials. The object is to throw the frisbee on the square on the wall at a height of 4 feet.

Volleyball Frisbee

Two teams are placed on either side of a 4' to 6' high net. Each player on each team is given one frisbee. Team one starts first. Each player on the team tries to throw the frisbee over the net in order. When the last player finishes throwing his/her frisbee, the teacher counts the total number of frisbees thrown over the net. The same is repeated for the second team. Points are given according to the number of frisbees crossing over the net. The winner is the team with the most points. Try to vary the distance from the net according to ability.

Variation: Light balloons could be used or light balls, beanbags, balloons, etc. This activity is good for teaching throwing, arm extension, etc.

KICKING

Cage Ball Soccer

Two teams face each other in the gym. Each team has half of the gym. (With a smaller group and with severely handicapped players, a smaller section of the gym might be used.) A 24" cage ball is placed in the center. At the given signal, the object is to see which team can push the ball and make it touch the opponent's wall area at the end of the field. Any time the ball touches the wall, the opposing team receives a point. This game involves vigorous movement, which develops teamwork and cardiovascular endurance. To assure success the following rules/modifications are needed: (1) Ball must be 24" or larger if any players are wheelchair-bound. (2) Groups should be given color identification (use pinnies). (3) State appropriate safety rules. (4) A non-ambulatory player may be pushed by an ambulatory player, provided the pusher never removes the hand from the wheelchair. (5) No lifting of the ball is permitted. Only pushing with the hands, legs, or any part of the chair is permitted. (6) Encourage students to spread out in the field to avoid over-crowding. (Rules may be created.) When overcrowding occurs or the ball is being trapped, stop the game and ask players to spread out. Enter the ball again.

Cage Ball Floor Soccer

Place a large number of gym mats together on the floor to cover a large area. Place traffic cones in each corner of the mat area, and on the center of each side demarcating the middle line. Arrange two teams, placing each team on a half. Ambulatory and wheel-chair-bound players should be lying on the floor facing the other team on their stomachs or any other comfortable position.

Figure 17.

More severely handicapped students could be placed in front, close to the centerline. A 24" cage ball is placed in the center. The object is to push the ball (using hands or head) toward the other team's goal-line. (See Figure 17.)

Variation: A player on an electric wheelchair may serve as a goalie at the end of the playing area outside of the mat. He/she can move horizontally, forward, and backward to stop the ball.

Knock the Bowling Pins

Arrange 6 to 10 bowling pins in a straight row for each player. Have players run or wheel from the starting line to a row of bowling pins, and attempt to kick or knock them down as soon as possible. This activity is appropriate for the wheelchair-bound, and is particu-larly helpful for those students on crutches, and those with limited balance and body coordination. Bowling pins may be placed at fixed distances. Individual times could be recorded and compared with future performances. (See Figure 18.)

ROLLING

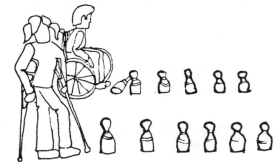

Figure 18.

Line Roll Ball

Players on wheelchairs or walkers stand at varied distances from a line marked on the floor, approximately 2' to 5' away from the wall area. The ob-jective is to roll the ball from a distance with the ball stopping or bouncing from the wall as close as possible to the line on the floor, or on the line itself. Players are to be placed at varying distances according to their ability. The player whose ball stops closest to the line receives a point. (See Figure 19.)

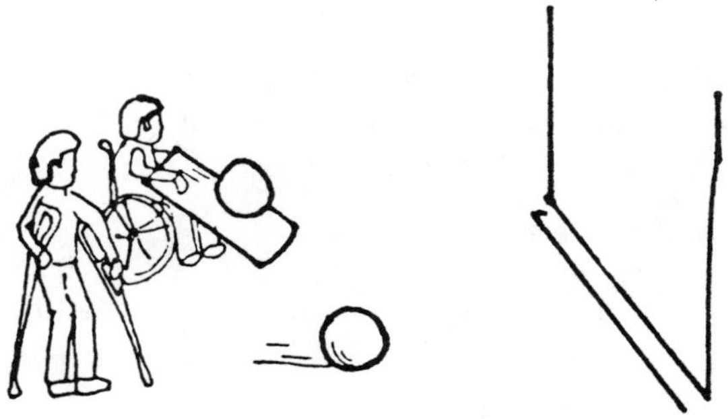

Variation: At a longer distance roll the ball to the wall. The closer to the wall the better.

Figure 19.

Line Bowling

Players are arranged in two groups facing each other from a distance of approximately 8'. Three to four feet in back of each team, a line of bowling pins is placed. (Plastic or wooden pins might be appropriate.) Each player gets a ball, or each player shares two to three balls, depending on ability. The objective is for each team to knock down the opponent's bowling pins at a given signal using the balls. The team to first knock down all of their opponent's pins is the winner.

Variation: Have one team start first, then count their points. Reset the pins for the other team and compare the number of points between the two teams.

EXERCISES/ACTIVITIES ON FLOOR MATS

Floor and Mat Activities

The following activities are best for those who have limited mobility, and who would benefit from a change in the routine of sitting constantly in a wheelchair. Activities are performed on a mat, and could be part of a well-balanced exercise program. Caution is needed, particularly in cases of certain conditions and specific types of cerebral palsy where activities might be contraindicated. The activities could be used individually, or with two or more participants on a competitive basis.

- Student lies supine, must turn quickly onto stomach, and then opposite.

- Student lies supine, lifts the head and neck to count of _____, then turns the head from side to side.

- As above, in a prone position.

- Student tries to sit up independently.

- Student tries to stand independently or with support.

- Raise leg to count of _____ (from prone or supine position).

- Bend, then extend knees.

- Crawl on floor or move body around (for a distance, or to reach a target).

205

• Touch each different body part (knees, legs, with left, right, etc.).

Body Bowling

A player with limited mobility or who is non-ambulatory is placed on the mat on the floor. Place 6 to 12 bowling pins around the player on all sides. Pins should be placed far enough from the student to elicit effort from him/her. The object is to knock all pins down using any part of the body. Two players or more may be placed at the above position, competing against each other to see who can knock the pins down the fastest. (See Figure 20.)

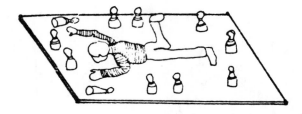

Figure 20.

Grab the Ball

Have a group of students of approximately the same ability level lying prone on a floor mat in a circle formation with a ball in the center. The object is to grab the ball or any other object as quickly as possible upon the teacher's signal. The teacher may place the student at different distances from the ball or object, according to individual ability.

Variation: Students may lie in a line formation and do the same as above.

Place It Around

Have the student lie on the floor mat at its edge, with a traffic cone placed at each end of the mat. Each student is given a hula hoop or small ring. The object is to see which student could crawl or kneel and place the hula hoop (ring) around the cone on the teacher's signal. They can also retrieve and go back to the starting point. (See Figure 21.)

Figure 21.

Weight-lifting--Poli

Windshield washer plastic bottles, or bleach bottles could be filled with sand. They should be varied in weight and sprayed with color to be more attractive. One end of the plastic bottle should be tied to a rope. Two plastic bottles should then be placed over a bar or basketball hoop, etc., so they hang down. A ring should be tied at the other end of the rope. This innovative equipment could be used for pulling weights. Amount of weight could be marked on the bottles. The above also could be permanently secured on two large rings, hooks, or two reels with tracks attached to a wall area. These pullies allow weight-pulling for wheelchair-bound or those on a floor mat, which always could be adjusted for best fit. (See Figure 22.)

Figure 22.

206

TABLE ACTIVITIES

Table Bowling

A long table is used for this game. One end of the table has to be raised approximately 1/2" by putting a book or other object under the two legs of the table. At the opposite end place 1 to 4 bowling pins (depending on table width and student ability). Provide student(s) with a heavy softball which is to only be released going toward the bowling pins and knocking them down. Each student may acquire points for each pin he/she knocks down at each attempt where he/she releases the ball. (Allow only releasing, not pushing of the ball.) Helper may

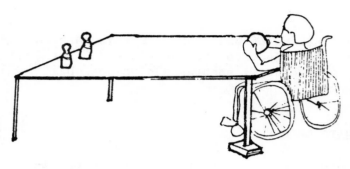

Figure 23.

be needed in ball retrieval. (See Figure 23.)

Table Shuffleboard

On a table surface, place a cloth or plastic which has a triangle with colors and numbers drawn on it. Students could be seated around the table. On the student's turn place the shuffleboard cloth in front of him/her at a distance according to ability. Give each student small wooden blocks, round checkers, or use marble for those players with extremely limited finger movement. Ask the student to flip with the finger or push the object onto the shuffle cloth. Each student has 4 to 5 trials, with points received per trial recorded for comparison. (See Figure 24.)

Figure 24.

Variation: Student may use a long stick to push the object or a communication board pointer elongated for the purpose. A triangle could also be drawn on a tennis table with yellow chalk or with masking tape, provided students are not restricted in movement.

Blowing Games

(1) Ping pong or regular classroom table could be used. Wooden boards, 2" wide, could be placed on either side of the table, leaving only the ends free. Two players, one on each side, blow a ping-pong ball to the opposite side. Players receive a point when the ball falls in the opponent's end. (2) Two or more players are seated at one end of the table. At the opposite end two paper cups are placed (the bottom one is upside down, and on top of that, one is placed right side up). The object is for the players to blow the top cup off the bottom one, receiving a point if he/she succeeds in doing so.

207

The Winning Edge

This is a table game where all students are at one end of each long table (or attached ones). Each student is given a bean bag. The object is to throw the bean bag to the end of the table as close as possible to the edge without letting it fall off. The player whose bean bag is closest to the table's end receives a point.

Variation: As above using checker in lieu of bean bag. In this case the player may flick his/her finger to push the object to the table's end. For those with limited finger movements a round object, such as a ping-pong ball or marble may be used instead of a checker.

WHEELCHAIR DRILLS

Wheelchair drills are activities provided for regular or electric wheelchairs. Drills could be executed by individuals, pairs, or a group. The larger the group of wheelchair students, the more the activities that can be performed. The drills are very similar to those done by marching bands. These drills are helpful to the handicapped since they teach movement efficiency and wheelchair operation facility, build cardiovascular muscle strength, teach organization, strengthen listening skills, build sensitivity to rhythm, and prepare the student for wheelchair folk and square dancing. Wheelchair drills with large groups could be used for demonstration at a school assembly or other events. Music in the background could be used in the drills.

● Wheel in a straight line to the end of the gym and back.

● Wheel in a circle in one direction then the other.

● Turn around in a very sharp turn in a designated circle.

● Wheel with a group at the same speed in a row, line, or circle.

● Wheel forward, inside the circle.

● Wheel backward, outside the circle.

● Wheel at moderate speed, stopping immediately on signal.

● Wheel in a zigzag fashion between cones in a circle, curve, or straight line arrangement.

● Two teams face each other, then move forward to meet each other and move backward away from each other.

● One team may stand still in a line while leaving sufficient space for the other team to wheel in between them.

One can come up with many possible variations borrowed from folk and square dancing. Cones could mark the drill area. Adaptation could include an ambulatory student pushing a non-ambulatory player.

AQUATIC GAMES AND ACTIVITIES

Wall Relay

This game could be played by two individuals or two teams competing against each other. The objective of the game is to move along the side of the pool from the starting position at one end of the pool to the other, and return to the starting line. The student should hold on to the side of the pool with one hand and move in this fashion as rapidly as possible. An individual having difficulty holding and swimming in a side position could be instructed to hold hands while in a position facing

Figure 25.

the side of the pool as he/she moves along. This could be done on the back or in a prone position. (See Figure 25.)

Adaptation: A line across the swimming pool could serve the same purpose as the wall.

Yellow Submarine

This is a chasing game wherein a player is safe if his/her face is submerged in the water. A group of players are scattered in a predetermined area. The size is according to ability and number of students. One player is designated as "it." At the signal "it" attempts to catch any of the players. The player is safe only if his/her face is submerged in the water and he/she is floating, while one of his/her hands is lifted above the water as a submarine. Players who are caught by "it" become the new "it."

Variations and Adaptations: One player, if able, is asked to catch all players in the pool before he/she is no longer "it"; two or more players could be "it" simultaneously with severely handicapped players. Players who are severely handicapped may use floating devices to help stabilize the body in water.

Breath-holding

The teacher gives the signal for players to submerge the head in the water and start the count for as long as they can hold. Who can last the longest in the group? Ask each player to remember to what count he/she held his/her breath. These are to be compared with additional trials in order to gauge improvement.

Whirlpool

The group forms a large circle in chest level water in the center of the pool. The group then starts walking in the same direction, holding hands,

maintaining the circle. Gradually movement is increased by running. This
movement creates a rip-
ple of water and the
current is built up.
When the current is
built up, ask some of
the players to float on
their backs as the rest
of the group keeps
moving. Continue the
same until all students
have had a few trials.
(See Figure 26.)

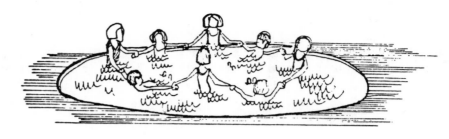

Figure 26.

Variations and Adaptation: At the end it is possible to ask all players
to float as they continue holding hands. A severely handicapped student may
need some of the adult support. Care must be taken that paraplegic individuals
will not drag their feet on the floor bottom, injuring themselves. A floating
device such as a tire tube might give them some support.

Object Retrieval

Different kinds of objects of varied textures, sizes, shapes, and color
could be placed in the pool and the swimmers would have to pick them up from
the bottom.

Fill a Bucket

Buckets are given to each swimmer. They are placed outside the pool at
the edge. Each player is given a large sponge, and at the signal submerges
the sponge into the water and then squeezes the water into the bucket. Who
can do this the fastest? This game is an excellent way to orient young
children to the water, and increase finger grasp and strength.

Walking Race

All students are lined up against one wall in shallow water, up to chest
level (dependent on ability). At the starting signal the students try to walk
to the other end of the pool as soon as possible. Who is the winner?

Adaptation: Handicapped students may use a floating device to give better
support, or could be placed close to the wall where they could move along it.

Water Valley

Two groups are arranged on opposite sides of the pool. In the center of
the pool, a rope line or imaginary marking is placed designating the halves.
Each group is given a number of objects (5 or more) such as balls, hoops,
sponges, swimming boards, plastic rings, etc. At the teacher's signal each
group tries to throw all the objects in its half to the opponent's half. Teams
stop playing at the second signal and the teacher counts the number of objects
on each half for each team. The team having the least objects left on its side
is awarded a point.

210

<u>Under or above the Hoop</u>

Students are arranged in a line along the side of the pool. In front of each student a hoop is placed at distances according to the player's ability. At the teacher's signal each student gets in the hoop by diving under it, or diving into the hoop from above and then out of the hoop.

Variation: For increased challenge a number of hoops may be placed in front of the more capable swimmers. They could be asked to dive under and through two hoops or more in sequence (one after the other).

REFERENCES

Adams, C.R.; Daniel, N.A.; and Rullman, L. *Games, Sports and Exercises for the Physically Handicapped.* 2d ed. Philadelphia: Lea & Febiger, 1975.

Aharoni, H. *Adapted Physical Education Manual: a Practical Resource Book for Initiating, Organizing, and Improving a Successful Program in Adapted Physical Education.* Columbus, OH: Columbus Public Schools, Special Education Department, 1981.

American Alliance for Health, Physical Education and Recreation. "Adapted Equipment for Physical Activities." *Practical Pointers* 1(5).

American Alliance for Health, Physical Education and Recreation. *Physical Activities for Impaired, Disabled, and Handicapped Individuals.* Washington, DC: AAHPER, 1976.

American National Red Cross. *Adapted Aquatics.* Washington, DC: Red Cross, 1977.

Cowart, F. *Instructional Aide for Adaptive Physical Education.* Hayward, CA: Alameda County Schools, 1977.

Cratty, J.B., and Breen, E.J. *Educational Games for Physically Handicapped Children.* Denver, CO: Love Publishing Co., 1972.

Croke, K.B., and Fairchild, B.J. *Let's Play Games.* Chicago: The National Easter Seal Society for Crippled Children and Adults, 1978.

Grosse, S.J. "Physical Activities for Children with Severe, Multiple Impairments." *Practical Pointers* 5(3).

Physical Education and Recreation for the Handicapped; Information and Research Utilization Center (IRUC). *Homemade Innovative Equipment for Activities in Physical Education and Recreation for Impaired, Disabled, and Handicapped Participants.* Washington, DC: AAHPER/IRUC, 1973.

Schultz, N. *Backyard Games.* New York: Grosset & Dunlap, 1973.

Sosne, M. *Handbook for Adapted Physical Education Equipment and Its Use.* Springfield, IL: Charles C. Thomas, 1972.

Section IV—
Practical Pointers for Adapted Aquatics

PRACTICAL POINTERS

ADAPTIVE DEVICES FOR AQUATIC ACTIVITIES
Jane Silverman Bradtke

Swimming, whether in lakes, ponds, oceans, or swimming pools is enjoyed by people all over the world. Successful aquatic experiences not only promote high levels of physical fitness and better health but provide enjoyable ways for participants to spend leisure hours while stimulating greater self-confidence and positive self-esteem. Individuals with handicapping conditions are not exceptions to this love of water. If individuals with handicapping conditions are not seen at community swimming pools on hot summer days or enjoying dips in nearby swimming holes, perhaps society has communicated to them by not providing opportunities for meaningful and adequate participaton in swimming programs that aquatic activities are dangerous, if not impossible, for them.

Increasing awareness of and sensitivity to interests, desires, and needs of individuals with handicapping conditions to join everyone else in all aspects of life--employment, education, and recreation--are evident. Legislation mandates that no person be denied benefits of, be discriminated against, or excluded from any program or activity solely because of a handicapping condition. Individuals with all types and severities of handicapping conditions take part in aquatic activities, from swimming to water skiing, wading to scuba diving, diving to water polo. For the most part there is nothing that cannot be accomplished by individuals who have the appropriate combinations of will, equipment, training, and opportunities. Water may be the only place a child with muscular dystrophy or cerebral palsy is able to walk--the only place to join able-bodied peers on equal bases physically.

Aquatic programs can become places for changing attitudes. Children with handicapping conditions can experience being equals or better with able-bodied peers in games and activities. Able-bodied children can see classmates with handicapping conditions excel, seometimes beyond what able-bodied children themselves can do. Such successes are good lessons for all involved, and can carry over into other activities at school, on the playground, and at home.

This Practical Pointer--Adaptive Devices for Aquatic Activities--presents information about commercial and homemade equipment which can be used in swimming programs by individuals possessing different handicapping conditions. Having proper equipment can make the difference between successful and enjoyable swimming experiences and frustration and fear at not being able to perform certain skills while learning to swim. This is true with all children, but especially with children possessing handicapping conditions as they work to overcome a variety of inconveniences and impairments.

GETTING INTO THE POOL

Commercial Equipment

The first step to being able to <u>swim</u> in a pool is, obviously enough, to <u>get into</u> the pool. This is an important <u>first</u> step because a teacher sets the tone for new students. Don't rush a non-swimmer into a pool--it's an awfully scary situation for a person to get into a body of water with a <u>stranger</u> if he/she does not know the first thing about keeping afloat! Methods and approaches for these situations are not dealt within this <u>Practical Pointer</u>--emphasis is on adaptive devices and equipment. A bibliographic listing on page 14 includes resources dealing with instructional aspects of aquatic programs.

Devices to assist persons with various physical conditions--i.e., obesity, amputations, paraplegia, quadriplegia, cerebral palsy--enter pools are available from different commercial sources. Following is information about selected commercial pool-entry devices with source names, addresses, and brief descriptions of equipment and their functions.

<u>Hydraulic Swimming Pool Lifter</u> (North American Recreation Convertibles, P. O. Box 758, 33 Knowlton Street, Bridgeport, Connecticut, 06601). This device makes it possible for individuals with physical or multiple handicapping conditions to get in and out of swimming pools easily. A simple hydraulic jack system combines sixty-two inches of lift with ninety inches of horizontal swing and supports up to 400 pounds. This device is especially useful with obese individuals who are unable to get in and out of pools by themselves.

<u>Vari Pod Platform</u> (Dominion Aluminum Fabricating Limited, 3570 Hawkestone Road, Mississauga, Ontario, Canada). This movable pool floor can be positioned for any desired height or depth, and is designed to accommodate individual pools according to their designs, needs and criteria. Costs vary from several hundred to several thousand dollars depending on size and sophistication of operation. Floors can be made from aluminum or fiberglass with total or just portions of floors moveable. Floors can be designed to manual or hydraulic power lifting. Hydraulically powered floors can be raised to deck level where wheelchairs and stretchers can be taken onto the floor before it is lowered for safe pool entry.

<u>Bath Trolly</u> (Ortopedia Gmbtt, D2300 Kiel 14, P. O. Box 6409, Germany). A plastic seat on four casters--resembles a gym scooter--was designed to help leg amputees move from changing areas to pool or lakeside by propelling themselves with their arms. The seat has a slightly curbed backrest for stability and comfort; slots cut into it allow drainage of water.

<u>G.E.G. Pool-Lift</u> (G.E.G. Ltd., P. O. Box 282, King of Prussia, Pennsylvania, 19406). This pneumatically operated elevator chair allows safe and convenient entry into pools. The <u>G.E.G. Pool Lift</u>, constructed of stainless steel and rust proof materials, features leg and headrests. It can lift up to 320 pounds and is permanently secured to the deck of a pool. An air compressor, located in an area remote from the pool, can be included.

<u>Hoyer Hoist</u> (Ted Hoyer and Company, Department AL, 2222 Minnesota Street, Oshkosh, Wisconsin, 54901). Canvas stretcher suspended on a track can be used with quadriplegics and severely involved persons who can be transferred directly onto it from litter or wheelchair after which the hoist is lowered directly into a pool.

Improvised and Homemade Equipment

Commercial devices for pool-entry can be assets in making public swimming pools accessible to individuals with handicapping conditions. However, many facilities do not have funds for what can amount to a sizeable expense for such devices. This does not by any means excuse a facility from not becoming accessible. There are ways to assist in pool entry with no more expense than cost of a towel or chair!* Following are suggestions for adapted and homemade devices. It is hoped that they trigger more ideas from readers--remember chairs are not just for sitting and towels not just for drying!!!

Chair Lift. A wooden chair with a clear varnish or plastic finish and four helpers are all needed to accomplish this transfer. With the student seated in a chair, a helper on each side and one at the back of the chair, and a helper waiting in the water, the chair is picked up by the three out of the water helpers and placed with back legs at the edge of the pool; the helper in the water helps secure the chair. Helpers at the sides of the chair now enter the water. The three helpers now in the water lower the chair while the back person lends support and control. To get an individual out of the pool, simply reverse these procedures.

---

*Policy interpretations of Section 504 of the Rehabilitation Act of 1973 prohibit lifting or carrying individuals to circumvent requirements to make facilities barrier-free and accessible to all. Some procedures presented in the following section involve lifting and/or carrying individuals. The Office of Civil Rights has indicated that such procedures are acceptable during the transition period ending June 3, 1980. However, whether such procedures continue to be legal or not after the transition period can only be determined in terms of individuals with whom they are proposed for use. Individuals with severe handicapping conditions who require lifting in a variety of situations can also be lifted into and out of swimming pools in ways presented. However, these decisions cannot be generically or categorically determined but only in terms of individuals with whom they are proposed for use.

Towel Lift. A large beach towel or blanket is all that is necessary for this transfer process. A towel is placed so that half supports the student's back. The towel is gripped securely by two people at the sides who hold the edges close to the student's thighs with one hand and the back edges at the corners with their other hands. A person at the back holds the upper edge close to the student's shoulders. On signal all lift together with arms straight and move smoothly to the pool to lower in towel and student. Another helper waiting in the water lifts under the student's thighs with one hand and supports legs with the other hand. The student is lowered until sitting on the pool edge at which time the helper in the water places one arm at the student's back and the other around his/her knees and pulls as other helpers lift slightly. To get out of the pool, the water helper pulls and slips towel into position before handing ends to helpers on deck. Care must be taken to make sure the towel is well placed and the student balanced.

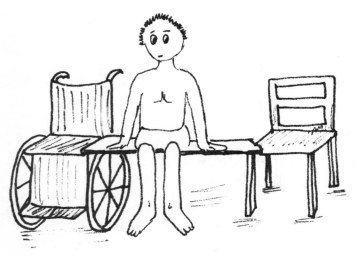

Transfer Board. A 12 inch by 33 inch board provides an excellent means for transfer to either a swimming pool or from one surface to another--i.e., from wheelchair to wooden chair. Place one end of the board underneath a student in a wheelchair and the other end on the surface to which he/she is to be transferred so that the student can slide across with as much or little assistance as necessary. A board with formica surface is excellent to facilitate sliding whether the student is wet or dry.

Ramp. For an outdoor swimming pool with surface at ground level, a ramp can be dug with the bottom of the slope ending nineteen inches--height of standard wheelchair seat--below the surface of the pool. The student can then slide from wheelchair to the edge of the pool and then lower him/herself into the pool.

Stretcher. A stretcher used to bring a student to the pool area can simply be lowered into the pool. Once in the pool the stretcher is slipped away and the student is then often the most independent and mobile of any time or situation.

Commercial Equipment

Getting into the water is the first step. Now, instruction in swimming skills can begin. In the process of learning specific swimming skills, confidence and a love for water should also result not to mention improved levels of physical fitness, better muscle tone, greater range of motion, and more flexibility. Positive attitudes and good teaching techniques are important; inventive activities with proper equipment can assist in this process. Several companies produce equipment, toys, and assistive devices to aid in the instructional process. These companies are listed along with specific devices each manufactures and distributes.

Pull-Buoy Inc. (2511 Leach, Auburn Heights, Michigan, 48057).

. Water Saucers

Made from Ethafoam and bound with colored plastic tape Water Saucers can be used in playing a variety of pool games, including water polo, saucer tag, keep away, and catch. They can also be used as a small kickboard or in water ballet routines.

. Unbreakable Arm Floats

Made from Ethafoam these solid arm floats are held on with surgical rubber tubing. Once adjusted they easily slip on and off a learner's arms. These floats will not leak and thus last longer than inflatable versions; they can be used for extra buoyancy and help instill confidence in beginning swimmers.

. Kick Roller

Used like a kickboard this aid looks like an oversized rolling pin made of Ethafoam with plastic handles. It is used to develop kicking skills necessary for independent floating.

. S-Board

Designed to make a swimmer kick or sink, this device is made of strong white styrene; it is 1/8 inch thick, 12 inches wide, 16 inches long, and has two lengths of rubber tubing at its midsection to hold the hands in place. The top of the board is bent upwards and the bottom bent downwards to give the S shape. Although not suitable as a buoyancy aid, this board can spur swimmers to kick harder and thus develop greater leg strength.

. Kickboard Plow

Similar to the Pull Buoy Drag this styrene plow fits onto any kickboard so as to help the user build leg strength while swimming. While the kickboard keeps the upper body on top of the water without arm movements, this plow makes the swimmer use more kicks per length of the pool.

- <u>Thong Hand Paddles</u>

These rectangular paddles have two rubber thongs in a V-shape to fit easily between middle and ring fingers. In swimming these paddles increase surface areas of the hands pressing against the water so as to improve efficiency and arm strength in strokes.

- <u>Pull Buoy Drag</u>

This strong white styrene drag fits onto any of the company's <u>Pull Buoys</u> to help swimmers build arm strength. The <u>Pull Buoy</u> itself keeps legs afloat without kicking, while this drag requires about one-third more arm pulls per length of the pool.

- <u>Lap Counter</u>

Large number boards are designed to stand at the end of a pool as easily visible indicators of numbers of lengths done by a swimmer. Plastic numbers are flipped over to count numbers of odd laps up to seventy-one that have been completed. These can be adapted for use in other physical education, recreation, or sport activities.

- <u>Unbreakable Line Floats</u>

These floats can be used for dividing different sections of a swimming area. Most common use is to divide shallow from deep ends; they can also be used to separate stations when swimmers of different abilities are receiving instruction in several classes simultaneously. Made from Ethafoam each has a 3/4 inch plastic insert through the middle to keep the rope from wearing away. Floats are four inches in diameter and can be ordered in six, eight, ten, or twelve inch lengths.

- <u>Kickboard</u>

Made of Ethafoam these kickboards will not break when bent, thrown, or jumped on, and will not flake off in the pool. Boards have rounded tops and squared-off bottoms; they can be used as swimming aids with reluctant and/or physically impaired swimmers. Gripping near the top of the board and keeping arms straight, a swimmer remains buoyant and can concentrate on strengthening leg muscles and improving technique without simultaneously having to think about arm strokes.

. Training Kit

Collection of training aids also sold separately by the company are
contained in this kit which includes <u>Thick Kickboard</u>, <u>Swim Goggles</u>,
<u>Thong Hand Paddles</u>, and <u>Pull-Buoy</u>. Swim goggles help protect
swimmers from burning eyes and can make putting faces in water more
acceptable for reluctant swimmers. All other items in the kit are
mentioned above.

<u>Cosom</u> (Airlake Industrial Park, P. O. Box 701, Lakeville, Minnesota, 55044).

. Float Ball

These 3 3/4 inch diameter floating balls can be used in various
activities by beginning and advanced swimmers. The balls which
are red/white or blue/white have holes to accommodate up to a
1/4 inch line so as to make them servicable as markers. They
can be used in swimming pool obstacle courses, relay games,
various tossing and retrieving games, and various other activities.
Bulk economy packs are available.

. Pool Toss-Um Game

This floating version of a lawn dart game can be played by
participants who throw from different distances while treading
water or while standing on the pool bottom or deck. This game
consists of two twenty-four inch target hoops and four <u>Toss-Ums</u>
which are weighted missles with rounded tops that float on the
surface of the water. A variety of playing and scoring options
are possible depending on participants and their skills. Because
<u>Toss-Ums</u> have long handles, players can retrieve them in their mouths
if they have limited use of hands.

. Diving Rings

Six yellow polyethylene rings are numbered and weighted. One
suggested use for rings involves tossing them into the pool so
that each swimmer in turn can dive and retrieve as many rings as
possible. Numbers on retrieved rings are added with the first
player socring a designated number of points winning. Each ring
measures 7 1/4 inches in diameter and weighs 1 2/3 pounds.

<u>GSA Athletic Equipment</u> (600 North Pacific Avenue, San Pedro, California, 90733).

. Kik Board

Molded of polyethelene this aid has handles molded into the sides
of its flat torpedo like shape. This is similar to <u>Pull-Buoy</u>
<u>Kick Roller</u> (page 7) in use and purpose.

Belleair International (1016 Ponce De Leon Boulevard, Belleair, Florida, 33516).

- Schwimmflugel

Made in West Germany, these inflatable cuffs can be worn around arms above the elbows to help keep non-swimmers afloat. Cuffs are slipped on, inflated by blowing air into a valve, and then valves closed and pushed into air chambers so they do not protrude from the surface of the cuff. They can also be worn on thighs, lower legs, or combinations of arms and legs to assist in attaining independent functions in water. These are available in three sizes to fit infants, children, and adults.

Hilsinger Corporation (Plainville, Massachusetts, 02762).

- Eyeglass Floats

For persons who wear glasses these floats, about four inches long and one inch wide, can be fastened onto temples of eyeglass frames. It is recommended that one float be worn on each temple for glasses weighing less than 1 5/8 ounces and two floats on glasses weighing more.

Blue Grass Industries (Carlisle, Kentucky, 40311).

- Speedo Aqualift Swimsuit

This one piece nylon tricot swimsuit is constructed with an air bladder inside the front of the suit which is inflatable by blowing into a double safety valve located on the center front of the suit's scoop neck. When inflated this suit supports up to a 200-pound adult. An optional flotation collar attached to the suit can offer added support to the neck and prevent the wearer from flipping over. As experience, ability, and confidence increase, the collar can be removed and the suit gradually deflated.

Recreonics (6202 La Pas Trail, Indianapolis, Indiana, 46268).

- Pull-Buoy

Two cylinders of Ethafoam are connected with one nylon cord through their widths at the top and bottom. The cord may be knotted to adjust space between the buoys to fit user's legs which are closed with one cylinder in front and the other in back. Swimmer can float in a horizontal position--face down or face up--and swim using only arms for propulsion. These can be used in combination with hand paddles for variation.

Suspended Aquatic Mentor (4022 Bedford Avenue, Brooklyn, New York, 11229).

- Suspended Aquatic Mentor

This easily assembled portable tripod has a canvas support suspended from the top. It allows complete freedom of movement and a full range of motion as the student who lies across the support is able to

practice movements without concern or fear of sinking. This can
be used on deck as well as in water.

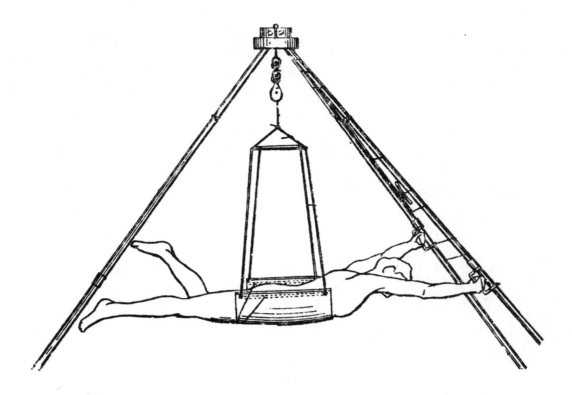

Stadiums Unlimited (Box 374, Grinnell, Iowa, 50112).

. Tot Dock

This is an underwater portable swimming pool platform which rests
on the swimming pool floor at heights of six to twelve inches. This
sturdy base is quite useful, especially in pools which have inadequate
shallow areas. It can be assembled and disassembled in a matter of
minutes. Sections stack upon each other for easy storage on deck
when not in use.

Improvised and Homemade Equipment

As discussed in the section on pool entry devices, a facility may not have
adequate funds to purchase much extra equipment or specific assistive devices.
Certain items listed may not be necessary in the sense that an individual can
learn to swim without them. However, considering that such devices help make
instruction a more enjoyable process and give teachers new ways to teach old
skills, they certainly add much to swimming programs. Many items can be
constructed in a matter of minutes from the most common household items. Cost
is negligible--results and rewards priceless!

Wash Cloths. Many times if a child will not submerge under water, a simple wash cloth provides all the help needed. By holding the cloth over his/her own face, many children will put their faces under water.

Boards/Towels. For improving certain strokes or body movements in water, boards or towels provide effective and inexpensive assistance. With aides holding both ends of a towel or board, a student can lie lengthwise and practice desired movements. Gradually lower the board or towel into the water until it can be removed makes for a smooth transition from out of water swimming to in-water swimming.

Broomstick with Plastic Bleach Bottles. Plastic Bleach bottles attached in barbell fashion to a broomstick make effective floatation devices to allow for free movement through water.

Bleach Bottles. Bleach bottles themselves attached to arms or legs make effective floatation devices. By gradually increasing amounts of water inside the bottles, reduction in buoyancy results and provides excellent muscle-building activity.

Ropes. Ropes attached to one side of a pool can be used by students to pull themselves across. This approach can be used to help build confidence in going across a pool and moving through water. Tying pieces of rope into loops provides rings for various ring-toss games, or dive-and-retrieve activities.

Wooden Bench. A wooden bench placed in the water provides an interesting object and challenge for students to swim under or over. Several benches in a pool make fun obstacle courses of circuit games which can include different tasks to be accomplished at each site.

Plastic Bottles, Coins. Diving and swimming underwater can be challenging for a student, but diving to find a coin or other small object can be down-right fun! Almost any small object can be used effectively and successfully for this particular activity.

Water Wings. A piece of foam flutterboard laced around the arms will make excellent water wings, or floatation devices. Larger pieces of foam flutterboard can be used as floatation devices which can be strapped with clothesline around the waist.

Floor Mat. Outside of the water, strokes can be practiced on a floormat. These same activities can be practiced directly on the floor, a bed, or chair. In fact, students can be encouraged to practice on their own at home using a bed, chair, or floor.

Exercise Bars. Lowering exercise bars into the water provides stable handrails for students to hold onto while practicing kicking or breath control.

Ping Pong Balls. A very nice characteristic of ping pong balls--besides the fact that they're rather useful in a game of table tennis--is that they are buoyant. A student can practice breath control by blowing a ping pong ball across the pool. In a very different setting--the ocean--a ping pong ball attached to a string can be tied to the wrist of a blind scuba diver.

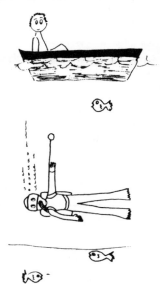

This can provide immediate answer to
an important question --

Which Way is Up?!?!

RESOURCES FROM AAHPERD AND IRUC

The Information and Research Utilization Center in Physical Education and Recreation for the Handicapped (IRUC) functions within the AAHPERD Unit on Programs for the Handicapped. Major purposes of this Center are to collect, categorize, describe, interpret, package/repackage and disseminate information about all aspects of physical education, recreation, and related areas for impaired, disabled, and handicapped persons. As a part of the Center's operation, IRUC Reprint Services functions to make available information about unpublished materials such as curriculum guides, program descriptions, conference proceddings, research reports, and selected journal articles. In addition, Topical Information Updates are published based on demand for a subject area. Below are listed selected reprints dealing with aquatic activities for the handicapped. Cost for items is based on 10 cents per page and all order must be prepaid except for official purchase orders over $10. Two Updates dealing with Aquatics for Handicapped Persons are available also (Update Number 16, December 1976, and Update Number 27, October 1978.) Each sells for $2.00.

Selected Reprints

Aquatics for the Impaired, Disabled, and Handicapped: Information Sheet. Washington,
    D.C.: IRUC, 1972. 31 pp. (IRUC Order # 2, $3.10).

Weiser, Ron, ed. Swimming Manual. Pomona, California: Pacific State Hospital, n.d.
    57 pp. (IRUC Order #130, $5.70).

Lathy, Laurel, Monica Young, and Claudia Clarke, compilers. Programme Handbook:
    Swimming for the Disabled. Vancouver, British Columbia: Red Cross Society,
    Water Safety Service. B.C. Yukon Division (4750 Oak Street). (IRUC Order # 271,
    $2.90).

Aquatics Workshops. Longview, Washington: YMCA of Southwest Washington, 1975. 157 pp.
    (IRUC Order #278, $15.70).

Watch Me Learn to Swim--Instructor's Record Sheet. Town and Country, Missouri:
    Special School District of St. Louis County, n.d. 1 p. (IRUC Order #280, $.10).

Watch Me Swim--Instructor's Record Sheet. Town and Country, Missouri: Special
    School District of St. Louis County, n.d. 1 p. (IRUC Order #281, $.10).

Watch Me Swim. Town and Country, Missouri: Special School District of St. Louis County, n.d. 5 pp. (IRUC Order #282, $ .50).

Watch Me Learn to Swim. Town and Country, Missouri: Special School District of St. Louis County, n.d. 8 pp. (IRUC Order # 283, $ .80).

Allen, Rosemary B. Selective Swim Program 1975-76. Bremerton, Washington: the Author (11330 Kitsap Way, 98310), 1975. 18 pp. (IRUC Order #285, $1.80).

Patrick, George D. Behavior Modification Techniques in Aquatics. Paper presented at Council for National Cooperation in Aquatics Closed Workshop, Fort Lauderdale, Florida, November 14, 1975. 12 pp. (IRUC Order #290, $1.20).

Melvin, Linda. The Use of Games in the Aquatic Environment. Atlanta, Georgia: Georgia Retardation Center, n.d. 8 pp. (IRUC Order #302, $.80).

Noble, Susan. A Guide to Swimming Instruction for Developmentally Disabled Children. Boston, Massachusetts: Developmental Services Resource Project, Massachusetts Department of Mental Health (190 Portland Street, 02114), n.d. 128 pp. (IRUC Order #389, $12.80).

Martin, Peggy and Madeline Nichols. An Innovative Swimming Program for the Severely and Profoundly Mentally Retarded. Pineville, Louisiana: Pinecrest State School (P.O. Box 191), n.d. 24 pp. (IRUC Order # 516, $2.40).

National Multiple Society Guidelines for Development of Chapter-Sponsored Group Aquatic (Swimming) Programs for Persons with Multiple Sclerosis. New York (205 East 42nd Street, 10017), National Multiple Sclerosis Society, n.d. 7 pp. (IRUC Order #544, $ .70).

Melvin, Linda. Adapting Perceptual Motor Programs for the Aquatic Environment. Atlanta: Georgia Department of Human Resources (1260 Briarcliff Road, 30306), n.d. 34 pp. (IRUC Order $547, $3.40).

Therapeutic Swimming for the Multi-Handicapped. Final Report 1975-76. Clark County School District. Las Vegas, Nevada: Helen J. Stewart School, 82 pp. (IRUC Order #555, $8.20).

Wolf, Jan. Elementary Forms of Water Rescue. Minneapolis, Minnesota: Joint Independent School District # 287 (1820 Xenium Lane, 55541), 1976. 11 pp. (IRUC Order # 559, $1.10).

Canoeing. Minneapolis, Minnesota: Joint Independent School District # 287 (1820 Xenium Lane, 55441), 1976. 11 pp. (IRUC Order # 560, $1.10).

American Red Cross Swimming Color Book. Minneapolis, Minnesota: Joint Independent School District # 287(1820 Xenium Lane, 55441), 1978. 43 pp. (IRUC Order # 561, $4.30).

Fender, Linda. Aquatic/Swimming Orientation Manual. Bethany, Oklahoma: Children's Convalescent Hospital, January 1975. 29 pp. (IRUC Order # 1174, $2.90).

Horton, Patricia S. Development of a Swimming Program for a Children's Developmental Clinic Applied Project in Physical Education. Athens, Georgia: University of Georgia, Physical Education Department, 1973. 112 pp. (IRUC Order #1189, $11.20).

PRACTICAL POINTERS

INDEPENDENT SWIMMING FOR CHILDREN WITH

SEVERE PHYSICAL IMPAIRMENTS

Susan J. Grosse
Christine D. McGill

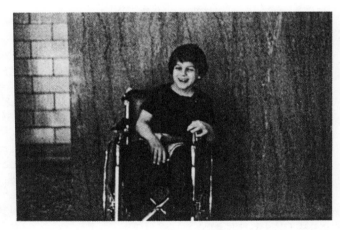

This is Mark--our subject for demonstrating
swimming for an individual with a severe
physical impairment.

Note: A one-half inch black and white video-cassette, Independent Swimming for the
Child with a Severe Physical Impairment, shows procedures and practices
presented in this Practical Pointer. This video-cassette is available for free
loan from Department of Physical Education, Division of Curriculum and
Instruction, Milwaukee Public School System, P.O. Drawer 10X, Milwaukee,
Wisconsin, 53201.

It started with curiosity about how a young boy with severe impairments from cerebral palsy could function in water. One doesn't usually think of a quadriplegic whose voluntary movements are extremely limited and whose speech is impaired as being a candidate for swimming instruction! Rather, such an individual is usually recommended for <u>recreational</u> water activities in which he/she is carried around in the water and/or supported by buoyant aids. Generally the individual has good social experiences but learns little, if anything, about swimming. However, <u>severe physical impairments do not mean that individuals cannot become independent swimmers</u>. It means that <u>instructors</u> must keep open minds to the potential for skill development, and develop highly individualized programs of instruction for each of these students.

WATER ADJUSTMENT

The place to start is with water adjustment. Many individuals with severe handicapping conditions have had little or no contact with swimming pool settings. Actually this is an ideal way to start! It is much more difficult to work with someone who has been in several different swimming programs or who has been exposed to a variety of aquatic instructors, especially if those programs and instructors had not stressed student independence. Because of such limited experiences, it is necessary to start at the very beginning -- the physical fact of being in water. Many individuals with severe physical impairments have either extremely limited movements or a great deal of extra, unwanted movements due to unpredictable muscle spasms. Nervousness, excitement, fear, or just concentration can increase muscle tensions, limit further voluntary movements, and increase involuntary actions. Therefore the primary goal in water adjustment is to make the individual comfortable in water.

Progressions in Water Adjustment

1. While the individual is still on land have him/her lie or sit on the edge
    of the pool, whichever is more comfortable for the student.

    . Explain to the student that you will...

       ...tell him/her ahead of time what is going to happen, what you are going
       to do and what the student will be doing.

       ...not do anything to the student that you do not tell him/her about.

    . Ask the student to show you...

       ...how he/she will indicate to you <u>yes</u> or <u>ok</u> if the student is not
       verbal.

       ...how the student will indicate to you <u>no</u>.

    . Get the student wet by cupping pool water into your hands and rubbing them
      over his/her body. Ask how it feels. When the student is wet over most
      of the body tell him/her that you are now going to help him/her get into
      the water!

2. Lift the student into the pool. An easy method is to turn the student on
    land so that he/she is lying on the stomach with feet toward the edge of the
    pool, head away from the pool edge and body perpendicular to the side. Then
    gently pull the individual backward, supporting him/her first at the waist
    and then at the armpits as the body is lowered into the water. <u>Be sure you</u>
    <u>do what you promised earlier--tell the student what is happening and what is</u>
    <u>going to happen</u>.

3. Once in the water, position the student with his/her back to you; support
    the student under the armpits with his/her back against the front of your
    body. <u>Be sure the student's head stays above the water</u>.

4. While maintaining this vertical position, carry the student around the pool
    area. Move relatively slowly, talk to the student as you move, and tell
    him/her what you are doing. While walking make mental assessments of...

       ...the student's general reactions to water;

       ...amount of excessive, involuntary muscular activity taking place; and

       ...any voluntary actions done by the student.

5. If voluntary movements are excessive at this point it helps the student
    if you aid in containing them. The student can only concentrate on one
    thing at a time. If you assume responsibility for taking care of extra
    movements, the student can focus attention on the water. If extraneous
    movements are...

...in the arm and shoulder area, first use your hand position under the student's armpits to curl his/her shoulders slightly forward; then tuck one or both of his/her arms under yours to pin them down.

...in the lower trunk and or legs, curl the student's upper body forward while at the same time placing an arm under his/her knees and curling them towards the chest so that the student is sitting in your arms in almost a ball.

The first carrying position-- help the student control excessive body movements.

In either or both of these positions extra movements are contained and the student can return attention to the water.

6. While carrying the student in the water, swish his/her body back and forth, turn in circles, bounce gently--vary movements so that the student can feel water moving in many different ways over his/her body.

7. As student relaxation in the water increases, gradually release the containment position until just the armpit support is used--this may take several sessions in the water.

8. While carrying the student in water gradually get his/her entire body wet, head and face included.

   . Gently rub water onto all dry surfaces.

   . Sprinkle water over the student's head as if he/she were in a shower.

   . Wash his/her face with a wash cloth.

   . Pour water from your hand over the student's head.

   . Ring out a sponge over the student's head.

   . Wash his/her face with a sponge.

   . Have a sponge fight.

   . <u>Be creative</u>!

230

BREATH CONTROL

Comfort and relaxation in water develop over time. While a student is working on water adjustment he/she should also be working on breath control. Any form of independent swimming involves submersion of the face and breath holding. The time to start developing this is during the very first lesson.

Progressions in Developing Breath Control

1. Have the student practice opening and closing his/her mouth with the face out of water; be sure the student knows which position is which. Check to see that when his/her mouth is closed it is in a natural closed position, not with one lip tucked in or the teeth showing.

2. Tell the student that he/she is going to dunk all the way under water—be sure to emphasize closing mouth before going down and not opening it again until the head is up and out of water. Explain that you will say, ready, at which point he/she should take a breath and close the mouth. The student then dunks quickly and comes right back up.

Bobbing—ready, lift.
Mark knows he has to
take a breath.

Bobbing—the quick
dunk under.

. Hold the student under the armpits in water that is deep enough for him/her to be dunked without hitting the feet on the bottom of the pool.

. Explain the dunk procedure.

. Say ready and watch to be sure that the student opens his/her mouth, takes a breath, and then closes the mouth.

. Lift the student up slightly.

. Quickly dunk the student under water, just to the top of his/her head.

. Bring the student up and tell him/her to take a breath--smile, praise the individual and tell him/her it was _fun_.

Lifting the student slightly before the dunk serves as a last reminder that he/she is going under--this is a _kinesthetic_ ready signal and should be used before _every_ dunk.

3. If the student swallows water or coughs...

    ...don't make a big thing about it.

    ...wait until he/she gets a breath and then remind him/her to close the mouth next time.

    ...after several dunks the student will get the idea and either close the mouth, or if that is not possible, learn to close off the back of the throat.

4. If the student cries...

    ...tell him/her what a goood dunk was accomplished.

    ...do something with which he/she is already familiar--play with a sponge or swish in water.

    ...do not tell him/her there is nothing of which to be afraid--in fact, _do not mention fear at all_. Assume that it is all right and the student will soon come to think this way also.

5. Repeat the quick dunk procedure several times throughout each lesson, doing it _everytime_ the student comes swimming.

6. Help the student do bigger dunks. Use the same general procedure as for quick dunks, only go further under water and move just a little slower in the process.

7. Have the student practice holding the breath for several seconds. Keep his/her head out of water initially and check to see that the breath is actually being held. Have him/her take a breath, close the mouth, and hold the breath while you count to three--later count to five, seven, ten, or more to extend the time.

8. Do a big dunk and tell the student you will count to three and then bring him/her up. Remind the student to hold the breath while under water. Count loudly so the student can hear you under water; when you get to three bring him/her up immediately.

9. Extend gradually time under water during big dunks. Always tell the student how high you will count and then bring him/her up promptly.

10. As the student becomes familiar with the procedure for timed dunks, ask how high you should count before bringing him/her up. This places part of the situation under student rather than instructor control. It also begins the transition to independence while at the same time helping the student build accurate assessments of his/her own abilities. If the student should make an unrealistic request, don't tell him/her that this is wrong. Try it anyhow and let him/her have difficulty. Then bring the student up and talk about it. Ask if a mistake was made and if he/she would like to change the amount of time for the next dunk. Students need to have experiences of doing what they thought could be done so that they can determine for themselves their own capabilities.

Body positioning for breath control activities is basically the same as for water adjustment parts of lessons. The student should be supported under the armpits with his/her back to the instructor. Amount of freedom of movement allowed depends on voluntary muscle control of each student.

MOBILITY

After the student is relatively confortable in water and can hold the breath for at least a count of seven or eight, it is time to introduce mobility in the prone position.

Developing Mobility in the Prone Position

1. Tell the student that he/she is going to go under water in almost the same way as for timed dunks except that instead of being held upright while under water, he/she is going to be held on the stomach. While supporting the student under the armpits say, <u>ready</u>. Then lift him/her slightly as a breath is taken before placement in a prone position with the face in water. Count to five--or whatever number to which the student agrees--then lift him/her back to vertical by using leverage of your hands under his/her armpits and your outside elbow on his/her buttocks.

Prone floating--hold
the swimmer in the
float and count to
five before picking him up.

Prone floating without
assistance--count to five
and then pick him up.

2.	When the student is comfortable in the prone position while being held, tell him/her that when placed on the stomach you will let go while counting. When reaching the recovery number, put your hands back in place and lift up.

3.	When the student can float independently for at least a count of five on the stomach, it is time to try movement while in this position--when you let go the student should try to move the body any way that feels good. The student can kick legs, wiggle the body, move arms, do anything he/she wants.	Do not give specific directions about a swimming stroke--if the student had movement control to learn a regular stroke, you would not be using this procedure!

4.	Give the student several tries over a period of time to experiment with movements in the prone position.	Some things make the student move through the water, some do not; provide verbal feedback about what looks successful. Most individuals have some movement, though it may be random and erratic. This movement is what you want the student to develop in water.	If such movement keeps the student relatively close to the surface of the water and in some way, shape or form moves the body forward, it is acceptable.

5.	While the student is experimenting with movement be sure to continue to count floating time so that he/she does not have to worry about when to come up for air.

	When the student begins to develop some movement is the time to start developing recovery skills.	In this case recovery means the position the swimmer uses for getting a breath of air and for resting.	The recovery position should not depend on the bottom or side of the pool as the student may not be able to reach either when needing them.	For most students recovery is accomplished in a supine position.	Very few students float vertically; for those who do, the vertical position can be used for recovery.

Developing a Supine Position

1.	The supine position is introduced during water adjustment period.	While the student is working on breath control, floating, and movement in the prone position, all water adjustment activities should be continued to keep the swimmer familiar with different positions.

2.	Stand behind the student's head, support him/her under the armpits, and tip him/her gradually backwards until the body approximates a supine position. If the student shows a lot of random movement, use your own body for partial support under him/her until he/she gets used to the feeling of being on the back.

3.	When the student is relatively comfortable on the back with armpit support it is time to work on correct head position.	If the student is already focusing on the ceiling with the head tilted back and the chin out of water, do nothing--this position is fine.

4. If the student is in the supine position with the chin in the water, eyes focused on the feet or lower body, and the head tilted forward, the position needs to be corrected. Release your grasp under one armpit and use that hand to take a light chin pull position--student's chin cupped in the palm of your hand and his/her jaw wedged between your fingers and the fleshy part of your hand. Then tilt the student's head back into the desired position; use the elbow of the chin pull arm in the middle of his/her back--between the shoulder blades--for support and leverage.

The first supine position--hold the student's chin to help position the head.

5. Once the chin pull position has been established, the hand holding the other armpit can be relased and the student can float with just chin support.

6. Gradually loosen the chin pull as the student learns to keep the head back by him/herself.

7. Once the head position is established the chin no longer needs to be held. At this point several means can be used to provide support until the student can float independently...

    ...light support under one or both armpits.

    ...several fingers under the chin as a reminder.

    ...a hand under the back of the neck to provide head stability.

    ...selection of position depends on degree of control the student has in maintaining the supine position.

8. Do not be too concerned if the student's body does not float horizontally on top of water--few people do. If the head is in the correct position let the body seek its own level of buoyancy in water.

9. If the student's arms are flexed at the elbows so that the hands are placed next to or over the head, a reflex pattern on which the student must concentrate to minimize has been activated.

    . Have the student try to keep hands and arms under water.

    . Work gradually to lower the arms so that elbows are close to the body.

    . When the elbows come closer to the body gradually have the student concentrate on extending the elbows.

    . Breaking any reflex pattern takes considerable time and concentration on the part of the student, and even then it may not be possible to achieve the desired position.

10. As the student becomes relaxed in the supine position with some support, gradually lessen the amount of help given until he/she is floating unsupported for brief periods of time. Remind the student to try to stay still and move the body very gently only when necessary for balance. It is all right if some water washes over the student's face in this process. Students need to experience this happening to learn how to adjust balance to movements of water.

Back float and just a hand under the back of the neck as a reminder to keep the head back.

Back floating alone.

Developing Movement in the Supine Position

As in the prone position students need to experiment with various movements to learn what moves them in water while allowing them to keep heads up enough to get air. Keep in mind that an individual's head does not have to be above water all the time. If the student has breathing difficulties because water has been swallowed or inhaled, try to leave him/her on the back while coughing and getting breath. When swimming alone an individual will not have anyone there to pick him/her up so that he/she needs to learn to use the supine position for emergencies. Students can learn to recover breath in the supine position if given chances to learn by doing.

236

Again, any movement is acceptable. Do not expect a regular stroke to be the end product of the student's efforts. After an individual starts experimenting with movement, your comments should concern how actions can be made more efficient, not how to conform to accepted patterns of swimming.

Developing Recovery

Once the student has established a position on the stomach and a position on the back, he/she needs to learn how to get from one position to the other. The easiest way to do this is by rolling over along the longitudinal axis of the body. This keeps the student relatively horizontal in water and makes it easier to stay afloat. Though more difficult, some students go from front to back by letting their feet sink, tilting their heads back, and letting their bodies pass through the vertical. Usually obese students prefer this method. To teach students to recover by rolling on the horizontal axis--

1. Be sure that both prone and supine positions are well established.

2. Explain to the student that he/she is going to float on the stomach. However, this time instead of you picking him/her up, the student should try to roll over as soon as starting the float. At this point don't tell the individual how to roll over; most students have already done this in some way or other on land and have their own particular methods. Place the student in a prone float, stand close to his/her head and shoulders, and assist him/her complete the roll; most students will probably be able to start alone. A hand under the back of the neck helps the student finish with the head in a position in which he/she can take a breath. As the head clears the water, tell the student to take a breath.

3. After several tries at rolling over you should be able to assess the efficiency of the roll. If the student is having extreme difficulty--

    .   Check to see that the student is starting the roll by turning his/her head in the direction he/she wants to go.

    .   Have the student kick or move the body in a supine movement pattern as the roll is completed to help him/her get the body into alignment.

    .   Use the chin pull at the end of the roll if the individual has difficulty in getting the head back.

    .   Try to roll to the opposite side even though one side will probably be much easier to roll toward than the other.

4. After the pattern for the roll is established, practice it in several settings--

    .   Immediately after being placed in the prone float position.

. Set the student on your knee--place the bottom of one foot on the thigh of the opposite leg--and elevate him/her above the water slightly. Have the student fall forward and then once in the water, roll over for recovery.

Sitting support--ready to jump-in.

Jumping-in--Mark will then recover to a back float position.

. Have the student sit on the edge of the pool and fall in and roll over for recovery.

. Have the swimmer use a prone movement pattern for a count of five and then roll over for recovery.

. Toss the student from your arms into the water and have him/her roll over for recovery; toss the student into a variety of positions.

5. Continue to provide a helping hand under the neck and a reminder to breathe as soon as the student comes up until this can be done consistently alone.

6. Repeat this whole procedure teaching the student to roll from back to stomach. The procedure includes...

...while lying on the back, the student takes a breath;

...turns the head in the direction he/she wants to roll;

...brings arm opposite to the rolling side across the body--not all students are able to do this;

...initiates a prone movement pattern as the body completes the roll.

Provide help if needed by turning the shoulders using the armpit position. Pick the student up as soon as he/she has achieved the prone position.

7. After the student can roll front to back and back to front, chain rolls together—front to swim and back to rest—and have the student swim a short distance.

8. Increase distance gradually and reduce support given until the student is swimming independently.

FINAL STEPS TOWARD INDEPENDENCE

Independence means being able to swim without support from another person or object, being self-sufficient, and being able to take care of one's own needs. Once a student can swim and recover by him/herself, only a few final steps must be taken to make this individual totally independent.

1. Pool entry by falling in from the side of the pool may be sufficient. However, some students find this position extremely difficult without support. Try having students fall directly into the water from their wheelchairs. Pull the chair up to the edge of the pool, swing away footrests, take off the seat belt, set brakes, and have someone hold the chair; now have the student fall forward into the pool. Be sure that as the student falls his/her feet and legs clear the gutter and edge of the pool.

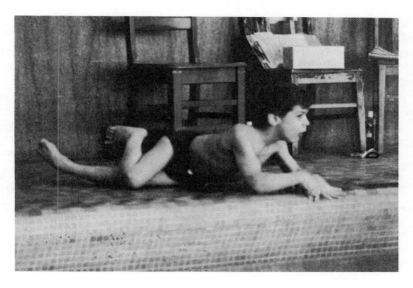

Getting ready to get into the pool.

2. Gradually move further and further away from the student while he/she is swimming until you are no longer looked upon for psychological or physical support. Eventually watch from the deck.

3. Teach an independent resting position at the side of the pool.

. Hang on to the gutter or pool edge—be sure to approach from both prone and supine swimming positions so that the student learns how to grab from both positions.

Practicing a safe position at the side
of the pool.

. You may wish to provide a resting platform suspended from the side of the pool and just slightly below water level so that the student can swim up and onto it to rest.

4. Pool exit is always hardest. A deck level hoist that the student can swim into and then be lifted out gives much more independence than having someone lift or carry the student out of the pool.

Independent swimming is possible for almost any person willing to take time and put forth effort. In working with students possessing severe handicapping conditions who have independent swimming as their goal—

. Keep an open mind about what constitutes <u>swimming</u>.

. Allow students to participate in goal setting and decision making about their efforts.

. Provide direct feedback to students about efficiency of their efforts.

. Be willing to let students experiment; even if some things tried don't work out; everyone involved has learned something in the process.

. Take time to practice, repeat, and try again everything that is happening.

. <u>Be committed to the goal of independence—don't settle for anything less.</u>

PRACTICAL POINTERS

MOVEMENT EXPLORATION AS A TECHNIQUE
FOR TEACHING PRE-SWIMMING SKILLS TO
STUDENTS WITH DEVELOPMENTAL DELAYS

Joyce M. Buis   Catherine S. Schane

Movement education continues to be an effective method for teaching physical and motor skills to students with developmental delays. While movement education has been used in swimming pools as well as in gymnasia and on playgrounds, little specific and definitive have been written about its uses in aquatic environments. Information and materials on movement education for aquatic programs and activities can be found in several publications on adapted physical education and instructional swimming in general, and for teaching mentally retarded students in particular. At least one publication deals in depth with applying movement education to aquatic programs and activities. However, all of these sources are rather general in their approaches to and applications of movement education to swimming.

This _Practical Pointer_ on the other hand is _developmentally_ approached. Activities are presented in terms of developmental levels, whether or not they are appropriate for non-ambulatory participants, and include ways to individualize and personalize activities and approaches according to _each_ participant's needs, abilities, and disabilities. Values of each activity and an easy to use index add to practical and functional contributions of this publication. With this organizational approach activities presented can be used as means to reach goals and objectives related to pre-swimming and swimming skills as well as goals and objectives related to various perceptual-motor functions and traits.

<u>Movement exploration</u> offers exciting possibilities for adapted aquatics programs, particularly for individuals whose disabilities include poor development in perceptual-motor patterns and functions related to mastery of swimming skills. Not surprisingly, use of movement exploration for fostering fundamental movement abilities in water has received increasing attention over the last decade (American National Red Cross, 1977; Moran and Kalakian, 1977; Hackett, 1970); this approach is congruent with the growing humanistic movement in psychology and education.

In this <u>Practical Pointer</u>...

...reasons for using movement exploration in teaching beginners with developmental delays in swimming programs are given;

...appropriate objectives are listed;

...particular needs of students that can be met with this approach are explored; and

...specific activities illustrating how the technique can be used to help meet listed objectives and needs are described.

The term <u>developmental delays</u> is used in the broad sense to mean <u>any</u> mental or physical developmental level that is below what is normally seen in a person of like age, and that impairs an individual's functioning in some important ways. Mental retardation, emotional disturbances, and learning disabilities are conditions likely to be accompanied by delays in development; such delays can also be associated with cerebral palsy, sensory impairments, and a variety of other handicapping conditions.

Developmental delays accompanying or resulting from these disabling conditions can have several causes. <u>Physical causes</u> include objective results of trauma or inherited impairment, secondary weakening of other body systems, and time lost due to confinement. <u>Psychological causes</u> of delay include poor self-perceptions and unfavorable perceptions of others. <u>Physical and attitudinal barriers</u> in the environment can also delay development.

Short attention span, poor spatial awareness, and unusually awkward, ineffective movement skills are among the most obvious indicators of developmental delays. Other signs which point to delayed development are poor memory, need for frequent encouragement, weak self-identity, and poor body image. A student who consistently displays several of these characteristics and to considerable degrees may lack necessary basic movement skills for learning to swim. Such an individual can benefit from participating in types of activities presented.

Rationale

Rationale for using any method must include answers to three basic questions--

. Are program and/or activity objectives worthwhile?

. Is there specific need for action?

. Why use this approach?

Perhaps not every person needs to know how to swim, but every person needs to know how to move effectively. Movement is considered by some educators to be an excellent learning route to all behavioral domains (Feldenkrais, 1977, p. 15). One of four basic elements of the wakeful state of human behavior, movement exists in dynamic interaction with feelings, perceptions, and thoughts. These last three named processes, however, are internal. Only through some type of movement can we consciously express our feelings, respond to situations as we perceive them, and make others aware of our thoughts. Without movement we would be unable to act on our choices or achieve the slightest control over our lives. Physical educators understand readily how important fundamental movement education is to individuals whose development has been delayed.

But why swimming particularly? Swimming has all physical, psychological, and social benefits that vigorous movement activities have for anyone, plus some unique to itself. Competence or mastery over one's environment is an important human need according to humanistic psychology (Maslow, 1968). Competence in water may very well have greater benefits for self-concept than other kinds of mastery over physical environments because water is not Homosapiens' natural habitat. Relaxation is best aided by rhythmic, free-swinging movement, stretching, and improved breathing according to a report from the American Medical Association's Committee on Medical Aspects of Sports. Swimming provides all three and is extraordinarily beneficial in the last respect--improved breathing--because extra pressure exerted by water additionally strengthens respiratory functions. The popular attitude toward swimming, especially among young people, is that it is a cool sport, thus providing motivation for learning the skills. Swimming, unlike many sports learned in childhood and youth, is especially suitable and available as a lifetime recreational pursuit.

Swimming has even more pronounced rewards for individuals whose disabilities limit other forms of exercise. Cushioning effects of water provide support for weak limbs and break falls. Because gravity is not the problem it is on land, physical skills may be easier to perform in water, particularly for individuals with severe motor impairments. Water offers greater resistance to movement than air, so movements made in water result in stronger kinesthetic and proprioceptive feedback and a surer sense of where the body is and what it is doing. Added resistance also strengthens and tones muscles to relatively greater degrees than movements on land. Even muscles not actually used are benefitted by movement and pressure of water surrounding them. Finally, water literally as well as figuratively hides disabilities. When people are swimming, each moves independently though they are together, and it may not be readily apparent if some have impairments or disabilities.

A problem suggested here is that swimming is potentially very beneficial to many persons with disabilities, but that many of these individuals may not have fundamental movement abilities needed to learn skills required for safe, independent functioning in water. Movement exploration as an approach for teaching basic movement skills has three main activities...

...aids initial mental and physical adjustments to water;

...is effective in teaching desired skills; and

...has widely recognized psychological values beyond those implicit in successful experiences.

Movement exploration is a problem-solving or guided discovery technique. A challenge is presented -- "Move around in your (marked-off) space without going outside it."* A participant may respond by circling inside the periphery of the space, moving back and forth across it in an orderly way, walking, swimming, going backwards or sideward, moving rapidly or slowly. Any movement that does not cross boundaries of the designated space accomplishes the task that was presented. Whatever the challenge, every response is individual and none measured against a norm. The method is characterized by informal but carefully planned, progressive activities that involve participants in successful, non-competitive movement experiences.

Adjustment to an aquatic environment is made easier because participants are involved at their own levels and without pressure to perform. The playful attitude of this approach releases tensions and alleviates fear of failure. Inactivity is minimized and practice time increased.

Movement-exploration allows some autonomy, some choice. Accomplishments therefore build self-esteem, confidence, and courage. Through greater self-acceptance an individual finds more acceptance in other areas, greater cooperation is fostered, and the positive spiral continues. Satisfying peer interactions increase rewards. The participant feels a sense of control resulting from increased competence, and self-concept is further improved.

Positive values of developing and applying a problem-solving approach to tasks,** other people, and life cannot be overemphasized. However, problem-solving is an enormously complex process. Although only a few values, usually based on skills important for swimming are listed for each activity presented, a participant's responses to movement-exploration tasks are always neuromuscular patterns that include as a minimum...

...perception of a challenge;

...comprehension of its meaning;

...conceptualization of possible solutions and outcomes;

...choice of solutions;

...motor responses to choices; and

...evaluation of outcomes.

---

* Avoid introducing problems with phrases such as "Can you" -- this can back teachers or leaders into a corner if a participant answers, "No!"

**Problem solving techniques and approaches can be used for many different purposes. To change focus, simply change emphasis or problems posed. Problem solving through movement exploration is a method, a technique, an approach -- not a goal or an objective.

Using the movement-exploration approach is not difficult, nor does it demand extensive technical knowledge. It does require a clear understanding of objectives, an appreciation of each student's needs, and a repertoire of activities that can be used for movement education.

Objectives

Safety, support, and skill are chief objectives of any swimming program. Safety must always come first--(1) safety of all involved while in a swimming program, and (2) teaching water-safety practices. A good aquatics leader wants to prevent any possibility of drowning, and avoid any trauma that might cause a participant to be more fearful in water or elsewhere. Support involves personal respect that a teacher gives a student as a right due another human being, plus nurturing one owes to anyone for whom he/she is responsible--efforts to develop, insofar as possible, each person's potential. Movement exploration, based on the theory that problem-solving aids growth more directly than rote learning, is compatible with both ideas of support.

Desired skill development is in psychomotor functions which underlie ability to control breathing, balance in water, use water for locomotion, and finally master more-advanced swimming techniques. Many basic movement skills needed to learn to swim are identified as values in Suggested Activities (pages 9 to 22). Other motor functions as well as many social and preacademic skills can be promoted by these activities, but are not listed. The following outline shows major perceptual-motor traits that suggested activities can foster and further.

Body Awareness

- Image - body parts, shapes, surfaces
- Functions - what the body does (see Movement, below)

Spatial Awareness

- Laterality/Directionality - right, left; up, down; forward, backward, sideward
- Pathways - straight, curved, zig-zag
- Levels - high, low, middle
- Relationships - over, under; in, out; around; together; beside

Movement

- Types of Movements
  -- Axial movements* such as bending, stretching, twisting, pushing, pulling, kicking
  -- Locomotor movements such as walking, running, jumping, hopping, climbing

---

*In swimming, normally axial (non-locomotor) movements such as pulling, pushing, and kicking become chief means of locomotion.

. Qualities of Movements
-- <u>Timing</u> - fast, slow; simultaneous, sequential
-- <u>Force</u> - strong, weak
-- <u>Flow</u> - continuous, interrupted

Perceptual-Motor Functions

. <u>Breath Control</u> - ability to hold breath and control exhalation in water
. <u>Balance</u> - using the body's buoyancy and properties of water to achieve stability in various positions
. <u>Manipulation</u> - controlled handling of objects through throwing, catching, hitting, turning, pushing, pulling
. <u>Responding to sensory cues</u>
-- <u>Auditory</u> - following directions; moving on signal
-- <u>Visual</u> - eye-hand coordination; eye-foot coordination; visual tracking (following a moving object with the eyes)

Special Needs

Myriad adaptations can be made to meet special needs of individuals having all types and severities of disabling conditions. The full range of applicability in adapted-aquatic activities is suggested in general requirements and typical techniques.

Needs of students with developmental delays are primarily the same as those of any student--<u>acceptance and respect, attention to physical well-being, and opportunities to grow</u>. In working with special populations, swimming instructors may have to adjust teaching methods to meet those needs. That is partly what is meant by <u>adapted</u> programing. For example--

. Students with large deficits in either motor or behavior control may require one-to-one aides while in water.

. A hyperkenetic child may also require one-to-one supervision.

. Students with severe physical impairments can be given independent mobility with inflatable swimsuits and other wearable flotation devices, but safety considerations demand constant companionship.

. Mentally retarded students may need assistance to overcome lack of communication skills. In many cases having one aide for every two or three mentally retarded students should be enough; the aide can repeat directions when needed and promote learning by encouraging student movements and verbal responses.

. Mentally retarded adults should <u>be</u> treated as <u>adults</u>--they don't play <u>tea party</u> even in water--although some individuals can benefit from participating in selected activities that children do.*

The problem-solving approach used in movement exploration, together with the novelty of the aquatic environment, take boredom out of doing simple things. Many students with developmental delays can be served well with kinds of general adaptations described in the Suggested Activities section (pages 9 to 22). However other individuals have special needs that must be assessed by professionals responsible for overall education and treatment programs.

Activity Guidelines

A partial list of activities which can help develop or reinforce fundamental movement skills follows. These activities are preceded by information on how they are arranged and classified.

Descriptions of some activities include specific ways to vary called for basic movements, adding different elements of time, force, or distance to original problems. Some entries give directions for adaptations. These adaptations are suggestive only, for all activities can be varied and adapted, most in many different ways.

A progression of breath-control activities heads the list; remaining activities are given by levels in ascending order of breath control required for comfortable participation. Good breath control is essential to safety in water and for developing locomotor skills there. Every swimming period should include appropriate level breath-control activities. Control of balance and body position is the second most important aquatic skill, so several activities are suggested for its practice. Other problems concern body awareness, locomotion, qualities of movements, manipulation of objects, and other functions outlined previously (pages 6 and 7). Many activities are useful for improving perceptual traits basic to movement skills--visual, auditory, tactile, and kinesthetic.

Activities should be chosen and adapted as necessary to be...

...suited to each participant's level of breath control and adjustment to an aquatic environment;

...appropriate for developmental needs of students; and

...compatible with conditions of staff, place, time, and other resources.

Some aides should be in the water at all times to lend hands in recovering unexpectedly lost footings and reassure frightened participants. Even

---

*Logical and simple adaptations can make many children's activities appropriate for and appealing to adults. Changes can be in such things as approach, manner, terminology, name of the activity, music used. Do not insult an adult's intelligence, age, experience, maturity, or size by treating him/her as a child.

momentary submersion can cause panic in the uninitiated because breathing is shut off. Other important general considerations in programing include--

. Demonstrate what a word means, but don't show how a movement-exploration problem is solved. Evidence suggests that in terms of overall development, correction and formal guidance may be counterproductive at this stage (Laban, 1975, p. 20).

. Increase structure in some activities when needed for emotionally disturbed or learning disabled participants.

. Provide each mentally retarded or emotionally disturbed participant with his/her own equipment when manipulative skills are being developed.

. Start unfamiliar movements slowly; build up speed, vary force, and/or increase distance after a pattern becomes familiar.

. Increase time to build attention span; use favorite activities for this purpose.

. Verbalize frequently what students are doing, especially for individuals who are non-verbal.

. Encourage students to verbalize their own responses to reinforce conceptualization.

. Refer to previous activities briefly even when they are not to be repeated to fix learning and establish habit or recall.

. Play music with simple rhythmic patterns during activities to foster rhythmic ways of moving.

. Remember that safety of students is always an instructor's first responsibility.

Suggested Activities

Movement-exploration activities presented are in no way all inclusive--countless others are suitable for aquatic use, and many variations and adaptations can be found for those both named and unnamed in the following pages. Possibilities are virtually limitless because most movement activities can be adapted in some fashion to water.

This listing is designed as follows--

. The top line of each entry gives a Level number, type of Task, and information about its usefulness for Non-Ambulatory participants.

. Major skills or traits that may be enhanced by this activity follow; these are called Values.

. Description gives basic information for developing the activity.

. Any needed special Information, Precautions, Adaptations, and/or Variations are provided.

Definitions for several abbreviations and specific terms used in entries help in understanding the information. Unless otherwise designated, level to which an activity is assigned presupposes an ambulatory participant is unassisted and in water no deeper than chest-high.

. Level 1 includes activities involving little splashing of water and no locomotion in water more than waist-high.

. Level 2 denotes considerable possibilities for splashing, but has the same locomotor requirements as Level 1.

. Level 3 participants may move through water above waist-deep, but not more than chest-deep.

. Level 4 activities involve both splashing and locomotion in water up to chest-high.

. In Level 5, letting the nose and mouth go under water is either encouraged, invited, or likely to happen because of the nature of movements involved.

. Total submersion is planned or considered likely in Level 6 activities.

. A participant should have good breath control and moderately good balancing skills before being asked to do Level 5 and 6 tasks.

Conditions in a particular situation can raise or lower the level of an activity. For any participant in water more than chest-high, unassisted locomotion must be considered Level 5 or above. In water deeper than waist-high, an activity becomes at least Level 5 if it involves taking both feet off the bottom at the same time, e.g., jumping. Any Level 3 or 4 activities become Level 2 for a participant who is assisted.

NA in the first line of an entry means the activity is suitable as described for non-ambulatory participants who are able to hold on to a side or ladder or sit on steps. When an adaptation for non-ambulatory use is given at the end, or when a non-ambulatory participant can do the activity with assistance of an aide, designation is NA. A participant who is assisted always has a one-to-one aide at hand, even when no active help is being given. Participant is abbreviated in these entries as P, the plural being Ps.

Some general considerations for choosing, developing, and directing movement exploration exercises in water are listed in the section on Activity Guidelines (pages 8 to 9); these should be kept in mind when using the following activities.

249

1

Level 1   Breath Control Task   NA

Values   Controlled exhalation

Description   Direct Ps to wet shoulders, arms, entire body up to neck;
                then blow on skin making each breath last a long time;
                have them wet skin again before each exhalation.

Special   Watch for Ps who duck down without holding on to side or
Precaution   who lean over to blow into the water as near-complete
                submersion may cause loss of footing.

2
Levels 1 and 2   Breath Control Task   NA

Values   Controlled exhalation

Description   Challenge Ps to make ping-pong balls move on water
                surface by blowing on them, first through straws,
                then without straws.

Special   Ps who stoop down to get mouth close to ball become
Precaution   less stable and can lose footing.

3
Levels 1 and 2   Breath Control Task   NA

Values   Controlled exhalation
                Mental adjustment to exhaling into water

Description   Have Ps make bubbles in cups or bowls of water by
                blowing through straws; then use straws to blow
                bubbles in pool water.

4
Level 2   Breath Control Task   NA

Values   Breath-holding
                Manipulation of objects

Description   Station Ps in water beside individual collections on
                deck of objects such as wash cloths, sponges, small
                plastic bowls, plastic cups, nonbreakable funnels,
                jug-showers; have Ps find all the different ways they
                can wet their faces.

Special   Jug-showers can be made from plastic milk containers—
Information   cut out below the neck on one side to fill the jug;
                punch several holes in the bottom of the jug for a
                shower.

5

Level 3   Breath Control Task   NA

Values   Repeated inhalation and controlled exhalation (rhythmic
                breathing)
                Locomotion
                Balance

Description   Challenge Ps to blow ping-pong balls across pool with-
                out letting balls stop.

                                6
Level 4   Breath Control Task   NA

Values   Exhalation in water
                Balance
                Locomotion

Description   Have Ps get in a tight circle and make a nest of bubbles
                in the middle by blowing into water; next call for each
                P to make his/her own small nest.

                                7
Level 5   Breath Control Task - Assisted   NA

Values   Breath-holding with face submerged
                Balancing body in horizontal position

Description   Have each P place hands on aide's shoulders (aide
                is low in water) and let body float; make straight
                line with body; later, ask each P to get a breath
                without standing up.

                                8
Levels 5 and 6   Breath Control Task   NA

Values   Rhythmic breathing
                Balance

Description   Challenge Ps to go in and out of water in time to
                music.

Special   Holding on to side of pool makes this a Level 5
Information   activity; free-bobbing is Level 6.

                                9
Level 6   Breath Control Task

Values   Breath-holding with face submerged

Values (cont'd)	Balance Responding to visual cues (eye-hand coordination)
Description	Challenge Ps to see how many objects they can pick up from pool bottom.
Special Information	Objects can be such things as smooth stones, pucks, weighted plastic flowers, plastic juice cans, and/or sinkable, nonbreakable toy animals.

Remaining activities are listed according to levels of breath-control required.

10
Balance Task

Level 1   NA

Values	Use of arms in maintaining balance Locomotion
Description	Give Ps float-rods (barbells) and challenge them to walk around, make turns, back up, change levels, and do other movement tasks while holding on to the rod. Float-rods are excellent for developing a sense of how to use water for balance.
Special Information	Some otherwise non-ambulatory persons find it possible to walk in chest-deep water with float-rods which are often effective in getting them started. A float-rod is made with two empty half-gallon plastic jugs stuck tightly on the ends of a broom handle.

11
Body Awareness Task

Level 1   NA

Values	Body image Axial movement Quality of movement (timing)
Description	Say to Ps, "Partners stand shoulder-to-shoulder-- now stand shoulder-to-shoulder with your partner." "Stand shoulder-to-shoulder another way." "How about back-to-back?" "Hip-to-hip." "Arm-to-arm." "Nose-to-nose." After Ps have done a series of relation-ships two or three times, call them out double-time; then do a series that speeds up and slows down--let voice indicate speed.
Adaptation	Non-ambulatory Ps may be assisted, hold on to wall or ladder, and/or have ambulatory Ps as partners.

<table>
<tr><td>Level 1</td><td style="text-align:center">12
Movement Task</td><td></td></tr>
</table>

Values	Locomotion Directionality Quality of movement (timing)
Description	Challenge Ps to walk the pool wall; have them change directions, name directions in which they are going; have them go more slowly at one time, faster at another; walk up the wall and then down.
Special Precaution	Frequent rests may be needed, especially by Ps with weak arms.
Variation	This can be a children's game with Ps in a train, engine at its head and caboose at end.

<table>
<tr><td>Level 1</td><td style="text-align:center">13
Body Awareness Task</td><td>NA</td></tr>
</table>

Values	Use of body parts Manipulation
Description	Ask Ps to find different ways to send their balloons from water up onto deck; no restrictions on method at first; then with one hand, both hands, no hands.

<table>
<tr><td>Level 1</td><td style="text-align:center">14
Spatial Awareness Task</td><td>NA</td></tr>
</table>

Values	Spatial relationships Manipulation
Description	Tell Ps to find different ways to be close to their hoola hoops--behind, in front of, inside, outside, going around, under, on top.

<table>
<tr><td>Level 1</td><td style="text-align:center">15
Movement Task</td><td>NA</td></tr>
</table>

Values	Axial movements (pulling, pushing water to develop balance and locomotor [stroking] skills) Quality of movement (timing, force)
Description	Have Ps pull water towards body; then push water away from body--with hands and arms; with feet and legs; from/in different directions; with different forces; at different speeds.

Level 1	Body Awareness Task	NA

Values   Body image

Description   Two people make <u>twin</u> shapes--each partner in turn creates a shape for the other to copy.

17

Level 1	Body Awareness Task	NA

Values   Use of body parts

Description   Two <u>P</u>s find different ways to hold a balloon between them, at first without restriction, then with qualifications such as with only one arm, no hands, no hands or arms, hands clasped behind you, hands on top of head, heads only, legs only.

18

Levels 1 to 3	Spatial Awareness Task

Values   Spatial relationships (around)
Pathway (curved)
Locomotion

Description   Have <u>P</u>s move from wall, out to and around a buoy or object on bottom of pool, and back to side; challenge <u>P</u>s to find different ways of moving.

Special
Information   A weighted traffic cone makes an attractive, easily visible object in the pool.

19

Level 2	Movement Task	NA

Values   Axial movement
Quality of movement (force, timing)
Body awareness

Description   Say to <u>P</u>s, "Be a funky chicken. Flap your wings like a chicken." Later tell <u>P</u>s to flap only one wing, then the other; then add qualities of force and timing to vary movements.

20

Level 2	Body Awareness Task	NA

Values   Body image

| Values (cont'd) | Responding to auditory cues |

Description

Ask Ps to relate various body parts and name them with such questions and commands as, "What do you clap with?" "Hold them up." "Now put them together." "Put your hands on what you hear with." "What are your hands on?" "What do you point with?" "Use them to point to what you see with." "What are your fingers pointing at?" "What are your eyes in?" "Use your head to turn your eyes from side to side." "What do you smell with?" "Draw an imaginary circle with your nose."

21
Movement Task - Assisted

| Level 2 | | NA |

Values

Locomotion with arms
Balance

Description

Have one P at a time hold on to lifeline; start from increasingly greater distances from side, and pull to side; challenge P to pull so that body is balanced above or beside rope and face stays above water.

Special
Precautions

This is a worthwhile safety skill, but at this level any P trying it must have an aide at hand constantly. If, as is likely, the rope is near a sudden drop-off to deep water, anyone who is not a good deep-water swimmer must be assisted whenever this task is attempted.

22
Body Awareness Task

| Level 2 | | NA |

Values

Use of body parts
Quality of movement (force, timing)

Description

Isolate body parts by naming them sequentially; have each P hold that part up, then put it in the water or touch it to the water in case of ear or tip of nose; later ask Ps to vary force and speed of movements.

23
Body Awareness Task

| Level 2 | | NA |

Values

Use of body parts
Quality of movement (force, timing)
Manipulation

Description   Give each P an easily handled, floatable object such
as a medium-size rubber block; challenge P to find
different ways to push the object under water, move
the object through water, move water with the
object.

24
Manipulation Task

Level 2   NA

Values   Manipulation of object
Spatial awareness
Axial movement

Description   Give each P a hoola hoop; challenge Ps to make their
hoola hoops do different things such as lie on the
surface of the water, stand on their sides, circle some
part of the body, go under the water, spin circles;
ask Ps to make hoops go from one side of the body to
the other to encourage twisting movements.

25
Movement Task

Level 3

Values   Locomotion
Spatial awareness (straight, zig-zag pathways)
Responding to visual cues (eye-foot coordination)

Description   Use ladder placed on bottom of pool as an obstacle
course; challenge Ps to step between rungs of the
ladder without touching them, find different ways
to travel the course; then direct them to do it
straight, from side-to-side, backward, crossing
the ladder at each rung.

26
Sensory Response Task

Level 3

Values   Responding to visual cues (eye-foot coordination)
Balance
Directionality

Description   Challenge Ps to move along line painted (placed) on
bottom of pool without stepping off line; challenge
Ps to find another way to move along the line--
backwards, sideward, cross over, giant steps, baby
steps, heel-toe, scissor steps.

Level 3

27

Movement Task

NA

Values
Quality of movement (speed, force)
Responding to tactile cues

Description
Work with partners so that one P leads another across pool, then is challenged to lead partner in another way; partners switch roles; vary speed and/or force of movements.

Special
Precaution
Remind Ps always to latch on to someone else in non-hurtful ways.

Level 3

28
Body Awareness Task

NA

Values
Body image
Use of body parts
Responding to visual cues (visual tracking)
Quality of movement (force)

Description
Give each P a balloon or beach ball; challenge each to tap his/her object into air with one hand, then the other; Ps later are asked to tap the balloon more than once before it hits the water; tap it without using the hands; tap it with head, elbow, shoulder, and other parts of the body in various combinations.

Level 3

29
Spatial Awareness Task

Values
Directionality
Locomotion

Description
Have Ps cross the pool facing the side they are headed towards (forward movement); then come back facing the side they are going away from (backward movement); challenge Ps to cross facing in still-different directions; ask, "What direction are you going when moving like that?"

Adaptations
Non-ambulatory Ps can be assisted or they can be individuals who call out directions in which they see others moving.

Level 3

30
Movement Task

NA

Values

Axial movement
Manipulation

Description

Give each P a balloon on a short string; ask Ps to find different ways of moving balloons over the water; have Ps name ways as they use them; aides can label movements for non-verbal Ps. Later direct Ps to make balloons move with different force and/or follow different pathways.

Level 3

31
Movement Task

NA

Values

Axial movement
Balance
Manipulation
Responding to visual cues (visual tracking)

Description

Have P throw large ball into net; ask, "Did you use lifting (underhand) or pushing (overhand) throw?" Challenge P to do it the other way; then practice each method several times.

Special
Information

Net should be large and close to P when this is first attempted; distance can be increased as skills improve. Hoop resting between two chairs can substitute for net.

Variation

Use small ball and one-hand throws.

Level 3

32
Manipulation Task

NA

Values

Manipulation (pushing, pulling)
Locomotor movement

Description

Have pairs of Ps work together to find different ways of moving tires or hoola hoops across pool; ask them to verbalize what they do; one partner and then the other acts as leader.

Level 3

33
Spatial Awareness Task

Values

Spatial relationships
Responding to visual cues (visual tracking)

Description	Have Ps walk across pool in pairs with partners staying exactly beside each other all the way. While moving, ask Ps to say who is on the right, left, on which side the partner is; switch sides, repeat, and name positions again.
Variation	Use in front of and behind for spatial relationships. Ask, "Who's in front?" "Who's behind?"

34
Movement Task

Level 4	
Values	Locomotion Balance
Description	Challenge Ps to move across the pool in as many different ways as they can find; name each way of moving as it is done; watch for and direct attention to hopping (pre-skipping) and skipping movements; music with strong four beat and simple rhythm is good for this activity.

35
Manipulation Task   NA

Level 4	
Values	Manipulation (throwing, catching, hitting) Responding to visual cues (visual tracking, eye-hand coordination)
Description	Give each P a balloon or beach ball; challenge each P to "See how long you can make your balloon/ball stay in the air without touching the water." "Try tapping it back up instead of catching it."

36
Balance Task

Level 4	
Values	Balancing on one foot Responding to visual cues (eye-foot coordination) Spatial awareness (pathways--straight, curved)
Description	Have Ps move objects on bottom of pool without touching them with their hands; challenge Ps to push objects in straight lines, circles, triangles, squares, rectangles, zig-zag lines.

37
Movement Task

Level 5	
Values	Locomotion

Values (cont'd)	Balance
Description	Have each P step onto and off a low, weighted plastic stool placed on bottom of pool; then, step off with both feet at the same time; have Ps name different locomotor movements.

38
Movement Task

Level 5	
Values	Locomotion Balance
Description	Challenge Ps to move from wall to middle of pool on one foot, without letting the other foot touch the bottom; ask them to label movements; repeat on the other foot.
Special Information	This difficult motor task is often easier to do in water than on land, so the activity is especially good to use.

39
Spatial Awareness Task   NA

Level 5	
Values	Directionality Object relationships Balance
Description	Have two aides hold a float-rod or broomstick about six inches above the water; challenge each P to see how he/she can get under the rod.
Variations	This can be a Level 4 activity if the rod is held farther above the water, or a Level 6 if the rod is on the surface.

40
Movement Task

Level 5	
Values	Locomotion Balance Directionality Object relationship
Description	Ask Ps to find all the ways they can go through hoola hoops which are held vertically, partly above and partly below the surface of the water.

Level 6   41
                      Balance Task - Assisted   NA

Values   Balance (pre-floating skill)
                  Breath control

Description   Challenge Ps to hold breath and try to fall down in
                  the water; make body stay under for five seconds;
                  sit on pool bottom; describe what happens when the
                  body is submerged.

Special   Each P must have an aide at hand when this activity
Precaution   is first attempted to help P recover to feet if
                  necessary.

Level 6   42
                      Balance Task - Assisted   NA

Values   Balance (floating skill)
                  Breath control

Description   Give these directions to Ps--"Hold breath and roll
                  your body up into a ball. Let the water hold your
                  body-ball for a moment."

Special   Be certain each P has an aide at hand until it is
Precaution   clear that P can recover to feet unassisted.

Selected References

American National Red Cross. Adapted Aquatics. New York: Doubleday and
      Company, 1977.

Feldenkrais, Moshe. Awareness Through Movement. New York: Harper and Row
      Publishers, 1977.

Hackett, Layne C. Movement Exploration and Games for the Mentally Retarded.
      Palo Alto, California: Peek Publications, 1970.

Laban, Rudolf. Modern Educational Dance (3rd ed.). Revised by Lisa Ullman.
      London: MacDonald and Evans Limited, 1975.

Maslow, Abraham. Toward a Psychology of Being. New York: D. Van Nostrand
      Company, 1968.

Moran, Joan M.; and Kalakian, Leonard H. Movement Experiences for the Mentally
      Retarded or Emotionally Disturbed Child. Minneapolis: Burgess Publish-
      ing Company, 1977.

PRACTICAL POINTERS

ADAPTING AQUATIC CIRCUIT TRAINING
FOR SPECIAL POPULATIONS

Kathleen Thome

Aquatic environments have long been recognized among the most complete settings for individuals possessing handicapping conditions. These environments can be used for rehabilitation and therapy, instruction and education, recreation and leisure, competition, and FUN. Various methods, techniques, and teaching strategies used successfully in the gymnasium, on the playground, and on the field of sport can easily be adapted for and used in aquatic environments of different types and descriptions.

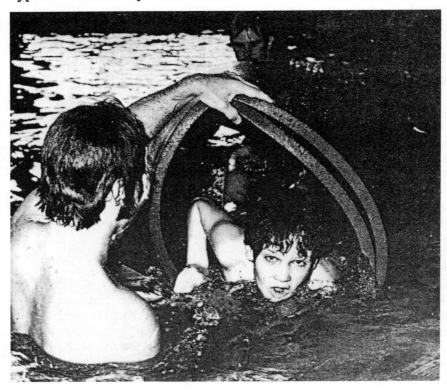

Land activities and exercises can be adapted to water so that individuals with handicapping conditions can participate in circuit training activities.[1] Movement in aquatic environments provide periods of training and relaxation for improving and maintaining balance, gait, muscular and cardiovascular strength and endurance, power, agility, coordination, and flexibility. Stations developed to enhance water adjustment and swimming skills are also appropriate for special and mainstreamed classes including swimmers and non-swimmers of all ages, types, and severities of handicapping conditions.

Continuous rotation to activity stations for pre-determined time periods allows every performer to be active at the same time. Adjusting performance standards when designing each station allows for individualization and personalization.

ORGANIZATIONAL PROCEDURES

Organizational procedures for aquatic training circuits include --

. Develop one activity or exercise station per participant so that each station has specific goals and objectives.

. Place stations in shallow water for accessibility to non-swimmers and swimmers of all ability levels.

. Fasten weights on light equipment that may float out of position and cause difficulties for performers.

. Space stations to insure sufficient performance areas.

. Specify work period times--i.e., two or three minutes; base these times on performer ability levels and difficulty of exercises and activities.

. Provide vocal and/or visual cues for start, stop, and rotation signals.

. Describe stations and direction of rotation in the circuit to assistants and performers before activities begin; demonstrate as appropriate and necessary.

. Use signal to start performers at initial stations; stop on signal after designated time has elapsed; allow time for rotation to the next station before activity time period starts again.

. Have assistants accompany the same performer throughout the circuit or stay at a specific station and assist performers at that station and during rotation to the next station.

_____

[1]Circuit and Station Activity Approaches (Practical Pointer Volume 1, Number 2, #245-26128, August 1977) presents circuit and station approaches that can be adapted and organized so individuals with handicapping conditions can participate actively in any setting--gymnasium, playfield, playground, swimming pool, athletic field, and classroom. Copies can be obtained for $2.00 from AAHPERD Publications, P.O. Box 704, 44 Industrial Park Circle, Waldorf, Maryland 20601.

- Keep stations consistent over a period of time so performers become familiar with the circuit and its activities.

- Complete the total circuit and note number of repetitions performed at each station.

- Repeat the circuit after all stations have been completed; attempt to surpass previous records at each station.

- Modify activities by moving backwards or sidewards through all exercises.

- Perform exercises as quickly as possible and note numbers completed in each time period.

- Keep records of performances at each station for comparison and evaluation, to show personal progress, and for necessary documentation of individual achievement and growth.

- Alter patterns, directions, and speed of movements to increase difficulty of the total circuit and activities at individual stations.

- Develop performance goals based on numbers of repetitions or sets of exercises that can be performed over the entire circuit in all-out efforts at each station; increase these goals--based on each individual's capacity--for new performance goals.

- Challenge performers to complete as many stations as possible in specified time periods.

- Increase clarity and understanding of circuit activities by pre-teaching water circuits on land.

- Reinforce activities through drawings and simplified written directions of the total circuit; post cards describing each station in writing, drawings, or visual cues on pool walls and/or in plastic bags or bleach bottles sealed with water-proof plastic tape.

- Repeat the circuit until a thorough understanding of procedures is assured; alter or add new stations in successive lessons and repeat them for performer familiarity.

- Develop stations with advice and assistance of medical professionals, adapted physical education specialists, therapeutic recreation personnel, physical and occupational therapists, and certified swim instructors.

- Devise stations with multi-purpose equipment to insure individualization and personalization. Use of special aquatic therapy equipment is not necessary. Equipment used on land can be adapted to water by...

    ...weighting down rust proof plastic or aluminum chairs, tables, and benches for activities performed in sitting, prone, and supine positions;

    ...using hula hoops, unfilled plastic bottles or jugs, plastic cones

264

or markers, buckets, and poles for aquatic therapy and skill training; and

...using non-rust weights, bricks, and similar heavy objects wrapped, tied, or sewn into material sacks with strings as weights for all equipment.

- Devise your own aquatic circuit activities by using and adapting land exercises, activities, and equipment.

- Use each station as an activity or exercise station rather than as part of a circuit.

- Select activities for conditioning or practicing specific aquatic skills by setting-up stations for kicking, bobbing, treading, bracketing and doing crawl arm stroke, diving for weighted objects, diving, or stroking (complete crawl or backstroke); establish stations to meet needs of individual performers.

SAFETY CONSIDERATIONS

Bouyant properties of water make aquatic settings suitable training environments for individuals with impairments, disabilities, and handicapping conditions. Resistance of water helps participants develop muscular strength and endurance as well as restrains individuals needing to relax and decrease movements. Aquatic environments can equalize performance and challenge levels for participants with and without handicapping conditions. Properties of water can be enjoyed by everyone providing safety is a major concern of all involved. Representative of types of information necessary for safety of participants in aquatic programs and environments include --

- Health history of each participant. Does the individual have any reactions to water--i.e., skin, eye, nose, throat sensitivities? Seizures? Fear?

- Does the participant have previous water or swim experience?

- Are assistants and instructors aware and trained in basic water safety and first aid? Are they aware of signs of fatigue? Seizures? Medical complications? Limitations of performers?

Similarly, performers should be aware of basic safety practices in water --

- Recognize fatigue and chill as signs to stop performances.

- Be knowledgeable of and skilled in arm and leg movements to recover from prone and supine float and submerged positions.

- Understand pool entries and exits and be familiar with depth and properties of water for ease in water adjustment.

A MODEL AQUATIC TRAINING CIRCUIT[1]

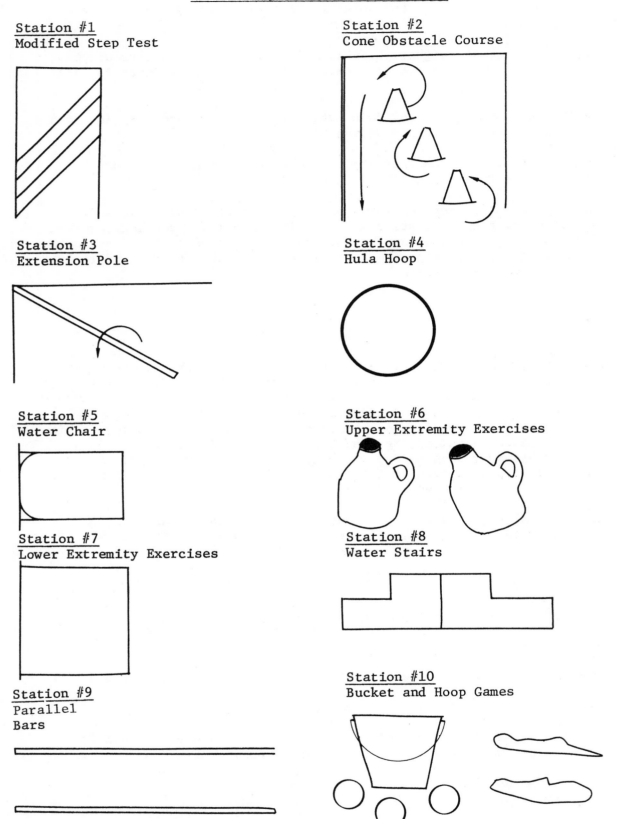

Station #1
Modified Step Test

Station #2
Cone Obstacle Course

Station #3
Extension Pole

Station #4
Hula Hoop

Station #5
Water Chair

Station #6
Upper Extremity Exercises

Station #7
Lower Extremity Exercises

Station #8
Water Stairs

Station #9
Parallel
Bars

Station #10
Bucket and Hoop Games

[1]See pages 7 and 8 for specific information about equipment, training benefits, and activities associated with each station.

Station	Equipment	Training Benefits	Activities
#1 Modified Step Test	Pool stairs into the water; low bench; aluminum therapy stairs.	Cardiorespiratory endurance. Balance. Agility. Coordination. Lower extremity strength and endurance.	Record number of completed climbs of one step-lift one foot up, follow with second foot, place one foot down, follow with second, continuing for 60 (30,15,90) seconds. Compare pulse rates before and after activity; record pulse recovery time.
#2 Cone Obstacle Course	Plastic cones, markers or sand filled plastic jugs; lines on pool bottom.	Balance. Agility. Gait training. Locomotor movements and patterns.	Place markers in an irregular pattern. Walk in forward, backward, and sideward fashions between and around markers. Use lines on pool bottom as balance beams.
#3 Extension Pole	Fasten reaching assist pole to pool wall and weight end down in water to form a sloping angle.	Lower extremity strength and endurance. Gait training. Agility. Coordination. Submerging.	Step over pole at various heights. Move in forward, backward, and sideward fashions. Duck under pole. Step over pole in one direction and duck under in the other direction.
#4 Hula Hoop	Hula hoops; rope tied in a circle; garden hose shaped as circle and held with wooden pegs or dowels.	Upper extremity flexibility-- for enhancing daily living skills requiring reaching. Agility. Coordination.	Lift hoop over head--one or two hands--and draw down to feet. Step out of hoop. Repeat starting from feet to head.
#5 Water Chair	Water table; chairs adapted equipment to provide needed flat surface.	Trunk, abdominal, and lower extremity strength and endurance. Cardiorespiratory endurance. Range of motion.	Kick with extended or flexed knees from sitting, prone, or supine positions. Kick at a moderate (slow, fast) speed for total time period or at maximum speed for 30 seconds; rest 10 to 15 seconds; repeat kicking for 30 seconds.

Station	Equipment	Training Benefits	Activities
#6 Upper Extremity Exercises	Unfilled plastic jugs; inflatable plastic floats.	Upper extremity strength, and endurance. Flexibility. Range of Motion.	Add resistance for arm exercises by grasping unfilled plastic jugs or inflatable floats when performing exercises described on page 9. Increase or decrease resistance by size of jug or float, or by amount of air in the object.
#7 Lower Extremity Exercises.	Water chair; table; inflatable floats that can be placed around the ankles.	Lower extremity, trunk, and abdominal strength and endurance. Range of Motion. Flexibility.	Add resistance for lower extremity exercises by placing floats around ankles when performing exercises described on page 10.
#8 Water Stairs	Water stairs; adapted benches.	Gait training--ascending and descending stairs. Balance. Locomotor movements and patterns.	Ascend and descend water stairs.
#9 Parallel Bars	Aquatic parallel bars.	Upper extremity and trunk strength and endurance. Coordination.	Perform exercises described on pages 11, 12, 13.
#10 Bucket and Hoop Games	Plastic bucket--place weights in bottom to hold it down; rubber rings; small towels.	Foot and lower extremity flexibility, strength, and endurance. Balance.	Place rings and towel on bottom of the pool floor with the bucket in the middle. Use feet to pick-up and place articles into the bucket.

268

Weight Training

Exercises performed with water floats as additonal weights benefit muscular strength and endurance and range of motion. Increase work load by adding additional floats; increase speed and repetitions; require use of two limbs at the same time while keeping the body in a well aligned and balanced position.

Arms and Shoulders
Drag floats through water and lift them up and out of water in these directions --

Front to Back

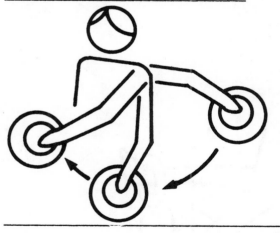

Lateral

Single arm abduction/adduction

Double arm abduction/adduction

Shoulder elevation-depression

Wrist--smooth water out with hand

Twist-turn float over with hand under water

Lower Extremities
Perform the following exercises in sitting positions in directions and ways shown (add floats around ankles for additional resistance and training benefits) --

Abduction/adduction.

Knee flexion/extension.

Single extended leg flexion/extension.

Double extended leg flexion/extension.

BAR EXERCISES

Illustrations below depict adapted gymnastic activities for use in aquatic programs. Exercises using simple equipment and exercise parallel bars can benefit and maintain muscular strength and endurance, range of motion, flexibility, coordination, and cardiorespiratory endurance.

Although many of the following exercises require performance by strong individuals, adaptations in repetitions and times of performances can allow for success by individuals with less strength and endurance. Perform these exercises with the trunk of the body in a straight, stable position, arms extended, and if possible, knees flexed and drawn up to the chest.

Arm Supports
Hold for X seconds; shift weight to the right, left, forward, backward, up, and down.

Arm Walk
Walk with arms in forward, backward, sideward, and hand-over-hand fashions.

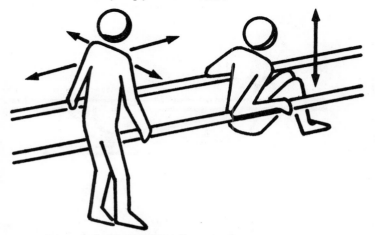 

Arm and Shoulder Support
Support body on the bars in a prone position with extended arms (Fig. 1); roll to supine by lifting one arm up and over to bar (Fig. 2); re-grasp bar with hands (Fig. 3); and roll to supine by lifting over hand up and over (Fig. 4); roll back to prone position in the same manner.

Fig. 1   Fig. 2

Fig. 3   Fig. 4

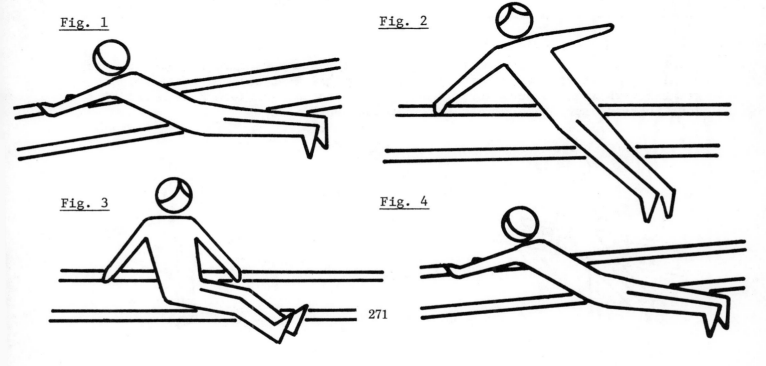

271

Sit Ups
Start in a relaxed position with arms at sides, knees flexed, bottom on bar, and feet under side bar; provide assistance if necessary.

Lift up to a sitting position and lower back down to a sitting position on the parallel bar.

The Bananna
For upper extremity and trunk strength and endurance. In a prone position with hips on the bar and legs under the bar, clasp hands behind head and lift trunk upward and hold; lower back to prone position.

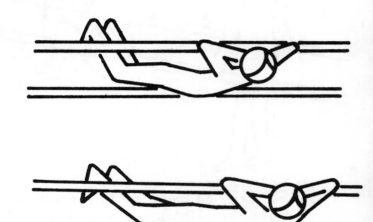

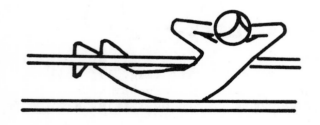

The Bell
For lower extremity and abdominal strength. With extended arms, trunk, and legs, draw legs in designated direction by using abdominal muscles; add extra weights if greater work load is ncessary; draw legs up-front-diagonal-back in a pendular motion; increase speed and trials for increased work load.

272

Interval Training on Parallel Bars

Benefits cardio-respiratory endurance, upper and lower extremity strength and endurance. Cycle or kick legs (from hips) while in a prone, supine, and neutral positions (at top speed for 10/15/20 seconds with extended arms on bars and then slowly for 5/10/10 seconds); repeat intervals of desired times for 4/4/3 repetions.

The Frog Walk

Start with legs extended and swing them up and back from a straddle position and then place legs forward on the bars; shift weight forward and grasp bars with hands between bars; lift legs off and over bars and back to neutral position.

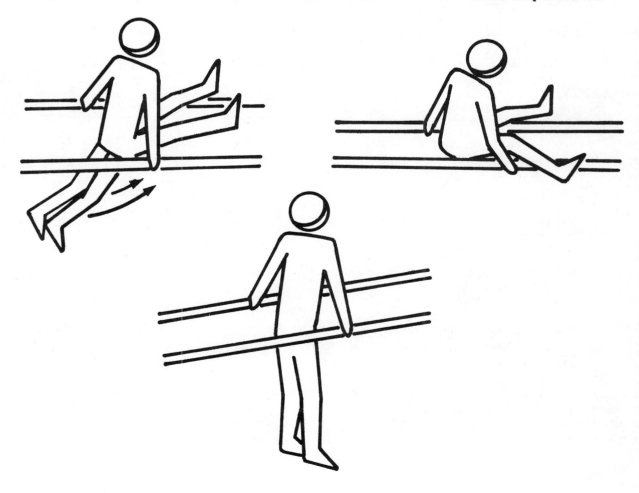

INTERVAL TRAINING

Swimming for physical conditioning and competition can be accomplished through interval training. This training, performed in a strict manner which can include taking pulse and swimming times, requires a highly disciplined and motivated performer for continuing such a program. Interval training can consist of--

. Recording resting pulse before swimming a designated distance--i.e., from one to eight lengths or 12.5 meters to 100 meters.

. Recording swimming time and pulse after swimming.

. Resting for one-half the swimming time.

. Repeating training distance using alternate swimming strokes.

Interval Training Record Sheet

Swim Stroke	Distance	Pulse before	Pulse after	Swim time
Back Stroke				
Front Crawl				
Breast Stroke				
Butterfly				
Sidestroke				

Interval training can also be used to fit conditioning objectives and needs of individual performers by --

. Increasing number of repititions.

. Varying distances swam--one/two width(s), one/two length(s), 25 yards, 50 meters, 100 yards.

. Regulating speed of swim.

. Shortening rest intervals between swims.

. Controlling action during rest or recovery intervals-- walk, float, bob, tread; discourage sitting or lying down during rest or recovery intervals.

Emphasis in interval training can be upon swimming speed and pace so timing widths, laps, and recovery intervals can become an important part of these activities. It should be noted that walking, running, other basic locomotor activities, and various exercises in water can be used in these same ways by

nonswimmers.   Examples of interval training routines that can be done following
a thorough warm-up are --

Crawl stroke two laps.

Rest stroke one lap.

Bob or rhythmic breathe two minutes.

Repeat pattern three or four times

Back stroke kick two laps.

Rest stroke one lap.

Backstroke arm stroke one lap.

Tread water one minute.

Repeat pattern three or four times.

Crawl stroke 50-yards 2 seconds
slower than best or goal time

Float or rest stroke
2 minutes.

Repeat pattern three
times.

ALTERNATE SWIMMING

Alternate swimming is a variation of interval training that allows for
swimming conditioning for one or several performers and the trainer (if possible)
in a highly motivating manner. Less time is spent recording pulse rate and
swimming time for individuals who are not in need of such stress. Alternate
swimming can be one station in an aquatic circuit.

Training begins with X lengths of swimming by Performer 1 (P1). Performer
2 (P2), swims X lengths following completion by P1. Training continues with
performers alternating and decreasing distance by one length on each alteration
of swimmers. Times can be recorded for trials on daily, weekly, or bi-weekly
bases. Key to this training approach is physical conditioning through competition in which each performer strives to give the other swimmer the least
possible resting time. Repetitions of sets are determined by individual needs
of performers.

PERFORMER 1

Rest

Return

PERFORMER 2

Rest

Return

PERFORMER 1

Rest

PERFORMER 2

Rest

Alternate Swimming Record Sheet

Swim Stroke	Swimming distance and time of swim							
	P1 100 m	P2	P1 75 m	P2	P1 50 m	P2	P1 12.5 m	P2
Back Stroke								
Front Crawl								

Section V—
Practical Pointers for Organization
and Administration

PRACTICAL POINTERS

TIPS ON MAINSTREAMING:
DO'S AND DON'TS IN ACTIVITY PROGRAMS

REFLECTIONS ON MAINSTEAMS*

It occurs to us that mainstreams do not necessarily run a smooth, tranquil, straight course across the landscape. Mainstreams may follow a twisting, winding, or even tortuous route. They may have eddies, whirlpools, rapids, falls, dams, and dikes, and you can never tell what you'll find in the bullrushes.

The Stream itself will not get the children where they need to go. It also takes the craft best suited to each individual's plotted course, with pilots equipped to aid him to avoid the shoals and un-navigable currents, to prevent him from coming to harm, or from drifting aimlessly into the pounding surf of the sea of life.

---

*CANHC-Gram (Vol. 10, No. 9), September 1976, page 1.

TIPS ON MAINSTREAMING:
DO'S AND DON'TS FOR ACTIVITY PROGRAMS

Accept me as I am is the first step in our working together.

Legislation and litigation mandate greater inclusion of individuals
with different handicapping conditions in regular school programs and
community activities. This procedure is called by many different names--
least restrictive environment, most normal setting feasible, normalization,
mainstreaming, zero-reject principle, deinstitutionalization, integration,
right to community services. Regardless of terminology, people from many
different walks of life--providers of services, parents of both handicapped
and nonhandicapped children, and some handicapped individuals themselves--
are apprehensive and fear including individuals with different handicapping
conditions in programs and activities with nonhandicapped participants.

So often negative attitudes are caused by able-bodied persons who have
not had opportunities to meet and know impaired, disabled, and handicapped
persons as individuals. As a result attitudes and relationships continue
to be influenced by labels and categorical thinking; sterotypes abound.

```
                              LABELS

         There are labels in my shirts;
              They tell me front from back,
         My "P.F. Flyers" make me run faster on the track.
              "Billie the Kid" made my pants
         And "Bonnie Doon" my socks.
              Momma says "Matel" made my brightly colored blocks.
         There are labels on most all things,
              And that is plain to see.
         But Momma, why's there a label on me?


                                        Jean Caywood
                                        Physical Education Instructor
                                        Plano, Texas
```

When individuals with even the most severe handicapping conditions are known
as individuals--people with the the same ranges of interests, aspirations,
abilities, biases, problems, and hang-ups as their able-bodied counterparts--
the first and possibly most important steps have been taken toward acceptance.
Not only is acceptance gained, but appreciation and understanding developed
as individuals with various handicapping conditions are looked upon, liked
or disliked, loved or hated, accepted or rejected because of their own
personality characteristics, personal actions, and behavioral patterns.

Obviously the earlier this process begins the sooner impaired, disabled,
and handicapped persons are recognized as individuals and the less likely they
are to be rejected categorically. In schools and communities where children
with various handicapping conditions have participated in Headstart programs

or have been integrated in activities in natural and unpretentous ways, little if any rejection has been evidenced toward impaired, disabled, and handicapped children. Differences have been looked upon as a natural and expected part of life. Handicapping conditions are viewed and accepted in the same ways as other differences displayed by members in gangs, neighborhoods, or classes--some are boys, others girls; some are tall, others short; some are happy, others sad; some have dark skins, others light; some wear glasses, others do not; some have red hair, others blond or brunette; some are well coordinated, others have difficulties in fine motor activities. The process of recognizing differences is an important part of the maturing process in growing-up.

The situation is not so logical and easy when older children, adolescents, or adults face associating with and accepting impaired, disabled, and handicapped persons in school, work, or play. Attitudes and misconceptions have developed over the years--individuals without sight or hearing, people without arms or legs, persons with unsteady gait or speech problems, or those with intellectual, learning, or emotional problems are not only looked upon as different but often considered deficient, deviant, and not really whole persons. Unfortunately, the mass media often do little to reverse this process or to emphasize abilities rather than disabilities. In fact, many times television exposures, radio programs, magazine features, and newspaper articles directly or subtly reinforce attitudes that promote undesirable emotions such as sympathy and pity or even antagonism, prejudice, and further rejection. Consequently many--possibly a sizeable majority--of the general population not only do not know what to do when meeting handicapped individuals but often actively avoid them.

"I do not choose to be a common man. It is my right to be uncommon -- if I can. I seek opportunity -- not security. I do not wish to be a kept citizen, humbled and dulled by having the state look after me. I want to take the calculated risk; to dream and to build, to fail and to succeed. I refuse to barter incentive for a dole. I prefer the challenge of life to the guaranteed existence; the thrill of fulfillment to the stale calm of Utopia. I will not trade freedom for beneficence nor my dignity for a handout. I will never cower before any master nor bend to any threat. It is my heritage to stand erect, proud and unafraid; to think and act for myself, enjoy the benefit of my creations and to face the world boldly and say, this I have done."

MAINSTREAMING: A GOAL AND A PROCESS

Whatever the mind of man can conceive and believe, it can achieve.
                                                    Napoleon Hill

The word mainstreaming is often misunderstood and inappropriately defined. <u>Mainstreaming is both a goal and a process</u>. Mainstreaming and integration are not synonomous; physical proximity does not guarantee social integration; being together does not in itself bring about acceptance. However, both research and experience show that real understanding, true acceptance, and elimination of prejudices are enhanced by direct people-to-people contact--when people get to know each other as individuals, not as parts of categories. Putting individuals in programs or activities for which they are not ready is cruel; to keep them out of these same programs and activities when they are ready and can participate is criminal!

Mainstreaming represents one level in the continuum of services required by the <u>least restrictive alternative</u> mandate contained in the Education for All Handicapped Children Act (P.L. 94-142) and Section 504 of the Rehabilitation Act (P.L. 93-112). Rules and regulations for P.L. 94-142 require that each public agency insure a continuum of alternative placements to meet the needs of handicapped children for special education and related services. Instruction in regular classes, special classes, special schools, home instruction, and instruction in hospitals and institutions are all included as integral parts of this continuum of services. Provisions must also be made for supplementary services such as resource room or itinerant instruction in conjunction with regular class placement. These requirements are consistent with provisions of Section 504 that mandate <u>program accessibility</u> and appropriate accommodations so that handicapped individuals can participate to the maximum degree possible with their nonhandicapped classmates and peers. This process does not...

> ...suggest massive return to or placement of all children with learning problems in regular grades;

> ...refer to separate settings as equivalent placements;

> ...mean the end of all self-contained special classes as service vehicles for children.[1]

This process does suggest...

> ...a continuum of appropriate service alternatives to allow placement of children as individuals, not members of categories;

---

[1]Based on materials developed by Dale E. Coons, Department of Counseling and Special Education, University of Akron, Akron, Ohio, and appearing in <u>IRUC Briefings</u> (Vol. 1, No. 3), May 1976, page 5, published by Physical Education and Recreation for the Handicapped: Information and Research Utilization Center (American Alliance for Health, Physical Education, and Recreation, 1201 16th Street, N. W., Washington, D. C., 20036).

...some system other than the present dichotomy of either placement in regular classes or placement in categorically defined special classes;

...preventive services being as important for children with potential learning problems as intervention for children with identified learning problems;

...a need to integrate all levels and types of handicapped children with handicapped peers to the maximum extent possible even if initially integration is only possible in non-academic, play, or lunch areas, or through flexible scheduling to allow regular interactions between handicapped and nonhandicapped children;

...need for greater understanding of handicapped children by all school personnel;

...placement of handicapped children in their home school districts whenever possible to insure mutual home and school peer relationships;

...new roles for education personnel providing services to handicapped students.[2]

This process emphasizes procedures by which impaired, disabled, and handicapped children are placed in educational programs. Some readjustments are necessary in one's thinking and approaches when dealing with handicapped children, whether in a regular classroom, gymnasium, or swimming pool, on the playfield, in a drama class, or in recreational activities. In the past, the procedure was to <u>label</u> a child, <u>place</u> that child--usually categorically based on handicapping conditions--and then <u>program</u> the class. Often these programs had little if anything to do with needs, abilities, and interests of individual children in the class.

> *Teachers must really believe that the child rather than the curriculum should be the center of the school.*

Now the process is to <u>assess</u> each child's needs, <u>develop</u> a program for each child based on identified needs, and <u>place</u> the child according to individual needs for each activity included in his/her individualized education program. In fact, many of our ideologies and procedures regarding homogeneous and heterogeneous grouping must be carefully reviewed. Have these procedures been designed to help meet interests and needs of individual children or for the administrative and organizational convenience of program personnel?

> *Handicapped children have the right to grow up in a world which does not set them apart, which looks at them not with scorn or pity or ridicule, but which welcomes them exactly as it welcomes every child, which offers them identical privileges and identical responsibilities.*

---

[2]<u>Ibid</u>.

WHAT TO DO WHEN YOU MEET A HANDICAPPED PERSON.

You cannot individualize instruction
if you do not know the individual.

While each teacher and leader is going to have to deal with impaired, disabled, and handicapped children as he/she is confronted with them, the following tips and suggestions provide ideas as to what to do and what not to do when dealing with individuals having certain handicapping conditions, whether in teaching, recreational, social, or employment situations. These points and suggestions have for the most part come from individuals who themselves have had to deal personally with conditions being discussed. This in-and-of itself suggests an important yet frequently overlooked and neglected approach--involving impaired, disabled, and handicapped persons themselves in helping able-bodied individuals feel more comfortable and at ease in dealing with these populations. So often groups most directly involved and with greatest opportunities to provide important input of this type have been ignored.

"Never check the actions of the child; follow him and watch to prevent any serious accidents, but do not even remove obstacles which he would learn to avoid by tumbling over them a few times. Teach him to jump rope, to swing weights, to raise his body by his arms, and to mingle as far as possible in the rough sports of the older boys. Do not be apprehensive of his safety. If you should see him climbing in the branches of a tree, be assured he is less likely to fall than if he had perfect vision. Do not too much regard bumps on the forehead, rough scratches, or bloody noses, even these may have their good influences. At worst, they affect only the bark and not the system like the rust of inaction."

> Dr. Samuel Gridley Howe, patriarch
> in the field of education of the
> visually handicapped

For additional information see this reference by Harvey N. Switzky and Ted L. Miller:

The Least Restrictive Alternative. *Mental Retardation* (Vol. 16, No. 1), February 1978, pp. 52-54.

TIPS FOR DEALING WITH HANDICAPPED PERSONS

Today if a crippled child possesses normal intelligence,
is educated properly, and receives the faith he deserves,
it is no longer acceptable for anyone in placing a prop
under his body to place a ceiling over his potential.

Earl S. Miers

Anne H. Carlson, Director of the Jamestown (North Dakota) School for Crippled Children and herself a quadriplegic, provides the following Tips for Dealing with Handicapped Persons:

. Offer help when it looks as though it might be needed, but do not insist on it if an individual refuses aid.

. Don't hover--handicapped adults do not wish to be treated as babies.

. When handicapped persons fall, take it easy. Wait for them to give you a cue. If individuals can get up by themselves, they may prefer doing that. If they need a lift, they will tell you which is the easiest way to get them back on their feet.

. Crutches and wheelchairs are necessary accessories. Don't take them away from handicapped persons unless they indicate they would like to have them out of the way. Nothing is more irritating than to have your crutches grabbed quickly as soon as you hit a chair, leaving you stranded!

. Train, plane, and bus steps are hard even for the young and agile. Handicapped individuals often need help here. Again, let them tell you how to help. Those who do not need to be carried up the steps usually have methods of their own for making them. Do not pull an arm or push from behind unless such assistance has been requested. Precarious balance can be lost entirely with such tactics.

. Keep your perspective. As Gertrude Stein might say, "An arm is an arm is an arm," and "A leg is a leg is a leg." It is just that. An arm is an arm and a leg is a leg--it is not the whole person!

. Relax. No matter what you do, if you are friendly and kind, the handicapped person is going to like you.

. Have fun. Talk about the same things you would with any other person. A physical impairment or disability does not necessarily limit interests or dampen a sense of humor.

. Be yourself. Don't be sticky sweet; omit the pious note.

. Let common sense and consideration be your guide and you will never err seriously. Disabled individuals are just like you, only with a physical difference that does not have to make them feel or think differently.

RELATING TO ORTHOPEDICALLY AND VISUALLY HANDICAPPED INDIVIDUALS

If we accept the premise that all people are special, we are better able to deal with individual differences in different individuals.

Specific suggestions for relating to orthopedically and visually handicapped individuals based on materials developed by Susan Phillips, and Michael Ward, and Council for Exceptional Children (1920 Association Drive, Reston, Virginia) include:

. Ask the individual if he/she needs help. If so, what kind? Do not assume that the individual needs more help than requested.

. Ask the individual if he/she needs help when meeting that same person again. Do not assume that the individual needs help again or the same kind of assistance.

. Offer help in ways that deal directly with demands of specific situations; offer help in discrete ways.

. Do not be persistent; supply required help. If an individual does not seem to require further assistance, do not feel obligated to stay. However, you can check this out by asking something like, "Is there anything further I can do?"

. Do not assume that the way you help an individual with an impairment or disability will be the same for all people with similar conditions. Always ask what is the best way to help that individual.

. Recognize that handicapped individuals have different ways of doing things. What looks difficult or awkward may be the easiest way for the individual to perform that task or action.

. Do not be afraid to ask a handicapped person to repeat what he/she said. Most handicapped individuals would rather repeat what they said than to have an able-bodied person fake understanding and subsequent communication.

. Remember that blind or orthopedically handicapped individuals are not necessarily hard of hearing; therefore, there is no need to raise your voice!

. Be senstive to the fact that some handicapped people get tired of asking for help and may forget to say please and thank you. They are not necessarily being impolite.

. Engage in casual conversation to ease tensions if a helping situation lasts any duration of time.

MAKING RELATIONSHIPS MORE COMFORTABLE
BETWEEN BLIND AND SIGHTED INDIVIDUALS

I've never let stereotypes--like a blind
person can't do that--stand in my way.

Bill Schmidt

<u>Charles Buell</u>, pioneer in physical education, recreation, and sports programs for blind and partially sighted participants, suggests the following points of courtesy to make relationships more comfortable between blind and sighted individuals:

- Please address me directly and not through my guide or companion.

- I can walk more easily with you than with a dog or cane. But don't grab my arm or try to propel me; let me take yours. I'll keep a half step behind to anticipate curbs and steps. Going down stairs I may prefer to hold a railing. When giving me directions, make it plain whether you mean your right or my right.

- Speak to me when you enter the room and tell me who you are--don't play guessing games. Introduce me to the others, including children. Guide my hand to the arm or back of a chair.

- For me, doors should be completely closed or wide open--a half-open door is a hazard; so are toys on the floor. Warn me of coffee tables and projecting lamp shades--I hate to break things.

- At dinner time, tell me quietly how things are arranged. Perhaps my meat will be at six o'clock, peas at eleven o'clock, potatoes at two. And I may ask help in cutting my meat.

- Don't avoid words like see or watch--I use them too! I'm always glad to see you! I watch television!

- I don't want pity. But don't talk about the <u>wonderful compensations</u> of blindness--whatever I've learned has been by hard work.

- I'll discuss blindness with you if you are curious, but it's an old story to me. I have as many other interests as you do.

- If I'm your house guest, show me the bathroom, closet, dresser, window and outlet for my electric razor. The light switch, too-- I like to know whether the lights are on.

- Don't think of me as a blind person. I am an individual who happens to be blind.

WHEN YOU HAVE A HEARING IMPAIRED
PLAYER ON THE TEAM OR IN CLASS

*Our challenge in special education is to
reach the unhandicapped mind behind the
handicapped senses. To know is more important than to see. To understand is
more important than to hear.*

Dr. Richard Kinney

Personnel at Lexington (New York) School for the Deaf have developed
various <u>Ideas for Families</u> to assist in dealing with deaf and hard-of-hearing
children. The following hints, applicable to physical education, recreation,
and other activity programs as well as to sports have been adapted from a
list of suggestions entitled <u>Hey Coach</u> developed and distributed by personnel
at the Lexington School for the Deaf:

> You have an individual with a hearing impairment on
>   the team or in class!
> No, it's not going to affect how well he/she plays
>   or participates.
> But, it might be helpful to understand a few things
>   about hearing impairments that probably are true
>   for individuals on your team or in your class.

. A hearing impaired player is not going to get much out of group
  meetings, so coaches should make special efforts to have a team-
  mate or him/herself brief the player at some point--before or
  after a game. However, don't exclude the player from group
  meetings. Expect him/her to come and treat him/her the same as
  any other player.

. Remember, nothing is wrong with the intelligence of the individual
  although language may be simple and speech sound different. When
  explaining something new, speak as simple as possible. Avoid
  cliches and idiomatic expressions--tighten up on defense, don't
  bunch, stick 'em. If you use certain idioms, take time to explain
  them.

. Hand signals are imperative during a game. Try to use regular
  official hand signals even when playing without an official referee.

. When talking to the team or class out-of-doors, avoid standing
  so the hearing impaired individual must look into the sun. It's
  tough, if not impossible, to lipread that way.

. Don't expect a hearing impaired individual to lipread from the
  outfield, or across the tennis court, or from the other end of
  the track.

. When individuals wear hearing aids, it may not appear that they get
  much out of the aids, but wearing them gives additional clues to
  what's happening. If possible, a hearing impaired individual should
  wear an aid while playing in any sport <u>except</u> a contact sport or
  swimming--water ruins an aid; a tackle might break the aid.

- Be sure hearing impaired players have a list of all games and practices, with places and times. If schedules change, see that they get the new information correctly--it helps to have a pad and pencil handy.

- Check that hearing impaired individuals know exactly what they are to do to insure safety. Don't assume that they understand everything said the first time it is presented. You say, "Tuck your head," when demonstrating a forward roll. A hearing impaired individual might be embarrassed to admit he/she doesn't understand you and could injure the neck. Demonstrate physically whenever possible.

- Encourage parents to contact you in case of some misunderstanding. Be sure you know how to reach the parents or a relative, friend, or neighbor in case of emergency.

Here are a few ideas about problems that might arise in specific sports. This list obviously does not include every possible situation, but should alert you to other situations that may arise.

- Basketball. If a player does not hear a whistle in the middle of the game, he/she might continue to play. If a foul is called behind the player, he/she might not know and go on to make a basket that doesn't count. Hold your arms up to try to signal that play has stopped and ask others on the team to do the same.

- Bowling. Hearing impaired individuals are at no disadvantage at all.

- Dance. Hearing impaired students can learn folk dances or any dance by counting beats aloud. They should wear hearing aids, and the phonograph speaker should be put on a wooden floor so that vibrations can be felt. Dancing in bare feet or socks makes it easier to feel vibrations. Balloons can be used to facilitate feeling different rhythms and beats.

- Football. A hearing impaired player can't hear signals, so a system of hand signals has to be used. Some schools for the deaf use a base drum on the sidelines to initiate offensive plays.

- Gymnastics. The hearing impaired gymnast has to understand what has to be done. Don't give instructions while bouncing on a trampoline or while upside down on parallel bars, rings, or ropes. It's tricky enough to lipread when someone is standing still!

- Life Saving. All students have to do homework but a hearing impaired individual probably has to do more reading because of instructions missed in class. When practicing activities like the rear head hold, set up a signal system so that if a hearing impaired individual is in trouble, he/she can tap the hands of the partner, which means, let go!

. <u>Skiing</u>. Hearing impaired skiers should wear identification tags for their own protection in case of accidents. Little children should be tagged with name, address, and other pertinent information.

. <u>Soccer</u>. A player has to rely completely on what is seen and cannot rely on other players to call signals.

. <u>Swimming</u>. Be sure you have a way of attracting the attention of a hearing impaired swimmer. A buddy system works well. The life guard should know when a hearing impaired swimmer is in the pool. During instruction, if a hearing impaired student starts on a 25-yard lap, you can't catch his/her attention for corrections until the lap is completed. During meets, many hearing impaired swimmers cannot hear the starter's gun--a hand signal start is fairer.

. <u>Tennis</u>. Watch out for the sun when giving instructions.

. <u>Volleyball</u>. Hearing impaired individuals are at no disadvantage at all.

<u>Questions You Have Always Wanted to Ask About Integration !!</u>

Teachers, parents, administrators, and counselors continue to seek guidance and direction in determining children for whom integration is appropriate. Answers to certain key questions can assist in this process. Among key questions that can be asked to help determine if integration is feasible and appropriate are --

. For whom is integration appropriate? Is it appropriate for this child in these activities now?
. What personal characteristics make it likely that an individual child can be successfully integrated? Does this child possess these characteristics?
. Does this child have communication skills that enable him/her to function effectively in regular public school classes and/or community programs?
. Does this child have sufficient social and emotional maturity to be a part of an integrated group?
. Must a child perform at grade level? Activity level?
. Does assessment of this child's ability to learn equal or surpass that of other members of the class?
. At what levels and in what subjects and activities can this child be integrated?
. What supportive services are needed for this child? For his/her teacher?
. What is the result of a cost analysis of this educational practice for this child in terms of resources required and educational outcomes?
. Can this child participate in these activities safely, successfully, and with personal satisfaction?

Questions adapted from "Mainstreaming Deaf Students Using Team Teaching," <u>American Annals of the Deaf</u>, December 1977, p. 522.

COMMUNICATING WITH HEARING IMPAIRED
PERSONS IN ONE-TO-ONE AND GROUP SITUATIONS

*A difference is a difference only
when it makes a difference.*

Helen Keller said, "Blindness separates people from things; deafness separates people from people." Communicating with hearing impaired persons is crucial in whatever the setting or activity. The following suggestions for communicating with hearing impaired persons in one-to-one and group situations were developed by Lynn Smarte, Council for Exceptional Children (1920 Association Drive, Reston, Virginia):

One-to-One Situations

- Ask the individual, "Can you read my lips?"

  --If the individual says yes, continue your conversation in a normal voice and remember--

   --Don't shout.
   --Speak distinctly but don't over-enunciate your words.
   --Face the person.
   --Don't cover your mouth or speak with a pipe or other obstruction in your mouth.

  --If the individual does not seem to understand, offer him/her paper and pencil.

- Ask the individual, "Would you like me to speak louder?"

- If you can't understand a hearing impaired person's speech, ask him/her to repeat.

  --Don't pretend to understand.

  --Ask the individual to write it down if you still cannot understand.

Group Situations

- Inquire in advance as to whether the deaf person would like an interpreter.

  --Ask if the individual prefers an oral or sign language interpreter. Both may be needed since different deaf people have different preferences.

  --Decide in advance where interpreter(s) will stand.

- Blink lights to get attention.

- Try to arrange for seating of hearing impaired persons near speakers and interpreters.

. Make sure you have the attention of hearing impaired persons when important announcements are being made--e.g., changes of meeting room assignments announced during a luncheon.

Remember not all deaf people can lipread well.

Edward E. Corbett[3] raises a number of questions related to the ability of hearing impaired children to function in mainstreamed programs. What is needed if answers to listed questions for any given child are negative? What assistance in interpreting, tutoring, and communication training programs is needed to make answers affirmative? While these specific questions are posed in terms of hearing impaired children, similar questions can be raised for children with other handicapping conditions to assist in determining appropriateness of mainstreamed programs for specific individuals. Answers to some of these same questions can provide direction and assistance for formulating guidelines and practical procedures to facilitate the mainstreaming process. Corbett's specific questions follow:

Can the hearing impaired child...

...hear the teacher?

...hear classmates in front, behind, and all around him/her?

...hear the educational film being presented that day?

...hear the principal over the public address system?

...hear and participate in class discussions?

...hear the visiting speaker invited for the day?

...hear the guide on the class field trip?

...hear the TV or radio program assigned to the class?

...hear the exchange of friendly chit-chat at recess?

...hear the quick exchanges when going down the hall between classes?

...hear news and gossips during the lunch hour?

...hear sum up on the walk home at the day's end?

...hear debates of the student body government and run for office or participate in clubs and athletic events?

---

[3] Edward E. Corbett, Jr. "Mainstreaming--A National Perspective." The Deaf American (Vol. 30, No. 3), November 1977, pp. 9-12.

FIRST STEPS IN MAINSTREAMING

*The best reformers the world has seen
were those who began with themselves.*

Regardless of an individual child's specific condition, various strategies exist for introducing and improving relationships between handicapped and nonhandicapped children. For example:

- Arrange with parents for special needs and non-special needs children to play together outside of school.

- Individualize the curriculum for all children, not just special needs children.

- Establish respect for individuals as the prime classroom value.

- Create a safe, protected environment so that children can risk forming relationships.

- Explain individual differences to children in a neutral, value-free manner.

- Read aloud books and stories that deal with differences.

- Answer children's questions directly and honestly.

- Reinterpret actions for children in behaviorally observable terms--e.g., "His legs don't work very well," or "It's hard for him to hold your hand without squeezing it."

- Encourage children to use behavioral explanations rather than labels.

- Design and guide positive interactions between children based on a common interest or curricular experience.

- Encourage all children to talk about feelings such as fear and anger--and help them begin to understand and govern these emotions.

- Encourage spontaneous dramatic play and role playing to help non-handicapped children identify with the experience of special needs children--e.g., using crutches, walkers, hearing aids, crawling or limping.

- Create opportunities for all parents to meet with each other to discuss their reactions to mainstreaming.[4]

---

[4] Based on First Steps in Mainstreaming: Some Questions and Answers, by Samuel J. Meisels, Media Resource Center, Massachusetts Department of Mental Health, March 1977.

MAINSTREAMING DOES WORK [5]

IRENE M. KEHRT

When I first read this letter, I cried. My recurring, guilt-ridden, nagging regret returned. Many years ago it was so easy to give several rational reasons why a blind eighth grader could not participate in the regular junior high school physical education curriculum. Difficult, inconvenient? Yes. Impossible? Never!

Too often teachers are far more concerned with schedules, numbers, facilities, and activities than they are with the individual human being. Hooray for the emphasis on the "new" physical education. People, students, children are what it is all about.

Despite misconceptions and even past experiences, mainstreaming does work. Kevin sustained severe head injuries when he was a toddler. Now after four operations, a useless left arm, a plastic plate in his skull, a brace on his left leg, Kevin can talk and walk. His motor coordination is seriously affected, but not his desire to compete mentally and physically. Horribly frustrated and angry with his unsuccessful efforts to keep up with his peers, Kevin in the third grade was a candidate as an emotional stress victim. Supportive parents, an understanding teacher, a sound physical education program and a grade promotion resulted in Kevin's spending an evening composing this letter.

Dear Miss Neder,°

I have enjoyed the last three years verry much in P.E. I loved every sport and every event. I think I have learned a great deal of activity and have gained a lot of strength from you. From the begginning of 3rd grade to up to now I have learned a lot of recpect for others in sports as well as trying my hardest to get better each year in P.E.

I know now that from 3rd grade when I didn't get my way and just ran out and cried on the sidelines to the 5th grade, and haven't done it yet I have gained a lot of confidence in myself and to show leadership and cooperation to others. Now I can face a new life and show my ability to do things in the future and remember everything that you have taught me.

If it were possible I wouldn't want to loose you as a P.E. teacher because I have become so attached to you that I don't think that I will be able to get used to another teacher like you.

Learning from you I believe that every athlete should try his or her hardest to become a star in some sport that he or she likes and enjoys.

I never, ever, forget the moments that we have shared together. I don't think there another P.E. teacher around that tries as hard and has all the patients that you have.

Everywhere I go I am going to set an example to athletes exactly like you have taught me.

Do you know what I wish more than anything in the world?

I wish that everywhere I go you would be alongside with me teaching me knew skills so that we would never be apart.

But, I can't be that way and I still have to go to the Middle School and get accustomed to a whole new program. But I'll remember everything I have learned from you.

Going to the Middle School is not going to stop me from coming over and saying hello and tell you about the Middle School.

Well—I think I have said everything about my experiences that I have gained from you so I say goodbye before I shed in tears because I know I'll miss you and I ALWAYS remember you forever.

Sincerly yours,

Kevin Faulkner

Kevin wrote this letter before he was presented the fifth grade award for "Most Improved Athlete." His classmates, by a large majority, voted for Kevin from a list of seven nominees selected by the two physical education teachers.

Why didn't I take Peggy in my class those many years ago?

°Charlotte Neder, Physical Education Instructor, Lake Side Elementary School, Orange Park, Clay County.

5 Irene M. Kehrt, "Mainstreaming Does Work." *Florida Journal of Health, Physical Education, and Recreation*, November 1977, p. 7.

PRACTICAL POINTERS

ORGANIZING PLAYDAYS AND LARGE GROUP ACTIVITIES

Susan J. Grosse

The scope of a playday or large group activity involving a number of students encompasses almost everything regularly found in physical education classes in which these students participate in the same or similar activities. Great for boosting school spirit and togetherness, playdays and large group activities give students chances to relate to large numbers of peers, some of whom they may be meeting for the first time. Such activities also foster group interaction and cooperation as members of each team work toward common goals. Opportunities for participation in sports and games that can only be played by large groups are provided. Participants have the _fun_ of being involved in special events, are offered changes in daily class routines, and are given opportunities to apply many skills learned in physical education classes.

However, beneficial playdays and large group activities take a great deal more preparation than regular classes to make them successful. Several basic decisions must be made regarding students, activities, staff, and facilities. Additional details to be considered include those related to refreshments, transportation, lead-up and follow-up activities, scheduling, on-site preparation, publicity, direction of events, first aid availability, and last but not least, financing. No doubt about it, playdays and large group activities are hard work, but well worth it when one realizes contributions they make to physical educating the children involved.

Deciding Basics

Student Participant

Even though an event is planned to accommodate a large group of individuals, some selection should be made to insure that numbers don't become unwieldy and that age range included is not too great. Many persons planning their first playdays want to include as many participants as possible. While this is a generous thought, in reality some limitations should be brought to bear if all participants are to achieve maximum benefits. Consideration should be given to--

• Total number participating. Only as many students as can be kept active should be included. Nothing is more deadly than having large numbers of children sitting and watching because there are too many participants for the size of the facility and/or the amount of equipment. If an activity includes formal competition, particularly in individual sports some sitting and waiting can be expected and are necessary for recovery of athletes.

• Levels of physical and mental abilities. Even if play is just for fun, games are much more interesting when teams are reasonably evenly matched. If teams sent from different schools retain their own identities, organizers of the event should attempt to invite and seed competition accordingly. However, in many playdays students from different schools or classes are mixed into teams. In these cases students get changes to meet new people their same age. Whoever arranges teams should make sure that each team has a full range of abilities and is balanced against the others. This may take considerable time and effort but insures much more interesting play for participants. When there is an extremely wide range in abilities it may be advantageous to set limits as to who is included in a particular playday. However many students, even those more severely limited, can participate in and enjoy such events right along with their more capable peers.

- <u>Age span</u>. Ages of students invited in part dictate activities to be planned. Important differences exist in physical abilities, interests, and previous experiences of elementary school age youngsters, middle school students, high school age individuals, and adults. What age groups to include is a decision that must be made. The elementary school age group is probably least likely to benefit from playday type experiences. Children in this age range can function in large groups but often only for limited periods of time. These children are still learning basic skills and need more individual help than many large group settings provide. At this age children are not yet into the competitive phase of sports and therefore should probably not be included. Middle school, high school, and adult populations can all benefit from large group experiences. If the total population to be served is quite small, all three of these groups can be included in a particular event. However if the population is large it is probably best to limit groups included. Additional factors to consider include needs and interests of participants themselves. Many adults do not like to be included in kiddie events and most younger students do not have sports backgrounds to participate with adults. The more specific the age group the easier it is to tailor activities to satisfy needs and interests of participants.

- <u>Sex</u>. Is the activity to be co-ed? By rules of Title IX it should be. However, if dressing facilities are needed, for swimming particularly, be sure that everyone can be accommodated.

- <u>Who needs assistance?</u> Most handicapped students can participate in large group activities with minimal assistance. They can physically get themselves from place to place, follow simple directions, and possess behavior that is reasonably good. However, a segment of the population with severe involvements may need additional help. Some may be in wheelchairs and unable tp push themselves; they need help getting from place to place. Others may have severe perceptual problems and need a companion to help keep experiences organized. Behavior may be a problem for some students, particularily in new settings with more people than usual. For a large group of deaf students, additional interpretors may be necessary. Blind students may need assistance in getting around in different locations. Whatever the case, the number of students who require extra help needs to be determined ahead of time and enough people provided to give one-to-one help when and if needed.

Focus of the Activity

Free play is fine for recess but the larger a group, the more difficult it is for students to organize activities themselves. Any playday or large group activity needs careful structure and preplanning. Needs and interests of students must be considered. A balance must be achieved to accommodate <u>fun</u> activities in learning environments so that the specific natures of events can be determined.

- <u>Needs and interests of students</u>. An excellent source to provide input in this area is the physical education staff person currently working with individuals to be invited. From this person the following information can be obtained--

--Activities with which students already familiar. These make the foundation of the program. Starting the program with a game or sport already known helps students feel more at home and relaxed in new settings.

--New activities students like to try themselves or see others perform. It may be necessary to give teachers time to go back and survey their groups. Some programs have limited access to certain types of equipment, for example, and may not be able to offer a sport in school but can briefly acquaint students with it at a playday. This may also be the only opportunity for students to see live some little known sports such as fencing or riflery. If a playday is to take an entire day some time is needed for sit-down relaxation where demonstrations of these sports can be provided.

--Sports or activities teachers consider inappropriate for their groups. Again individuals in the best positions to judge needs and abilities of groups are regular teachers. In some cases students just may not be ready to try a particular sport. Some sports, because of dangers involved may be on a school's list of activities that are not allowed. A particular activity may be part of a school's curriculum but students have not come to that point in their instruction yet and the teacher may wish that it be put off. Whatever the case, a multitude of activities can be chosen so that exclusion of a few should not cause undue problems.

--Ability levels represented in groups. Regular teachers can help group teams if several schools or classes are to be mixed and can provide data on how many students need additional help to participate.

. Learning can be fun. A familiar comment heard in planning meetings is, "Let's get the kids together and give them a day that is really FUN!" The implication is that the rest of the time physical activities for these children are drudgery. Quite the contrary; most children with various handicapping conditions lead happy, healthy lives and are already participating in many fun activities. A playday will probably be an entirely new experience for them and as such a learning experience of vast dimensions. Whether or not it is fun depends on how successfully the student is able to function in a large group environment. This does not mean that students need to have everything done for them--to avoid frustration; that they need to be winners at everything--because they wouldn't understand losing even when a good effort is made or that they need to be given something because they participate--because they would not enjoy themselves otherwise. Children with various handicapping conditions do things for themselves and have fun at the attempt as well as the success; they can lose and enjoy competition because they know they did their best, probably better than ever before. The most precious thing they can take home is the happy feeling of having been a part of such a good time. Those memories will last long after a paper or ribbon is lost.

. Types of events. Large group activities can be grouped into four basic categories--

--Sports playdays provide a good format for first experiences with large groups. Several schools or classes are invited and for purposes of competition teams are mixed with students from every school on each team. Emphasis is on group interaction and cooperation, fun rather than serious competition.

--Sports competitions require that students have some previous sports experience. Schools or classes retain their own individual identities and compete against each other. More emphasis is on the competitive structure and each student's part in it.

--Special theme events are more suitable for in-school activities involving large groups of students. Activities usually center around special theme, such as a holiday or a different idea, like a Trivia Day.

--Special sports events consist of unique, one-of-a-kind activities such as sports competition between students and staff or students and local celebraties. This is also more suitable for in-school rather than inter-school participation.

Each of these events can be run on either a half day or a full day basis. Sample programs are included in the Appendix, pages 12 to 15.

Staffing

The larger a group of participants the larger the staff needs to be.

- Planning committee. This group should consist of regular physical education teachers of students to be invited and persons responsible for over-all administration of the event. Functions include deciding events and activities, scheduling and determining facilities, equipment, and additional staff needed to stage activities. Teachers are responsible for preparing their students (refer to the section on lead-up and follow-up activities, page 9) and people administering the program for taking care of the rest of the details (refer to the next section).

- Running the playday. Though job descriptions differ depending on types of activities the following represent tasks that may need to be considered--

--Setting up equipment and preparing the site.

--Pre-event paper work--i.e., programs, name tags, directional signs.

--Greeters to meet students and show them where to go.

--Someone to check in participants, hand out name tages, distribute programs.

--Announcer.

--Event directors--individuals to run each event.

--Officials--rated officials should be used if the event is interschool competition or competition against celebraties for example.

--People to provide one-to-one assistance where needed and as determined
  ahead of time.

--People to assist in moving groups from place to place.

--People to assist with toileting and feeding if needed.

--People to assist with dressing if a change of clothes is needed and
  to assist with wraps.

--Clean up crew.

Sources of help might include--

--Community volunteers.

--University students.

--Local sports personalities.

--Parent groups.

--Regular school personnel and administrators.

All personnel should be thoroughly briefed ahead of time regarding their
functions, supervised if necessary (depending on types of jobs and
experience of the person), and shown appreciation after events are over.

Facilities and Equipment

Part of the success of any large group event depends upon physical conditions.

. An appropriate facility should be accessible to persons in wheelchairs
  or on crutches if they are to be part of groups included. This means not
  just accessible entryways but also bathrooms and all areas of the
  building where activities are to be held. Facilities should also be
  large enough to accommodate group activities. If a school's gymnasium
  is small, adjacent halls can be used for simple games while students
  await their turns in the gymnasium.

. Equipment should be gotten out of storage rooms and readied ahead of
  time. Necessary modifications--based on recommendations of regular
  teachers--not guess--should also be made in advance. Items which need
  to be borrowed should be arranged for before the day of the event and
  returned to the lending agency promptly after the event. If any borrowed
  equipment is damaged, it should be so noted and the lending school
  compensated for repair.

Filling in Details

Refreshments

Activity makes participants hungry. Whether an all day event or just an afternoon, food may be a part of the program. When deciding whether or not to serve a snack or lunch the following guidelines may be helpful.

- Feeding help. How many youngsters need assistance with eating, either supervision or complete feeding? Check with regular teachers to find out.

- Allergies and alternate selections. Certain handicapping conditions result in dietary restrictions, sugar free diets, or calorie reductions for example. Arrangements should be made so that appropriate foods are available to these children.

- Special utensils. Many children with handicapping conditions can eat independently if adaptations are made in their eating utensils. Accommodations may be as simple as straws for drinking or bibs to take care of the mess to special silver. If advance notice is given regarding types of food, proper items can be brought along with students.

- Where to eat. Is there sufficient space to provide room for eating? Can tables and chairs be set up for those that cannot sit on the floor or bleachers?

- Who brings food? Three systems have been used with success--

  --Students bring food from home, either bag lunches and drinks if an all day event or sack snacks. A variation is to have each student bring a snack to share with the group--a bag of potato chips, a dozen cookies--and a mass feed is provided.

  --Students bring a specified amount of money ahead of time; this is collected and used to provide the same lunch for everyone--this takes a little more work on the part of staff. Sometimes a school can take regular lunch money so that the cafeteria staff can make sandwiches to replace the lunch students would eat if they had stayed in school.

  --The host institution provides lunches. If they are not capable of doing it themselves they can solicit contributions from local food chains.

- Clean-up. Be sure to allow time for clean-up. Students need chances to wash and trash taken care of before activities are resumed. Remember, these are learning experiences.

Transportation

If these activities are in-school events, transporation is obviously no problem. If travel to another site is necessary, special arrangements must be made. Each school system has its own intricate methods for getting busses. Keep in mind, however, that scheduling should be done well in advance and verified several days before the event to avoid problems with the bus company. Determine in advance who pays the cost of busing. Possible sources of funds include the sponsoring group, individual school's funds (field trip, booster club,), school system's funds (intramural or athletic budgets in addition to exceptional education), local community agencies, and the bus company itself. Before transportation of private cars is considered, careful note should be taken of local and state regulations on insurance and liability.

Lead-Up and Follow-Up

Once the program is established, regular teachers can plan lead-up and follow-up activities for involved students. These may include--

- Announcement of the special event. Let students know where they will be going, when, and what they will be doing once they get there. This information should go out as part of parental permission forms needed for all students who participate.

- Student planning. Involve, if at all possible, participating students in selecting activities.

- New games. If students are to play any new games or ones in which they might not have participated for a long time, it might be wise to teach or review these activities ahead of time. If events are designed for students to do for the first time, review and preteaching are not necessary.

- Rules review. If serious sports competition is to take place, students should be aware of rules which govern these sports, particularily rules affecting disqualifications.

- What to wear, what to bring. Once a program has been established, teachers can advise students about types of appropriate and safe clothing for participation. Directions can also be given for bringing anything else, such as lunches or snacks.

- Follow-up. After the playday teachers should sit down with students who participated and discuss their reactions to it. What did they really enjoy? What did they dislike? What would they like to do again? How could the day be improved? Make note of these comments for use in planning future events.

Scheduling

Once general program content has been decided, it needs to be put into a workable time framework. When making the schedule the following should be considered--

- Participation time. If more than one activity is to take place, be sure to allow sufficient time for students actually to do each activity. Explanations, group organization for participation, and distribution of equipment all take time. Students should have sufficient time to participate after all this is finished. Allow at least a half hour to forty-five minutes per activity; increase this to at least one hour for older students and adults whose attention spans are longer and who may have higher degrees of skill. It may also necessary to allow more time if students are trying an activity for the first time.

- Time for changing activities. If more than one event is to take place, schedule time to get from one group to another and to change teams on the floor. This time should not be taken from that allocated for actual participation.

- Refreshment time. If food is to be served, time must be scheduled for set-up, eating, and clean-up.

- Formalities of the occasion. At any special event have time for a short welcome, explanation of things that will take place, and general directions. At the conclusion of the playday take time for a few short closing remarks. If formal sports competition has taken place, allocate time for an awards ceremony.

- Bus loading. If a school has a set departure time to return to its home site, some time will be needed for bus loading. If all students are ambulatory this isn't much of a problem. Loading buses for children with physically handicapping conditions takes more time.

- Less active time. If an event is to last all day, it is difficult to keep students active the entire time; students will be worn out before noon! It may be necessary to pace activities so some less active things like a See Something Different sports demonstration--if only for twenty minutes--are scheduled between active parts of the program. If serious sports competition is involved, some recovery time is needed for athletes between events; break between preliminaries and final competition should be included.

On-Site Preparation

The day of the event several things must be done to prepare for the playday before participants arrive.

- Equipment set-up. All equipment to be used should be out and ready being sure balls are inflated and nets are up. Guest participants should not be expected to help set-up; participation time should not be taken for this purpose.

- Directional signs. If the facility is an unfamiliar one, large paper signs noting bathrooms, event locations, stairs, and elevators are extremely helpful.

- Spectator seating. Space should be provided for individuals who come to watch such as parents and additional staff.

- Public address system. If a public address system is used, it should be set up and tried out in advance. It is less confusing if an announcer can be seen by students as well as heard.

.   <u>Staff check-in</u>. If additional volunteer helpers are used, they should
    arrive ahead of participants and be ready to work when students arrive.

.   <u>Accessibility</u>. Be sure all building entrances, locker rooms, and elevators
    are unlocked and ready for use and that lights are turned on.

.   <u>Parking</u>. Be sure a loading space is clear and ready for buses.

Publicity

Any large group playday or interschool sports competition is a newsworthy
event. Announcements and requests for coverage can be sent to school papers,
system-wide newsletters, city papers, and local radio and television outlets.
Keep in mind, however, that not all students have permission for their pictures
to be used for such purposes. Before any picture taking is arranged, school
authorities should be contacted regarding rules on permission. For any serious
sports competition results should be sent immediately to persons responsible for
local sports coverage. If they have been advised in advance of the nature of the
competition they will probably be happy to print results.

Direction of the Playday

From the onset one person has to be responsible for pulling all loose ends
together. Such a person makes initial contacts, runs meetings in an organized,
constructive fashion, sees that all pre-event plans are carried out, supervises
site preparations, runs the total operation the day of the activity, sees to it
that the facility is left in the condition it was found, and makes sure that
appreciation is expressed to all who helped make the event a success. This job
needs a person who is willing to work with a variety of people who may have
differing opinions. This takes a responsible person who can get the job done,
not someone who will leave it to others. Direction an event receives often
determines its success or failure.

First Aid

Any large sports event necessitates availability of first aid supplies and
someone trained in their use. First aid services should be easily accessible
but in an area somewhat secluded so that an injured person can be cared for in
relative quiet. At the start of the activity, everyone should be made aware of
the whereabouts of the first aid area and it should remain open during the entire
day. The local chapter of the American National Red Cross may be contacted for
assistance as many chapters have groups of people who run mobile first aid stations
at community events.

Financing

Last but not least, what is all this going to cost? If all help is volunteer,
the activity run in school during school time, and all food and transportation donated,
it costs nothing! From there the price can rise indefinitely. Contributions can be
solicited from local community groups, school system athletic departments, parents
clubs, service and civic organizations. If necessary an entry fee can be charged.
However, this will probably limit the number of students who participate.

APPENDICES

Sports Playday

An all day interschool event was held at the field house of a local university. Three schools sent a total of ninety students, ten to fifteen years of age with various physical and multiple conditions.

9:30   Arrive and distribute name tags

9:45   Welcome

9:50-10:30   Play for Fun--Parachute Activities
                Three large chutes with three teams of ten students per team and three staff member to each chute.

10:30-11:15   Play for Fun--Relay Races
                Nine relay teams of ten students per team were prematched for ability; students from different schools were mixed. These same teams were used for parachute play. One staff member was assigned each team.

11:15-12:15   Lunch and Toileting
                Students brought bag lunches; soft drinks were donated by a local company.

12:15-1:15   Try a New Sport

                        Water Polo   Raquetball
                        Bowling   Golf
                        Disco Dance   Carnival Games
                        Frisbee

                Prior to the event students were asked their first and second choices; they were programed for one activity based on their choices. The list of activities from which to choose came in part from student selections.

1:25-2:00   See Something Different

                        Martial Arts   Afro Dance
                        Fencing   Wheelchair Slalom
                        Trampoline   Diving
                        Archery   Exercise Physiology/Weight Training

                Suggestions for sports in this category were also obtained from students ahead of time. They were then given two choices, of which they saw one.

2:00   Load buses and leave.

Of the ninety students, twenty-five needed one-to-one assistance; this was in addition to staff members assigned to activities in the morning. During the afternoon one staff member was also assigned to each activity group. Staff consisted of personnel from participating schools; university students provided one-to-one help.

Sports Competition

An all day interschool track and field meet was held at an orthopedic school with one visiting school. Approximately fifty students fourteen to eighteen years of age participated.

9:00   Arrive and check-in

9:15   Warm-ups

9:45   Preliminary Competition

            Wheelchairs - 50 Yard Dash
            Walkers   - 50 Yard Dash
            Crutches   - 50 Yard Dash
            Wheelchairs - 220 Yard Dash
            Walkers   - 220 Yard Dash
            Crutches   - 220 Yard Dash
            Walkers   - High Jump
            Walkers   - Long Jump
            Wheelchairs - Long Jump
            Wheelchairs - Slalom
            Shot Put
            Softball Throw

12:00   Lunch

1:00   Final Competition

            The top two finishers from each heat of dashes and top six from each field event qualified.

            Wheelchairs - 50 Yard Dash
            Walkers   - 50 Yard Dash
            Crutches   - 50 Yard Dash
            Wheelchairs - 220 Yard Dash
            Walkers   - 220 Yard Dash
            Crutches   - 220 Yard Dash
            Walkers   - Shuttle Relay
            Wheelchairs - Shuttle Relay
            Mixed Team - 440 Yard Relay
            Walkers   - High Jump
            Walkers   - Long Jump
            Wheelchairs - Long Jump
            Wheelchairs - Slalom
            Shot Put
            Softball Throw

2:30   Awards Ceremony

Staff members from participating schools served as timers and scorers with help from the school system's central office personnel.

Special Theme Event--Trivia Day

This was a half-day in-school event in which about sixty students ten to fifteen years of age with physical and multiple conditions participated.

12:30   Organization and team set-up.
Teams were pre-arranged so that they were evenly matched. At the start of competition each team was assigned a pie shaped portion of the floor, marked off with cones. Each team had to stay within its part of the floor the entire time.

12:40-2:20   Continous Trivia Competition.

- Clean the Yard. Every soft nerf and whiffle ball available was dumped onto the floor. Object was for each team to clean all balls off its section of the floor. All teams participated at the same time by throwing balls onto other teams areas. At the end of a specified time the winner was declared as the team with fewest objects in its section of the floor.

- Mat Stack. Each team got one five by eight mat. How many people could they get on it? To break ties, tape was used to reduce usable mat space.

- Balloon Break. Large container of balloons was placed in the center of the floor. Walkers ran and got one balloon which had to be broken by someone in a wheelchair.

- Rope Maze. Each team was tied up with a continuous rope. The first team getting free won.

- Mummy Wrap. Team picked a mummy and then wrapped it with toilet paper--neatest and fastest job won.

- Etc., etc., etc., etc., etc., etc., etc.!!!!

An infinite number of trivia type games could be described. They are fun things that students don't do everyday in physical education classes; by their nature they emphasize group cooperation. At the end of the afternoon the team with the highest total points--seven for first, five for second, three for third, and two for fourth and fifth--is the winner. Standings contribute towards intramural awards given at the end of the school year.

Special Sports Event

An all-school team of twelve students ten to twenty years of age with physical and multiple conditions played a regulation basketball game against local television news personalities who played in wheelchairs. The event was held at school with about 200 spectators. The team was picked ahead of time from open try-outs judged by persons in physical education and sports but not from the school itself. Prior to the game art classes made pep posters and home economics classes prepared refreshments. Invitations were sent to parents and special programs were printed. A cheerleading squad was also organized for the event.

12:30   Gymnasium open for spectators.

12:35-12:50   Home team warm-up.

12:50-1:00   Visiting team warm-up.

1:00-1:55   Basketball game.

2:00-2:30   Refreshments and autograph signing.

Rated officials donated time for the game and the television station gave several minutes of coverage on the evening sports show.

PRACTICAL POINTERS

MAKING OUTDOOR PLAY AREAS USABLE FOR ALL CHILDREN

Susan J. Grosse

     Research and experience both have shown that the <u>single</u> best predictor of
how successful a child with a handicapping condition can be integrated with able-
bodied classmates is how well he/she plays with abled-bodied peers in his/her
neighborhood. Foundations for these important interpersonal relationships are
often established on playgrounds. However, such interactions still are not
possible on many playgrounds which simply are not accessible to children with
handicapping conditions!

All children need places to play, yet how often is a child in a wheelchair seen at a neighborhood playground? Children love to run, climb, slide, and swing, but how frequently is the young retarded, blind, deaf or emotionally distrubed child seen at a tot lot play area? Though children with handicapping conditions have the same needs and desires for play as able-bodied peers, opportunities to engage in successful play experiences are few.

It may be that equipment is not accessible for someone in a wheelchair, on crutches, or in braces. Another possibility is that equipment is too difficult to use for the skill levels of a child. Even if equipment is accessible and could be used by the child in question, he/she might not understand what to do. Many children with handicapping conditions find it difficult to fit into neighborhood peer play groups. Successful playground experiences can not only satisfy these children's play needs and provide good exercise, but also aid in peer group acceptance. Once able-bodied children find that peers with handicapping conditions can do things just like they can, acceptance into their play groups is more likely.

Equipment available at play areas, whether at school, park, or neighborhood playgrounds, is important in determining which children have opportunities to play and types of activities in which individuals participate. Overall objectives of this Practical Pointer are to (1) provide a format for having all newly constructed play areas built so they are usable by all children, and (2) offer ideas for modifying existing play equipment to make it more suitable for use by all children. Making playgrounds specially for children with handicapping conditions is not part of this picture. This would only promote the very segregation that mainstreaming and integration efforts have sought to eliminate. Key is the term all children--the word all automatically includes anyone who happens to have an impairment, disability or handicapping condition, regardless of types or severities.

CRITERIA FOR SELECTING EQUIPMENT

Whether a play area is being designed from scratch or an already existing playground is being revitalized, decisions need to be made about equipment to be included. Ideally such equipment should meet movement needs of children in ways that are both safe and fun. Equipment should be easy to maintain, resistant to vandalism, and accessible to all children. Selecting and/or modifying equipment must, therefore be well thought out before actual work on a play area is begun.

Users of Play Areas

Children to use play equipment are the most important criteria in the selection process--their interests and needs must come first. Therefore, the initial step in the selection process is determining types of youthful populations to use equipment. Preschool children require different sizes and types of equipment than that needed by children in lower elementary school grades (ages six to eight). Upper elementary school age students--those in fourth, fifth, and sixth grades--need equipment that is larger in scale than that required by preschoolers. Both differences in sizes and activity levels among various age groups require that their play equipment be different. A play area for one specific age group--e.g., preschoolers located at a building used only for preschool children--can be constructed with equipment just for that age group. If an area is to be used by all age groups, then planners must make sure that selected equipment reflect traits of different age groups that are to use it.

Ability levels of students are also important factors. A playground to be used by all children should have equipment usable by children of all ability levels. Something should be available so a child with little movement capability can use equipment successfully. Equipment should be simple to figure out so mentally retarded children can go right to and use pieces of equipment. Some pieces should be scaled down and placed close to the ground so small and less able children can not only reach them but will be less likely to get hurt if they fall off accidentally. There should be something for an extremely capable child--places to climb, slide, and maneuver that make specific demands on his/her special capabilities. If there is no place for more able youngsters, it is possible they will intrude on spaces designed for less able children. More importantly, if a play area is for all children--and it should be--then needs of highly skilled children must be met.

A vertical ladder provides climbing experiences for challenging more able children.

Movement Needs of Children

Children playing on playground equipment use a variety of movements in their activities. Part of the reason for this is an inherent need in every child to be active. However the prime reason for such a variety of movements is that every piece of equipment demands particular types of activities. For example, to make a swing move, a child must push off with the feet or use the body to pump. To reach the top of a jungle gym a child has to climb. To get to the top of a slide and slide down a child must first go up the ladder. In each case movements are built-in. When selecting playground equipment, be sure as many different kinds of movements as possible are built into the total playground. Movements can be grouped into the following categories --

. <u>Movements in place</u>-- body stays in one place in relation to equipment.

-- <u>Movements by arm propulsion</u>...

...swings that can be <u>pumped</u> with the arms;

...merry-go-rounds that can be ridden by <u>holding on</u> with the hands.

-- <u>Movements by leg propulsion</u>...

...swings that can be <u>pushed</u> with the feet;

...equipment that can be <u>pedaled</u> to make it move.

-- <u>Movements by total body propulsion</u>...

...cars, trucks, or animals that a child can sit in or on and <u>bounce</u>;

...saucers that can be <u>turned</u> by moving the entire body;

...swings that can be <u>pumped</u> with the entire body.

Cars (foreground), saucers (to the right), and bouncing seats are ridden with whole body propulsion.

. <u>Movements through space</u>-- body moves in relation to equipment.

-- <u>Movements involving locomotor patterns</u>...

...ramps or inclined planes on which to <u>walk</u> up and down;

...mazes to <u>run</u> through;

...tunnels to <u>crawl</u> through;

...ladders or cargo nets to <u>climb</u>;

310

...tires to <u>jump</u> through;

...inclined planes or fireman's poles on which to <u>slide</u>;

...footprints on the surface to <u>hop</u> on and follow.

-- <u>Movements involving perceptual-motor functioning</u>...

...swinging bridges or balance beams on which to <u>balance</u> while walking;

...railroad tie fences to move <u>over</u> and <u>under</u>;

...free form sculptures to move <u>around</u> and <u>through</u>;

...very small spaces to move <u>between</u>.

. <u>Object manipulation</u>

-- <u>Movements involving interactions with natural elements</u>...

...ground boxes or elevated tables for play with <u>sand</u> and/or <u>water</u>;

...places to <u>garden</u>;

...<u>nature trails</u>.

-- <u>Movements involving outdoor games</u>...

...playgrounds for <u>ball games</u>;

...grassy areas for individual or dual play with <u>toys from home</u>.

. <u>Fantasy play</u>

-- <u>Movements involving structures that have places for hiding, climbing, and exploring.</u>

-- <u>Movements involving equipment that looks like animals, magic castles, cars, trucks, forts.</u>

-- <u>Movements involving free form equipment that encourages children to use their own imaginations.</u>

. <u>Movements structured to improve physical fitness</u>

-- <u>Movements involving equipment that demands both large and small muscle activities.</u>

-- <u>Movements directed by a specific exercise courses or trails.</u>

No one piece of equipment does everything for every child--there is <u>no perfect selection</u>! With a variety of choices most of the movement categories can be incorporated in any play area.

Making Play Areas More Accessible

Whether designing a completely new play area or working on improving an existing one, changes can make any area more accessible to children with handicapping conditions.

. **Ramps**

Usual methods of getting to the top of slides or onto structures include climbing stairs or ladders. Ladders can be replaced by inclined ramps with pitches to allow someone with balance problems or on crutches to walk up easily. Sides of ramps should have railings so that no child accidently walks or crawls over the edges. An adult can take a child

Many walkways provide access to all areas of the play lot.
Ramps (back left) provide access to bridges and slides;
long ramp (center) provides access to a circular slide.

in a wheelchair up a ramp, assist him/her out of the chair, and slide to the bottom together--the chair is retrieved later! Someone with crutches can go up a ramp, drop crutches over the side, come down the slide, and pick up the waiting crutches. The slide--with unaccessible ladder--is now easily used by <u>all</u> children.

. **Railings**

Steady hand holds on one or both sides of stairways, swinging bridges, balance beams, or uneven surfaces can provide needed extra support for children with balance problems; they can guide someone who is blind or partially sighted and support a child who otherwise needs crutches.

312

Railings can be added to many pieces of existing equipment.

Railings added to a swinging bridge or balance beam can
provide needed additional support.

. Height variance

Changing heights of pieces of equipment can many times move them into
functioning ranges of children with handicapping conditions. Large
climbing structures can be placed further into the ground when built
or supports can be shortened. This shortens access distance and makes
equipment easier to get onto as well as safer for a child who falls
off--the child is closer to the ground! Raising height of a piece of
equipment--putting a sand box on legs, for example--puts it into reaching range of someone in a wheelchair or makes it more usable for a
child who needs to be seated while working with the hands.

. Walk-ways

Wheelchairs are difficult to move on grass. Hard top walk-ways surrounding all pieces of equipment make it easier for a child in a wheelchair
as well as one on crutches to go from place to place. A child not likely
to use a specific piece of equipment because it is particularly difficult or just not something of interest should still be able to get to
it, if for no other reason than to be able to see what other children
are doing.

. <u>Specially designed equipment</u>

Increasingly many manufacturers are designing equipment with use by <u>all</u> children in mind. They have added special features that enhance use by children with handicapping conditions. A merry-go-round, for example, has been designed to accommodate wheelchairs. Before selecting new or replacement equipment check as many suppliers as possible to be sure equipment selected is the most usable and functional available.

Some merry-go-rounds are designed and built to carry wheel-chairs.

In addition to these general adaptations, attention to many small details can improve usability of any play area --

. Can stairs be used in place of some ladders? If so, are width and depth of steps appropriate for ages and ability levels of children using equipment?

. If pieces of equipment have seats--e.g., swing seats, riding seats-- are they all the same or are there different types? Different size children need different size seats. Children with sitting balance

314

Swing set with a variety of seats can meet needs of <u>all</u> children.

problems or those who have difficulty holding on need more secure seats than children with normal muscle control. Are seats easy for children to get in and out? Are seats easy for adults to place and remove children?

. Are there places where a child crawling on equipment can get fingers caught? Can a crutch tip be trapped? Perhaps a swinging bridge can be pulled up a little tighter so there is no space between slats.

. Are landing areas close to the ground? Coming down a slide is great fun, but with a sharp drop to the ground at the bottom of a slide some children can get unhappy surprises as they land on their seats on the hard ground. Not all children are coordinated enough to stand up as they come off a slide.

. Can seat belts or hand holds be added to riding equipment to assist children with poor balance?

Wide steps, handrails, and keeping the end of the slide close to the ground for soft landings are important <u>details</u>.

Many children of differing abilities can use the same play structures with just a few adaptations. A child with crutches drops one crutch over the railing before going down the slide. Ramp and railings make the equipment accessible for him.

Selecting Safe Equipment

<u>Actually no piece of playground equipment is safe</u>! Major responsibilities for safety rest with <u>users</u> of equipment. The <u>safest</u> piece of equipment can be deadly if used incorrectly. However several factors contributing to safe use should be considered when selecting equipment.

If adaptations are made, will they create safety hazards? Most manufacturers attempt to design reasonably safe equipment. If design of equipment is to be changed, will changes enhance or detract from safety? For example, a merry-go-round specially designed to carry wheelchairs is purchased. To make the merry-go-round more accessible a ramp is added so wheelchairs can be rolled right onto the equipment. However, when an ambulatory child rides the merry-go-round with feet and legs hanging over the edge, they will be smashed when the part on which he/she is sitting turns into the ramp. <u>A helpful adaptation for</u>

<u>one child can be a hazard for another</u>. Playgrounds should be for <u>all</u> children without hazards to any child.

Materials of which play devices are made can also contribute to their inherent safety--or lack of it. Factors to keep in mind about various construction materials include --

- ## Metal

  Resistant to vandalism and capable of withstanding heavy use, metals can be painted bright colors to stimulate children's interests and imaginations. However metals subjected to bright sunlight can become quite hot. Surfaces of slides are especially dangerous for children without complete sensations.

- ## Wood

  Many companies make complete play structures out of wood so that they blend into natural settings. However, these are more easily vandalized and may tend to <u>sliver</u> with wear. They should be checked periodically for large splinters that can cause injuries.

- ## Sand

  Sand, long time play favorite of children, can be kept in ground boxes or elevated tables. Sand, however, is also a favorite <u>litter box</u> substance for animals, and a substance that may harbor hidden articles of adult trash--e.g., broken glass and cigarette butts. Sand left open and uncovered when not in use should be sifted regularly to remove foreign particles. Preschool children cannot always differentiate what is and is not safe. An alternative solution involves covering the sand area completely when not in use or under supervision.

- ## Water

  Water activities can be provided in various ways. An elevated water table--much like a large sink--with drain and plug can be filled every day and emptied every night. Standing water invites bacteria and is unsafe for children who may accidentally drink it, lick their fingers, or put toys in their mouths. Small wading pools are good for water play but water must be kept chemically clean. Even the smallest wading pool must be supervised at all times; a child can drown in only a few inches of water if circumstances are right.

- ## Grass

  A favorite surface for play areas, grass not only looks nice but makes a soft cushion for landing areas. If an area receives heavy use, grass wears away to dirt. Grass is also somewhat difficult to maintain in play areas because of problems associated with cutting around all pieces of equipment.

. **Cement**

Cement is a particularly hard surface not especially suitable for equipment areas where children may fall; it does make excellent bases for sinking and anchoring support structures.

. **Fiberglass**

Fiberglass is being used in place of metal in many pieces of equipment. It is fairly easy to maintain and can be painted various colors. Main hazards to watch for are wear slivers. If equipment is vandalized or receives heavy wear and surfaces are nicked, slivers may result. Equipment should be checked periodically and any rough areas rubbed down.

. **Blacktop**

Blacktop provides for soft landings. However, in extremely hot weather blacktop surfaces can become soft so that wheelchair wheels make ruts and black surface material comes off on wheels and crutches. Care must be taken to seal the entire surface properly.

. **Rubber**

Tires are most frequently found rubber items on play areas. Companies and individuals build entire structures out of tires, securing them together, and then anchoring the entire structure in the ground. Tire devices have been painted bright colors and used in an infinite number of ways to stir children's interests and imaginations. They are easy to climb on because edges provide handholds and by nature they are relatively soft to land on or bump against. However, they present several maintenance problems; they are susceptible to burning by vandals. In addition, spaces inside tires serve as collection basins for rain water and debris. These areas need to be policed and cleaned regularly.

. **Rope**

Since ropes are used mostly for climbing and swinging rather than as supports for equipment, they need to be checked regularly for wear; frayed or cut ropes must be replaced immediately. Though ropes, cargo nets, and hanging ropes make for excellent climbing, they are easily vandalized.

. **Chain**

Chain is being used more frequently to support equipment that moves as a child uses it. Traditionally used on swings, chains can now be found as supports for swinging bridges as well. Any chain used should be heavy guage and resistant to rusting. Examine chains periodically for signs of wear and replace any links that show notches or indentations.

318

. Paint

Most commercial equipment comes already painted. If a play area is a
do-it-youself type or if repairs are being made on already installed
equipment, exercise caution in paint selection. Besides making sure
that all-weather paint is used, be certain that it is not paint which
easily chips and can poison children if eaten.

No equipment should have sharp edges or outcropings of metal or wood that
can injure a child. All stationary equipment should be well anchored in the
ground, and all parts of equipment firmly bolted together; bolts should be
recessed or countersunk. When equipment is installed these are responsibilities of companies doing installations. After equipment is in use, making sure
that each piece remains in good condition and proper working order are responsibilities of play area owners. Use sometimes loosens equipment parts; check
regularly to be sure everything is secure.

Laying Out Play Areas

Selecting equipment is only the beginning of developing a playground for
all children. After equipment has been chosen, decisions must be made regarding
where each piece is to be placed. If an original site has to be selected, an
already chosen site prepared, or equipment added to an existing site the following factors must be considered --

. Spacing

Pieces of equipment should be far enough apart so children playing on
one piece do not bump into those on other pieces. Particularly important is placement of swing sets. Space is needed for equipment to
swing, children to get on and off, and children to wait their turns.
Other equipment should not be so close that children come close to
swings when they are being used. Even with the need for adaquate
spacing, caution should be taken that equipment is not spread out too
far. Children with limited mobility require more time to get from
place to place; they should not spend more time traveling between
pieces of equipment than playing, learning, and having fun.

. Walks and parking areas

Walk ways leading to each piece of equipment have already been mentioned;
they make it easier for children in wheelchairs and on crutches to move
from place to place. A small parking area at each piece of equipment
provides space where a child can leave wheelchair, crutches, or walker.
Many children with handicapping conditions enjoy leaving their hardware
behind and crawling or using play equipment for support. It is advantageous if pieces of equipment can be placed where they are not hazards
to and cannot be tampered with by others.

. Grouping

If a play area is to be large some attempt should be made to group equipment designed for specific age groups. For example, all pieces specially designed for preschoolers--really small, scaled down items--should be separate from much larger pieces for older, more active children. When equipment is placed in random fashion very small children may get hurt by older children who often are not as careful as they should be.

. Natural elements

Take advantage of natural elements already on a site--trees provide welcome shade on hot days; natural hills are <u>fun</u> to climb up and roll down; large boulders make good seats. Natural hazards--and people made hazards--should be avoided; do not place any piece of equipment right next to a street or sidewalk--leave several feet of space for children to get off equipment safely without running into a pedestrian or car.

. Special additions

Are there special additions that will make a play area more accessible to <u>all</u> children? Perhaps signs with pictures to show how a piece of equipment is used so a less intelligent child can have a start on knowing what to do. Braille signs along walkways help blind children find specific pieces of equipment and get mental pictures of what each piece of equipment is like. If a play area is large, directional signs help children find their ways from piece to piece and to areas with picnic tables or bathrooms.

GUIDELINES FOR USING FACILITIES

Once equipment has been selected and installed the <u>real</u> work begins--<u>insuring that a play area is a fun place for all children all of the time</u>. Play areas should be places where children enjoy coming and can play safely. To have this happen, several procedures are helpful.

Teach Children How to Use Equipment

Children with handicapping conditions often have had little experience with playground equipment. Some able-bodied children may be at losses as to what to do and how to play safely on new and different pieces of equipment. Time should be spent explaining to <u>all</u> children how equipment can be used <u>safely</u>. This can be done on the spot by volunteers of neighborhood tot lots. As last resorts flyers explaining new pieces of equipment can be printed and distributed to children to take home and/or mailed to families in the neighborhood. Whatever methods used the following should be considered for each piece of equipment --

. Where to get on and off safely.

. Where to wait safely when awaiting turns.

. How to handle the equipment--e.g., stop the swing when getting off; do not leave it swinging.

. How to use equipment safely--e.g., come down a slide feet first.

Some of these helpful hints will be old stuff to able-bodied children; but for many children with handicapping conditions they are necessary to make these children safe users of play areas.

Maintain Safe Play Environments

Maintaining safe play environments are adult responsibilities. Children can help and be aware of safety precautions, but the over-all job is the responsibility of adults. Those responsible for a play area should --

. Check all pieces of equipment every day they are used. Keep eyes open for vandalism, general wear, and breakage due to use. Close any areas in need of repairs and see that repairs are made as soon as possible.

. Watch for dangerous litter--e.g., broken glass and beer cans--that children can pick up and from which they can get hurt--dispose of all dangerous litter immediately.

When adults are responsible for supervising children while they use play areas, either in capacities of teachers or playground workers, each should keep in mind the following --

. When students go to a play area in groups the faculty member or group leader is responsible for every child in that group--be alert for children who may wander off; be specific about pieces of equipment they may--and may not--use. It is difficult to watch a group spread out over a large area.

. Children who require seat belts while in wheelchairs should either have seat belts on while riding equipment or have adults holding them.

. If a youngster complains of dizziness or illness while on a piece of equipment, remove him/her immediately from the equipment. Be especially cautious if a child is known to have seizures.

. Metal surfaces get very hot in the sun--be sure to check equipment before used by children without complete sensations.

. Have a first aid kit readily accessible at all times.

Depending on equipment, it may be necessary to have special rules and safety hints concerning specific pieces of equipment. This should be at discretion of persons in charge of play areas. Procedures established when a play area opens are ones that determine its safe--or unsafe--use. Special care should be taken in developing these procedures which affect the fun of many important people--all the children who use these play areas.

SELECTED RESOURCES

The following two books contain extensive bibliographies which have not been duplicated here. Readers should consult these sources directly for more information.

Aitken, Margaret H. Play Environment for Children: Play Space, Improvised Equipment, and Facilities. Bellingham, Washington: Educational Designs and Consultants, (3259 North Shore Road), 1972.

Physical Education and Recreation for the Handicapped: Information and Research Utilization Center. Making Physical Education and Recreation Facilities Accessible to All: Planning, Designing, Adapting. Washington, D.C.: American Alliance for Health, Physical Education and Recreation, 1977.

In addition, readers may wish to refer to the following --

Ability Playgrounds. St. John's, Newfoundland: Newfoundland and Labrador Recreation Advisory Council for Special Groups, (Box 4385), n.d.

American Society of Landscape Architects Foundation. Barrier-Free Site Design. Washington, D.C.: U.S. Department of Housing and Urban Development, Office of Policy Development and Research (Government Printing Office), 1975.

Baker, Katherine R. Let's Play Outdoors. Washington, D.C.: National Association for the Education of Young Children, n.d.

Etkes, Asher. "Therapeutic Playgrounds." JOHPER, November/December, 1973.

Gallahue, David L. Developmental Play Equipment for Home and School. New York: Wiley, 1975.

Gordon, Ronnie. The Design of Pre-School Therapeutic Playgrounds: An Outdoor "Learning Laboratory". Rehabilitation Monograph 47. New York: Institute of Rehabilitation Medicine, New York University Medical Center, 1972.

Osman, Fred L. Patterns for Designing Children's Centers. New York: Educational Facilities Laboratories, 1972.

Playgrounds: Do It Ourselves Childcare. San Francisco, California: Childcare Switchboard/Single Parent Resource Center (3896 24th Street), n.d.

Playgrounds for All Children. Syracuse, New York: Playgrounds for All Children Task Force (Office of Parks and Recreation), n.d.

Reis, Michael L. Design Standards to Accommodate People With Physical Disabilities In Park and Open Space Planning. Madison, Wisconsin: University of Wisconsin Extension, Recreation Resources Center, 1973.

Seker, JoAnn. "A Scavenger Playground." JOHPER, May, 1971.

Stone Muntain Educational Projects Incorporated. Children's Things. Conway, Massachusetts: The Corporation (Roaring Brook Farm), 1975.

Werner, Peter H. and Simmons, Richard A. Inexpensive Physical Education Equipment for Children. Minneapolis, Minnesota: Burgess, 1976.

The following companies supply playground equipment and can be contacted for their current catalogs --

Bigtoys--3113 South Pine Street, Tacoma, Washington.

Burke Miller and Associates--Route 4, Box 17, Mauston, Wisconsin.

Creative Playgrounds--1234 East 99th Drive, Route 23, Terre Haute, Indiana.

Developlay--120 Hawthorne, Palo Alto, California.

Exceptional Play--Box 1015, Lawrence, Kansas.

Flaghouse--18 West 18th Street, New York, New York.

Game Time--Box 121, Fort Payne, Alabama.

Global Games Unlimited--4825 Penn Avenue South, Minneapolis, Minnesota.

Delmer F. Harris Company--Box 278, Concordia, Kansas.

Landscape Structures--Route 2, Box 26, Delano, Minnesota.

Mexico Forge Gerber Leisure Products--Box 5613, Madison, Wisconsin.

Miracle Recreation--Jerry Robinson and Associates, 6207 Mary Lane, Occomowoc, Wisconsin.

Parcourse--3701 Buchanan, San Francisco, California.

PCA Industries--2298 Grissom Drive, St. Louis, Missouri.

Quality Industries--Hillsdale Industrial Park, Box 278, Hillsdale, Michigan.

Recreation Equipment--Box 2188 Department 578, Anderson, Indiana.

Thera-Pla--Box 2186, Madison, Wisconsin.